THE
HISTORY OF
AFGHANISTAN

ADVISORY BOARD

THE HISTORY OF AFGHANISTAN

Second Edition

Meredith L. Runion

The Greenwood Histories of the Modern Nations
Frank W. Thackeray and John E. Findling, Series Editors

An Imprint of ABC-CLIO, LLC
Santa Barbara, California • Denver, Colorado

Library of Congress Cataloging-in-Publication Data

Names: Runion, Meredith L., author.
Title: The history of Afghanistan / Meredith L. Runion.
Description: Second edition. | Santa Barbara, California : Greenwood,
    an imprint of ABC-CLIO, LLC, 2017. | Series: Greenwood histories of
    the modern nations | Includes bibliographical references and index.
Identifiers: LCCN 2016054673 (print) | LCCN 2016055705 (ebook) |
    ISBN 9781610697774 (acid-free paper) | ISBN 9781610697781 (ebook)
Subjects: LCSH: Afghanistan—History.
Classification: LCC DS356 .R86 2017 (print) | LCC DS356 (ebook) |
    DDC 958.1—dc23
LC record available at https://lccn.loc.gov/2016054673

ISBN: 978-1-61069-777-4
EISBN: 978-1-61069-778-1

21 20 19 18 17   1 2 3 4 5

This book is also available as an eBook.

Greenwood
An Imprint of ABC-CLIO, LLC

ABC-CLIO, LLC
130 Cremona Drive, P.O. Box 1911
Santa Barbara, California 93116-1911
www.abc-clio.com

This book is printed on acid-free paper ∞
Manufactured in the United States of America

Disclaimer

*All statements of fact, opinion, or analysis expressed are those of the author and do not
reflect the official positions or views of the U.S. Government. Nothing in the contents
should be construed as asserting or implying U.S. Government authentication of
information or endorsement of the author's views. This material has been reviewed
by the U.S. Government to prevent the disclosure of classified information.*

This book is dedicated to all those who have served in the U.S. military to defend and protect the United States of America. Although your time away from your loved ones and family can never be replaced, the nation is grateful for your service.

Contents

Series Foreword

The Greenwood Histories of the Modern Nations series is intended to provide students and interested laypeople with up-to-date, concise, and analytical histories of many of the nations of the contemporary world. Not since the 1960s has there been a systematic attempt to publish a series of national histories, and as series editors, we believe that this series will prove to be a valuable contribution to our understanding of other countries in our increasingly interdependent world.

At the end of the 1960s, the Cold War was an accepted reality of global politics. The process of decolonization was still in progress, the idea of a unified Europe with a single currency was unheard of, the United States was mired in a war in Vietnam, and the economic boom in Asia was still years in the future. Richard Nixon was president of the United States, Mao Tse-tung (not yet Mao Zedong) ruled China, Leonid Brezhnev guided the Soviet Union, and Harold Wilson was prime minister of the United Kingdom. Authoritarian dictators still controlled most of Latin America, the Middle East was reeling in the wake of the Six-Day War, and Shah Mohammad Reza Pahlavi was at the height of his power in Iran.

Since then, the Cold War has ended, the Soviet Union has vanished, leaving 15 independent republics in its wake, the advent of the computer age has radically transformed global communications, the rising demand for oil makes the Middle East still a dangerous flash-point, and the rise of new economic powers like the People's Republic of China and India threatens to bring about a new world order. All of these developments have had a dramatic impact on the recent history of every nation of the world.

For this series, which was launched in 1998, we first selected nations whose political, economic, and socio-cultural affairs marked them as among the most important of our time. For each nation, we found an author who was recognized as a specialist in the history of that nation. These authors worked cooperatively with us and with Greenwood Press to produce volumes that reflected current research on their nations and that are interesting and informative to their readers. In the first decade of the series, close to 50 volumes were published, and some have now moved into second editions.

The success of the series has encouraged us to broaden our scope to include additional nations, whose histories have had significant effects on their regions, if not on the entire world. In addition, geopolitical changes have elevated other nations into positions of greater importance in world affairs and, so, we have chosen to include them in this series as well. The importance of a series such as this cannot be under-estimated. As a superpower whose influence is felt all over the world, the United States can claim a "special" relationship with almost every other nation. Yet many Americans know very little about the histories of nations with which the United States relates. How did they get to be the way they are? What kind of political systems have evolved there? What kind of influence do they have on their own regions? What are the dominant political, religious, and cultural forces that move their leaders? These and many other questions are answered in the volumes of this series.

The authors who contribute to this series write comprehensive histories of their nations, dating back, in some instances, to prehistoric times. Each of them, however, has devoted a significant portion of their book to events of the past 40 years because the modern era has contributed the most to contemporary issues that have an impact on U.S. policy. Authors make every effort to be as up-to-date as possi-ble so that readers can benefit from discussion and analysis of recent events.

In addition to the historical narrative, each volume contains an introductory chapter giving an overview of that country's geogra-phy, political institutions, economic structure, and cultural attributes. This is meant to give readers a snapshot of the nation as it exists in the contemporary world. Each history also includes supplementary information following the narrative, which may include a timeline that represents a succinct chronology of the nation's historical evolution, biographical sketches of the nation's most important historical figures, and a glossary of important terms or concepts that are usually expressed in a foreign language. Finally, each author prepares a comprehensive bibliography for readers who wish to pursue the subject further.

Readers of these volumes will find them fascinating and well written. More importantly, they will come away with a better understanding of the contemporary world and the nations that comprise it. As series editors, we hope that this series will contribute to a heightened sense of global understanding as we move through the early years of the twenty-first century.

Frank W. Thackeray and John E. Findling
Indiana University Southeast

Preface

Encapsulating the history of Afghanistan is one of the most complex feats to accurately summarize in a single manuscript. For a country which has been in existence for over 5,000 years, a great deal of history, religious influence, and civil unrest begs to be told. This vast treasure of life, history, and perseverance as a nation makes it nearly impossible to determine the most important aspects to include in this textbook, which is chartered with providing a brief historical account of the country. Regardless of the details included or omitted within this book, one aspect, however, is certain. Afghanistan's history is one of conflict, unrest, and social disparity. As of 2017, the nation has made great strides in uniting under a Democratic Republican government, even while the country continues to struggle with rebirth under a democratic regime. In order for Afghanistan to evolve into a true democratic republic and be able to resolve the many challenges facing the country, Afghanistan must grapple with how to stand on its own without NATO support, reduce the threats from the Taliban, increase social and economic harmony, and address a handful of pressures facing the nation. Even in the years after the death of the terrorist Osama bin Laden, other radical terrorist groups continue to thrive in Afghanistan or in the neighboring countries along its borders.

Although the United States (U.S.) ousted the Taliban in October 2001, the Taliban is still active in the country and continues to support other terrorist groups around the world. Once a diverse collection of quiet students fighting for the advancement of Islam, the Taliban joined forces with al-Qaeda and bin Laden in 1995. With this new alliance, this formerly peaceful group drastically changed course. The once-idealistic goals of the Taliban were forever skewed to a more radical way of thought. The result is a new draconian order for the advancement of Islam and desire to overthrow Western countries. The Taliban is still very much alive and active in Afghanistan. Even after key events such as the terrorist attacks of September 11, the U.S. occupation of Afghanistan, and the death of bin Laden, the resiliency of the Taliban is enduring. The Taliban continues to fight for their efforts to restore Afghanistan to the belief of a true "Islamic Emirate." The ongoing threat of terrorist insurgency is just a recent example which has occurred in the history of Afghanistan within the last 20 years. For centuries before the Taliban, countless leaders and countries have gloriously failed to break the hard-engrained Islamic principles and true roots of Afghan culture. It is this very foundation of unyielding Islamic faith that continues to fuel the Taliban and other extremists.

The purpose of *The History of Afghanistan* is to provide a sweeping account of the history of the country, portray an accurate picture of the state of affairs in Afghanistan, and outline some of the challenges facing the rebirth of the nation. There are deep, long-standing rifts among neighboring regions coupled with difficulties achieving tribal unity internal to the country. Afghanistan's continual overturn of leaders has perhaps hindered repair attempts within the nation, and many peace campaigns have regrettably been unsuccessful. Rebuilding Afghanistan will not be achieved overnight, or even in a few presidential terms under the new Afghan democratic assembly. In trying to understand the state of affairs in Afghanistan, several questions must be addressed. Why has the history of Afghanistan been so tempestuous? Why has Afghanistan served as a pawn for other cultures' advancement, including the British, Russians, and the United States? After the death of bin Laden, how has the seemingly rickety group of zealots known as the Taliban continued to sustain a hard grasp around the throat of Afghanistan? Why has Afghanistan continued to experience domestic instability and a lack of a cohesive rule of the country? These are just several of the questions that will be explored in *The History of Afghanistan*. This book is intended to provide a general overview of the country and insight into some of the deep issues that have plagued Afghanistan since the dawn of time. By having a deep understanding of Afghanistan's tumultuous past, readers of this book will be able to appreciate the struggles that continue to batter this war-torn land into the future.

Introduction

For more than 3,000 years, Afghanistan has been a battleground for invasion and conflict. Centuries before the death of Osama bin Laden, Afghanistan faced unrelenting years of turmoil and strife. The United States has held long-standing interests in Afghanistan, and has struggled with these relations just like many other countries. Afghanistan's history is one steeped in conflict, distress, and social unrest but, nonetheless, offers a wide-ranging, intriguing, and diverse narrative.

Due to the country's location along the crucial trade routes between Asia and the Middle East, Afghanistan has been repeatedly invaded and conquered by rulers and foreign governments for centuries. Yet, why have none of these invaders successfully sustained a lasting foothold in the country? Gaining control in the rugged and challenging terrain of Afghanistan is a challenge greater than many great rulers have salaciously imagined. As history has proven, any victory in Afghanistan should only be considered a temporary feat, for success will be taken almost as quickly as it was given. It is a scene that is all too common in Afghanistan for a nation that has watched so many newly conquering armies erect magnificent monoliths upon the crumbled ruins of previously defeated empires. Despite these ruins, which ominously foretold of the struggle to achieve long-lasting success in the country, many great nations have continued to try and fail to fully conquer Afghanistan.

In 2001, the U.S. military seemingly toppled the al-Qaeda regime and released modern Afghanistan from the control of the Taliban. Yet to this day, al-Qaeda and the Taliban continue to pose a threat to the success and future of the country. For many Afghan citizens, democratic hope was solidified when the country held elections in October 2004 that officially sanctioned Afghanistan as an Islamic republic. After 10 years as an Islamic republic, this democratically elected government has struggled to unite all Afghans under the new government and reconstruct the country. If truth be told, the road to recovery has not been easy. Afghanistan continues to face numerous obstacles and deeply constrained challenges across the country. These challenges include how to rebuild the crumbled economy, eliminate the continued opium drug trafficking (which is credited as the largest income source in the country), obliterate the country's large den of terrorist activity, recover buried landmines from constant wars, and the need to assist with the returning of home for millions of refugees after years of exile.[1] With opium records continually breaking previous years, 2016 resulted in some of the largest production totals yet. Many companies are hesitant to invest in such a troubled and problematic nation. Still, Afghanistan desperately needs this income in order to help increase and stabilize the economy. The continual threat and attacks by the Taliban are severe hindrances, particularly since the Taliban insurgents have become a way of life for extremists throughout South and Central Asia. These factors are only a handful of impediments facing the new Afghan democratically elected government. How will they overcome these challenges and face the arduous task of transforming this-war torn country into a land of peace and prosperity in the 21st century?

The hunt for Osama bin Laden, the terrorist behind the September 11 attacks and the leader of the Islamist militant group al-Qaeda, ended when bin Laden was shot and killed on May 2, 2011. The death of Osama bin Laden was a blow to the stability and future of the Taliban and al-Qaeda's extremist network. After a nearly 10-year manhunt to bring him to justice for the September 11 attacks on America, bin Laden and some of his family members were killed at their compound in Pakistan roughly 100 miles from Afghanistan. The al-Qaeda leader was killed by Navy SEALs in a CIA-led operation launched from Afghanistan. Referred to under the codename "Geronimo," bin Laden had been quietly living in a compound in Abbottabad, Pakistan, for several years.[2] After the raid, U.S. forces took bin Laden's body to

Afghanistan for identification, and he was buried at sea in accordance with Muslim tradition. Several days after his death, al-Qaeda officially confirmed the death of bin Laden via militant websites. However, some groups continue to promulgate conspiracy theories that Osama bin Laden is still alive. This is due to several factors, including the lack of sufficient evidence of his death, as well as clinging to the hope their leader could not have been killed in such a feat.

In response to the death of their leader, al-Qaeda and other Pakistani militant groups vowed to avenge the killing by retaliating against the United States and other countries that also championed for his death. In tandem, other radical groups have threatened attacks against Pakistan for not preventing the operation. The death of bin Laden after multiple terrorist acts that spanned across the globe was generally welcomed by the United Nations, NATO, the European Union, and a large number of governments. In contrast, some countries condemned the actions surrounding his death. Others questioned the legal and ethical aspects of his death, as well as the evidence used to identify the body. Controversy still surrounds the lack information released to the public regarding the data collected of bin Laden and his family. However, the al-Qaeda ideology did not die with bin Laden, and much like Afghan resistance to the Soviets during the Cold War, the struggle against radical Islamist terrorism will last for years. How will Afghanistan be shaped by these recent events?

One of the challenges facing Afghanistan is the preconceived notion many have regarding the country. While the current visualizations of Afghanistan may generate images of extremely rocky and jagged mountains, arid deserts with sparse vegetation, or the hot sun beating down upon the barren soil, Afghanistan used to look very different. Though it may be difficult to visualize, at one point Afghanistan was known as one of the most beautiful and prosperous locations in the world. It is the hope of many that perhaps one day this prosperous country will return amid a balanced state of affairs. Will Afghanistan ever recover and rebuild from centuries of devastation and turmoil?

The country faces political stability challenges as well. During the Afghan presidential elections in August 2009, President Hamid Karzai was reelected as the president of Afghanistan for another four-year term. Karzai's relationship with the United States deteriorated over the years, which many believe was a result of his handling of Osama bin Laden and responding to the strain on U.S. and Afghan relations. Further, President Karzai pledged to help rebuild Afghanistan, but many argue he failed to do so during his eight years as leader of the country. For the presidential elections held in June 2014, President

Karzai served his constitutionally allotted two terms and was unable to run for a third term. Dr. Ashraf Ghani Ahmadzai was elected president of Afghanistan on September 21, 2014, replacing Karzai in office and will continue the reform work Karzai started at the end of 2001. The elections may have indicated further strain occurring internal to the country as Dr. Abdullah Abdullah, who ran against Karzai in the 2009 election, received overwhelming Pashtun support for the presidency. Dr. Abdullah was defeated by President Ghani in the 2014 elections.

The transfer of the Karzai reign to President Ghani means he will oversee a tumultuous period as the country responds to the threat of insurgents as a result of the withdrawal of NATO forces from Afghanistan by the year 2020. The removal of U.S. forces has been delayed at the request of President Ghani, requesting that U.S. President Barak Obama allow troops to remain in the country and continue support to the Afghan forces into 2017. The Taliban insurgency has been on the rise, and the capture of the northern city of Kunduz in northern Afghanistan, which occurred seamlessly in a matter of hours, has increased concern on the preparedness of the Afghan forces. The Taliban and Afghan government held informal peace talks in the summer of 2015, which will be continued at a future date.[3] The Taliban has pledged to continue their crusade as long as foreign troops still occupy Afghanistan. This has created a significant challenge for the Ghani administration, and one that will continue to be a challenge in the years to come. In September 2016, the Ghani administration signed a peace accord with the country's second-largest militant group, Hezb-e-Islami. Will this unprecedented gesture of peace and amicability carry across other militant groups in Afghanistan?

The rise of the Taliban, the death of bin Laden, and neophyte political system are only a subset of the challenges facing the country. The Afghan government's difficulty in extending applicable laws and standards across Afghanistan challenges the future economic growth of the country. In tandem, Afghanistan's living standards are among the lowest in the world. The majority of the Afghan population continues to experience health and community issues such as shortages of housing, lack of clean water, running electricity, medical care, and stable jobs. Despite the help from many foreign countries, the government of Afghanistan will need to address a number of challenges and issues in order to rebuild the economy. This includes new methods to address low revenue collection, a reduction in corruption, threat of insurgency, and how to improve the poor public infrastructure. Despite these numerous challenges to be overcome in Afghanistan, many still remain hopeful that one day Afghanistan will be seen as a land of optimism, freedom, and new beginnings.

NOTES

1. Larry Goodson, *Afghanistan's Endless War: State Failure, Regional Politics, and the Rise of the Taliban* (Seattle: The University of Washington Press, 2001), 3–4.

2. Chris Martin, *Beyond Neptune Spear: The (Open) Secret History of SEAL Team Six, Post-9/11* (Unknown: Chris Martin, 2012), Kindle Edition.

3. A. Ahmed and M. Rosenberg, "Karzai's Secret Taliban Talks Put Strain on US Relations," *The Irish Times* (Dublin), February 10, 2014.

AFGHANISTAN

Timeline of Historical Events

EARLY HISTORY

3000 B.C.E.–2000 B.C.E.	The first true urban dwellings rise in two areas of Afghanistan.
2000 B.C.E.–1500 B.C.E.	The current capital of Afghanistan, Kabul, was established as a city. Afghanistan becomes the crossroads of Asia.
550 B.C.E.–331 B.C.E.	Afghanistan subjected to rule under the Achaemenid dynasty.
500 B.C.E.	King Darius I conquers the region of Afghanistan.
331–327 B.C.E.	Alexander the Great invades and conquers the region of Afghanistan. Greek and Greco-Bactrian rule in northern Afghanistan, and Mauryan Empire rule in southern Afghanistan. The spread of Hellenistic art and culture in the northern region.
255 B.C.E.	Emperor Asoka introduces Buddhism to Afghanistan.
150 B.C.E.–300 C.E.	Five merging tribes unite under the Kushan tribe, beginning the Kushan Empire rule in Afghanistan.
224–651	Sassanian Empire of Persia rules much of Afghanistan.

400	Invasion by the Hepthalites (White Huns) that leaves Afghanistan in ruins.
570	Birth of the prophet Mohammed, the founder of the Islamic faith.

RISE OF ISLAM

642–652	The Arabs introduce Islam to Afghanistan and rename the region Khurasan.
ca. 700–961	Muslim dynasties rule Afghanistan: The Abbasids (Arab), Saffarids (Persian), and Samanids (Persian).
962–1030	Afghanistan becomes the center of Islamic power and civilization under the Ghaznavid Empire.
1186–1219	Rule of the Ghorid dynasty in Afghanistan.
1219	Genghis Khan invades and conquers Afghanistan, killing thousands and leaving Afghanistan in ruins.
1370–1506	Mongol conqueror Timor-e-Lang defeats Afghanistan and leaves the region in destruction, and begins the rule of the Timurid dynasty. Afghanistan experiences its Golden Age (Timurid Renaissance).
1451	Ghilzai Pashtuns from southeast Afghanistan found the Lodi dynasty in Delhi.
1506–1747	Babur founds the Moghul dynasty and conquers most of Afghanistan and northern India. Afghanistan is split between the Moghul and Safavid empires. Moghul Empire rules Kabul and Pashtunistan; Uzbeks of Samarkand rule Balkh; Persian Safavid dynasty rules western Afghanistan.
1722	The Afghans invade Persia and overthrow the Safavid Empire.
1736	Nadir assumes power as shah by expelling the Afghans from Persia.

MODERN AFGHANISTAN

1747	Nadir Shah is assassinated, and Ahmad Shah Abdali (assuming the name Ahmad Shah Durrani) establishes modern Afghanistan under the Sadozai Durrani dynasty.

1747–1773	Rule of Ahmad Shah Durrani, known as the "Father of Afghanistan."
1773–1793	Rule of Ahmad's son, Timur Shah Durrani. During this time the capital of Afghanistan transferred from Kandahar to Kabul due to tribal opposition.
1793–1801	Rule of Zaman Shah Durrani.
1795	Persians invade the province of Khuasan.
1801–1803	Rule of Shah Mahmood Durrani during constant internal revolts in Afghanistan.
1803–1809	Rule of Shah Shuja.
1809–1818	Shah Mahmood returns to the throne and leads a war with Persia.
1819–1826	The sons of Timur Shah fight and struggle to seize the throne during a period of Afghan civil war between the Sadozai and Barakzai clans.
1826–1839	Dost Mohammad Khan takes Kabul and establishes control over Afghanistan.
1839	British troops invade Afghanistan.
1839–1842	First Anglo-Afghan War.
1839–1842	Shah Shuja is appointed king by the British and is killed in April 1842 by the Afghans.
1843–1846	Rule of Akbar Khan.
1846–1863	The once-exiled Dost Mohammad Khan returns to occupy the throne.
1863–1868	Death of Dost Mohammad; his son Sher Ali assumes power.
1872	Russians and British establish the northern border of Afghanistan.
1878–1880	Second Anglo-Afghan War.
1880–1901	Reign of Abdur Rahman Khan.
1888	Western border with Persia is finalized.
1893	Abdur Rahman signs the Durand Line agreement with the British; divides Afghanistan from India and would be a source of strife for years known as the Pashtunian issue.
1896	Kafiristan is converted to Islam and renamed Nuristan.

TWENTIETH-CENTURY MONARCHY

1901–1919	Reign of Habibullah Khan.
1903	Afghanistan's first secondary school opens.
1904	Persian border is demarcated.
1914–1918	Afghanistan remains neutral during World War I.
1919	Third and final Anglo-Afghan War.
1919	Afghanistan declares political independence from the United Kingdom and becomes an independent state in the Treaty of Rawalpindi. August 19 is commemorated as Afghanistan's Independence Day.
1923	King Amanullah proclaims Afghanistan's first constitution.
1923	Constitution document is signed on October 31; the Afghan National Bank, Bank-i-Melli, is established.
1926	Nonaggression treaty is signed between Afghanistan and the Soviet Union.
1927	The afghani is introduced as the first uniform currency.
1929	Civil War in Afghanistan; Habibullah rules for nine months.
1931	Nadir Shah signs the new constitution of Afghanistan
1933–1973	Reign of King Mohammad Zahir.
1934	Afghanistan joins the League of Nations and establishes diplomatic relations with the United States.
1940	Afghanistan declares neutrality in World War II.
1946	Afghanistan is admitted to the United Nations; Shah Mahmoud replaces Mohammad Haskim Khan as prime minister and introduces a series of liberal reforms; opposition newspapers, political groups, and student organizations form and demand additional reforms; brief liberal era ends in 1952.
1953–1963	Mohammed Daoud Khan replaces Shah Mamoud as prime minister; under Daoud the educational system, women's rights, and the economy

	improve; tensions escalate over the border dispute with Pakistan from the Durrand Line in 1893.
1954–1955	A series of trade, development, and military agreements are signed with the Soviet Union; more assistance is received from the United States.
1959	Becomes optional for women to wear the burqa, also known as the Chadari in Central Asia, a head-to-toe enveloping outer garment.
1963	Prime Minister Daoud resigns and is replaced by Mohammad Yousaf.
1964	The new constitution establishes a constitutional monarchy with a bicameral legislature.
1965	Following student protests, Yousaf is replaced as prime minister by Mohammad Hasim Maiwandwal, leader of the Progressive Democratic Party; Nur Muhammad Taraki founds the People's Democratic Party of Afghanistan (PDPA); women are allowed to vote for the first time in the national elections.
1967	Nur Ahmend Etemadi becomes prime minister.
1972	Musa Sahfiq becomes prime minister.

REVOLUTION AND THE SOVIET INVASION

1973	King Zahir Shah is overthrown and forced into exile, and the new ruler, Prime Minister Mohammed Daoud, declares Afghanistan a republic.
1977	Prime minister Daoud advocates for the new constitution and establishes a one-party state.
1978	Saur Revolution occurs, and Prime Minister Daoud is killed in a coup by communists, who then establish the Democratic Republic of Afghanistan; Nur Muhammad Taraki becomes the head of state; the new Treaty of Friendship and Cooperation is signed with the Soviet Union.
1979	President Taraki is assassinated by Hafizullah Amin; military invasion begins on December 24 by the Soviet Union, and the start of the Soviet Afghan War that would continue for 10 years; Babrak Karmal is appointed president.

1985	The Islamic Union of Afghan Mujahideen (IUAM) forms to fight the Soviet occupation; Mikhail Gorbachev comes to power in the Soviet Union.
1986	Gorbachev withdraws 8,000 troops from Afghanistan; Babrak Karmal steps down as president and is replaced by Mohammad Najibullah.
1988	The Soviet Union and Afghanistan sign the Geneva Accords; in August Osama bin Laden founded al-Qaeda in Peshawar, Pakistan, due to the Soviet War in Afghanistan.
1989	Soviet forces withdraw from Afghanistan; the interim Afghan government is created by Afghan exiles in Pakistan.

MUJAHIDEEN RULE

1992	Collapse of the communist regime by Mujahideen forces, who overtake Kabul; President Najibullah steps down; Islamic Republic of Afghanistan is established with an interim mujahideen government led by Burhanuddin Rabbani.
1992–1994	Afghanistan is fought over and ruled by competing local warlords.
1994	The Islamic group known as the Taliban establishes a campaign to overthrow Afghanistan, and captures the southern city of Kandahar with assistance from Pakistan.
1995	The Taliban seize control of Herat; Warlord Ahmad Shad Massoud wins control of Kabul.

TALIBAN

1996	The Taliban assassinate former president Najibullah, seize Kabul, and take control over most of the country.
1998	United States attacks al-Qaeda training camps in Afghanistan.
August 7, 1998	The U.S. embassy in Nairobi and the embassy in Dar es Salaam are bombed by al-Qaeda, as one of a series of U.S. embassy bombings; over

200 civilians were killed; the date marked the eighth anniversary of the arrival of American forces in Saudi Arabia; these acts resulted in the Federal Bureau of Investigation (FBI) placing Osama bin Laden on the Ten Most Wanted Fugitives list.

October 12, 2000   USS *Cole* suicide bombing while docked for refueling in Yemen; the event was the deadliest attack against a U.S. naval vessel since 1987; al-Qaeda claimed responsibility for the attack.

March 2001   Taliban fighters destroy the Buddhas of Bamiyan, two sixth-century monumental statues of standing Buddha carved into the side of the rockcliff in Bamyan valley. Mullah Mohammad Omar ordered the statues to be destroyed after saying they were false idols.

September 11, 2001   The World Trade Center in New York and the Pentagon in Washington, D.C., are attacked by airplanes hijacked by terrorists.

October 7, 2001   The United States and the United Kingdom begin an aerial bombing of Afghanistan under Operation Enduring Freedom and bomb terrorist training camps of al-Qaeda and the Taliban; shortly thereafter the Taliban is removed from power.

POST-TALIBAN ERA

December 22, 2001   Hamid Karzai is named as chairman of the interim government in Afghanistan.

June 2002   *Loya jirga* chooses Hamid Karzai as interim president of the Afghan Transitional Administration in Kabul.

January 4, 2004   *Loya jirga* participants adopt the Afghan Constitution and establish a presidential form of government with important powers reserved for the National Assembly; Afghanistan is declared an Islamic republic.

October 9, 2004   First Afghan presidential election in which more than 8.1 million Afghans participate and elect Hamid Karzai as president of the Islamic Republic of Afghanistan.

December 7, 2004	The inauguration of Hamid Karzai as the first democratically elected president of Afghanistan.
March 2006	President George Bush and the First Lady visit Afghanistan to inaugurate the renovated U.S. embassy in Kabul.
2006	More than four million refugees return from Pakistan and Iran after years in exile from the Taliban.
July 2006	NATO takes control of military operations in the south previously led by U.S. coalition forces.
May 13, 2007	Skirmishes begin with Pakistan.
2007	Mohammad Zadir Shah dies in Kabul.
February 2009	U.S. president Barack Obama orders 17,000 troops to Afghanistan.
August 2009	President Karzai is reelected.
December 2009	U.S. president Barack Obama triples troop strength in Afghanistan, bringing the total of American troops to about 100,000.
May 2010	Untapped mineral deposits of worth nearly $1 trillion are discovered in Afghanistan.
2011	Afghanistan National Front is created by Tajik leader Ahmad Zia Massoud, Hazara leader Mohammad Mohaqiq, and Uzbek leader Abdul Rashid Dostum.
January 2011	President Karzai makes the first presidential official visit to Russia since the end of the Soviet occupation in December 1989.
May 2, 2011	Osama bin Laden is killed in Pakistan.
July 2011	President Karzai's half-brother and governor of the Kandahar Province, Ahmad Wali Karzai, is killed in the Taliban's campaign against prominent Afghan leaders.
September 20, 2011	Assassination of Burhanuddin Rabbani, the former temporary president of Afghanistan and leader of the Islamic Society of Afghanistan.
October 2011	Afghanistan and India sign a cooperation agreement for security and protection after relations with Pakistan deteriorate over several attacks.
November 2011	President Karzai negotiates a 10-year military partnership with the United States which allows

	troops to remain after 2014, after foreign troops are planned to leave Afghanistan.
December 2011	Attacks occur at a Shia shrine in Kabul and a Shia mosque in Maza-i-Sharif in which almost 60 people are killed; after Pakistani soldiers are killed on the Afghan border, Pakistan boycotts the Bonn Conference in Afghanistan.
January 2012	Taliban agree to peace talks with President Karzai and the U.S. government.
February 2012	Protestors and soldiers are killed in response to the burning of the Qu'ran after U.S. officials believed Taliban prisoners were using the Qu'ran to pass secret messages back and forth.
May 2012	NATO plans to withdraw troops by late 2014 and turns control over to Afghan forces.
July 2012	The United States, Japan, Germany, and the UK jointly pledge $16 billion in civilian aid for Afghanistan.
June 2013	The Afghan army assumes control over security forces in Afghanistan from NATO.
January 2014	Taliban suicide bombing kills 13 foreign citizens in Kabul and has been the worst attack since 2001.
February 2014	Beginning of the Afghan presidential campaign; increasingly more attacks from the Taliban.
April 5, 2014	Presidential elections in Afghanistan are inconclusive; new election would occur between Abdullah Abdullah and Ashraf Ghani.
May 16, 2014	The remaining two candidates for President of Afghanistan, Abdullah Abdullah and Ashraf Ghani, admit they did not win sufficient number of ballots to claim presidential victory and new vote would take place in June.
May 31, 2014	Sgt. Bowe Bergdahl, the only U.S. soldier held captive by the Taliban, is freed in Afghanistan in exchange with prisoners held by the United States at Guantanamo Bay, Cuba.
June 14, 2014	Presidential elections are held between candidates Abdullah Abdullah and Ashraf Ghani. Due to a recount, the final results are delayed until September.

September 2014	Afghan Independent Election Commission determines the June election winner is Ashraf Ghani Ahmadzai.
September 29, 2014	Ashraf Ghani Ahmadzai assumes office as president of Afghanistan; it is the first time in the history of the country there is a democratically elected transfer of power.
October 2014	The United States and Great Britain remove combat forces from Afghanistan.
November 2014	Record-setting poppy cultivation totals result in the highest totals of opium production in the country.
December 2014	After years of planning, NATO officially ends a 13-year occupancy in Afghanistan. The country regains control of its security posture amid chaos and bloodiest totals since the NATO occupation.
January 2015	NATO begins training and transition support of Afghan security forces under mission "Resolute Support."
March 2015	President Ashraf Ghani requests extension of timeline for U.S. troop removal from Afghanistan.
May 2015	Representatives from the Taliban hold peace talks with Afghan officials in Qatar. Though the talks were not official, both sides agreed to continue the peace talks at a later date, in which Taliban representatives say they will continue to fight until all foreign occupation has ended and U.S. troops are withdrawn.
July 2015	Taliban forces continue to overtake territories across northern Afghanistan.
August 1, 2015	After Taliban forces acknowledge the death of former leader Mullah Mohammad Omar in 2013, the group announces that Taliban deputy Mullah Akhtar Muhammad Mansour is now the supreme leader of the Taliban.
September 2015	Taliban forces capture the city of Kunduz, with the attack lasting only a matter of hours. It is the most significant display of their power since 2001.
October 2015	Fall of Kunduz has many questioning the readiness of Afghan forces and the timeline for American withdrawal of troops.

July 2016
President Barack Obama pledges to leave 8,400 troops in Afghanistan until December 2016.

September 2016
Afghan leadership signs an unprecedented peace accord with Hezb-e-Islami, Afghanistan's second-largest militant group led by Gulbuddin Hekmatyar. Included in the peace agreement is a stipulation to grant Hekmatyar immunity from his involvement in warlord activities in return for his acceptance of the Afghan constitution and pledge to abandon all efforts of violence.

1

The Three Pillars of Afghanistan: Geography, People, and Islam

There are three main factors in the history of Afghanistan that have shaped the present-day environment, outlook, and political stance of the country. These factors are the backbone of the country and are the geographical characteristics, the diverse ethnic and tribal values of the Afghan culture, and a nearly 1,500 year-old belief in Islam. Any basic introduction to the country should include a brief insight into these three main facets, which provides greater insight into the convictions, culture, and beliefs of the Afghan people. The geographical terrain has allowed Afghanistan to remain at the forefront of political power and influence due to the country's location in the midst of several crucial trade routes between Asia and the Middle East. While this aspect has tempted many ancient rulers to seek control of Afghanistan and the remunerative Silk Route to China, the geography has also served as a paradox of enticement due to the harsh Hindu Kush Mountain ranges which geographically divide the country. This difficult terrain is one of the reasons why Afghanistan has been invaded and conquered for centuries without any enduring grip of control. Because of this continuous invasion by divergent ethnic groups which have each separately left a distinct mark on the country and its inhabitants, the geography has in effect influenced Afghanistan's people. As a result of the constant introduction of new cultures, the population is comprised of a multitude of varying civilizations due to this constant ebb and flow of foreign advancement and defeat in Afghanistan. This proclivity for invasion has not only resulted in the diverse ethnic culture which exists today in Afghanistan, but it has also molded the current emotional standpoint and hardened mental attitude of many Afghanis against foreign control and policy in the country. Lastly, the overwhelming influence of Islam is a core mind-set, and the belief in the Qu'ran is at the heart of nearly every Afghan citizen. Every Afghani is shaped and guided by Islam in emotional, spiritual, and moral ways. This religious pillar is observed in nearly every facet of daily life and interpersonal relationships. Working collectively as a complete system, the geographical terrain, ethnicity and tribal values, and the belief in Islam are the major historical forces that have significantly influenced Afghanistan for centuries. These fundamental aspects are crucial to understanding the present-day temperament, beliefs, and values of Afghan society.

GEOGRAPHY

Afghanistan is an entirely landlocked country located in southern Asia. Afghanistan is physically located to the east of Iran and both north and west of Pakistan. Other countries comprising the border of Afghanistan include Turkmenistan, Uzbekistan, and Tajikistan. On the eastern side of the country, Afghanistan also shares a small section of the border with China. Afghanistan is slightly smaller than the state of Texas and has a total land area of 252,072 square miles (652,864 sq. km). Historically, Afghanistan has thrived both culturally and economically because of its geographical location along the Silk Road, an early source of revenue for merchants between China and India. The Silk Road was a 4,000-mile stretch of trade routes so named due to the luxurious Chinese silk that was often carried along the main routes of the Silk Road for trade and barter. Even without access to a seaport, the country is perfectly nestled along the crucial trade routes between East Asia, South Asia, and the Middle East.

While gaining control of these lucrative trade routes has been a key reason for foreign conquest in Afghanistan, the harsh geographical terrain has been a hindrance to those vying to overtake the country.

The inability of foreigners to handle this terrain has been celebrated by the Afghan inhabitants. As such, this difficult environment is seen as a natural way to protect the country from foreign control. On the crossover from the 19th and into the 20th centuries, this period of time is commonly referred to as *The Great Game,* describing a time when the British and Russians jockeyed for control of Afghanistan. Ironically, neither country was able to fully gain control over Afghanistan. This inability for a foreign power to have lasting control in the country is not the first time, as many other rulers also were unsuccessful in trying to dominate an unyielding population living in the unforgiving terrain. The inability to overcome these geographical challenges, including navigating the Hindu Kush Mountains, has been a critical protection factor that Afghans celebrate. The topography of Afghanistan is divided primarily into three regions, from the pastoral farmland in the north, the central highlands in the middle region of Afghanistan (which include the majority of the Hindu Kush Mountains), and the mostly barren and wind-swept desert of the southern plateau.

The far northern terrain is the country's main agricultural region and is composed mostly of fertile grassy plains, cultivated fields, and rolling hills. The Northern Plains is a highly populated agricultural area where farmers cultivate such agricultural products as wheat, rice, and cotton. Shepherds and pastoral herders raise livestock such as sheep and goats in the grassy regions. This northeastern area of Afghanistan stretches approximately 40,000 square miles from the central highlands to the Iranian and Tajikistan border. Yet this fertile area still requires an adequate water source to allow for optimum cultivation and crop harvest since annual rainfall is scarce. Due to this shortfall, this lush farm region comprises only about 12 percent of the total land area in the entire country. Not only has drought taken a toll on the once-fertile soil, but landmines, remnants of the Soviet occupation, are still scattered throughout the region. Afghanistan has served as the battleground for many wars, and these landmines are a token of war from the decade-long conflict of the Soviet invasion which began in 1979. These impeding factors make farming increasingly difficult for the Afghans toiling to make a living off the terrain. Additionally, cropland once used for wheat is now primarily used for poppy cultivation, since harvesting wheat, rice, and corn does not compare to the profits received from the lucrative drug smuggling business. Due to these factors, Afghanistan largely relies on importing products, and traditionally the import totals have routinely exceeded the amount of the country's exports.

Translated as "Hindu killer," the treacherous Hindu Kush Mountains are the main mountain ranges of Afghanistan. (Dennis5514/Dreamstime.com)

The second region, known as the central highlands, encompasses the majority of Afghanistan and covers an area of approximately 160,000 square miles. As part of this region, and by far the most prominent geographical feature in Afghanistan, are the large mountain ranges that are part of the Himalayan Mountains. These long mountain series cover nearly two-thirds of the country and stretch from China into central Afghanistan. A section of this famously rough and rugged landscape is referred to as the Hindu Kush Mountains, which geographically almost separates Afghanistan into two distinct regions. This extremely jagged and legendary mountain range is just one of several mountain chains in Afghanistan. The literal translation of the name "Hindu Kush" is a true reflection of its forbidding topography, as this difficult and jagged section of Afghanistan translates to "Killer of Hindus." The Hindu Kush range is approximately 230 square miles (600 kilometers) in length, and stretches from Kabul westward. Other prominent ranges include the northwestward Turkestan Mountains, the Siah Kuh range, the northern-reaching Hesar Mountains, and the southwestern-reaching ranges of the Malmand and Khakbad Mountains. The Wakhan Corridor is an extremely narrow piece of land in the north-eastern Badakhshan region of Afghanistan, located between Tajikistan and Pakistan and geographically extends outward as a result of the British demarcation of the country's borders. This small section of land in the Pamir mountain region stretches out like a tentacle from the country toward China. The Wakhan Corridor was established at the end of the 19th century by the British Empire. The corridor was designated to be used as a buffer area against Russia's desire for expansion into India during "The Great Game," a time when both Russia and Britain vied for control of Afghanistan with neither achieving success. At the far eastern end of the corridor, the Wakjir is a narrow passageway through the Hindu Kush. This corridor, which is closed for five months of the year due to the severe climate, is often theorized as a frequent location for drug smuggling from Afghanistan into China. The majority of the central highlands experience desert-steppe types of soil, but snowfall is a typical weather condition in the mountains. Further, erosion is apparent in the mountainous areas that are affected by monsoons and heavy precipitation. As a natural result of the earth's shifting tectonic plates that form these mountain ranges, this area is prone to large-scale magnitude earthquakes. Yet even with this treacherous and unstable terrain, the deep valleys and high mountains have played a vital role in the struggle for control of Afghanistan, with this region serving as an important and natural way to defend the country.

The third region is a dry and arid desert plateau that comprises the southwestern area of Afghanistan, close to Pakistan and Iran. This predominately infertile desert is referred to as the southern plateau and comprises nearly 50,000 square miles. Several rivers cross the southern plateau, which allows for some fertile soil to thrive near the river's rich alluvial deposits. An important geographical feature in this region is the Helmand River, the largest river in Afghanistan. The Helmand River begins in the Hindu Kush Mountains, runs through the southern desert region, and ends along the border with Iran. The Helmand is the principal river in the southwest region, and being only 715 miles in length, the river serves as an imperative function for the country. The river and its tributaries operate as a major drainage source for more than 100,000 square miles of Afghanistan. Likewise in the north, the Amu Darya River forms the northern border between Tajikistan and Uzbekistan and also provides water and drainage for the northern plains.

Largest Cities

Afghanistan is governmentally divided among 34 provinces, referred to as *velayat*, and these provinces are more commonly recognized as administrative divisions. The major cities in Afghanistan

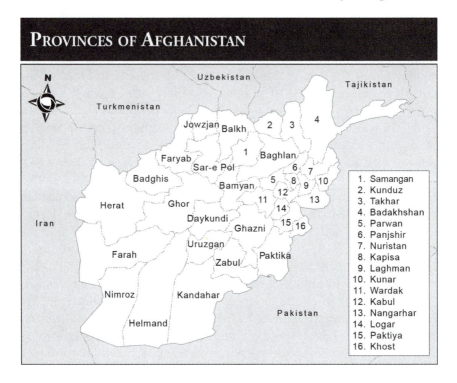

PROVINCES OF AFGHANISTAN

1. Samangan
2. Kunduz
3. Takhar
4. Badakhshan
5. Parwan
6. Panjshir
7. Nuristan
8. Kapisa
9. Laghman
10. Kunar
11. Wardak
12. Kabul
13. Nangarhar
14. Logar
15. Paktiya
16. Khost

include Kabul, Kandahar, Herat, Mazari Sharif (or Mazar-e-sharif), and Ghazni, as well as other populous cities such as Baglan, Jalalabad, Kondoz, and Charikar. Kabul, with a population of nearly three million people, is the largest and most populated city in Afghanistan.[1] Kabul is a central city of economic importance to Afghanistan, and the city's origins date back to more than 3,000 years ago. The city is tactically located between the Asmai and Sherdawaza Mountain ranges of the Hindu Kush and is also strategically positioned alongside the Kabul River. For as long as there have been wars in Afghanistan, civilizations have fought to gain control of Kabul due to its strategic location along the trade routes to Central Asia. Kabul has often served as the capital for many conquering empires and most notably was made the capital of the Mughal dynasty by Babur in the early 16th century. In 1738, the Iranian conquer Nadir Shah captured the city and overthrew the Mughal Empire. When Nadir Shah was assassinated in 1747, Ahmad Shah Durrani assumed the throne and continued to expand the country's borders, and through his actions he is credited in history as the father of Afghanistan. However, it was in 1776 when Ahmad Shah's son, Timur Shah Durrani, inherited the throne and moved the center of Afghanistan from Kandahar to establish Kabul as the official capital. Today, Kabul has an established business center and experiences continued urban development. In an effort to rebuild the struggling economy, President Hamid Karzai supported an effort to open a US$25 million dollar Coca-Cola bottling plant in Kabul in September 2006. In addition to President Karzai's efforts to increase local and foreign investments in Afghanistan, the government is working toward building an economy that is independent of Afghanistan's illegal drug trade. The Coca-Cola bottling plant was part of President Karzai and the Afghan governments' plan to rebuild the economy, and was also a symbolic gesture to show the government is making strides toward economic growth.

Kandahar is the second-largest city in Afghanistan and is also the capital of Kandahar Province. Located in the south-central region of Afghanistan, Kandahar is just over 200 miles from Pakistan. Kandahar is considered to be one of the wealthiest provinces in Afghanistan and is a major trade center for livestock, silk, and fruit from the region. As part of the historical origins of the city, researchers speculate it is possible this area was established as a farming village approximately 7,000 years ago. The area gained importance when Alexander the Great invaded the region in 330 B.C.E. and established the city of Kandahar. Much like Kabul, Kandahar was also fought over by conquering empires due to the city's imperative strategic location along the trade routes to Central Asia. Kandahar served as the capital of Afghanistan under Ahmad Shah Durrani in 1747, but 30 years later the capital was moved to Kabul. In an effort to return to original Islamic roots, Kandahar was the center of operations and the spiritual capital of the Taliban.

Often referred to as the "pearl of Afghanistan," Herat is widely known for art and culture and was established 2,000 years ago under the Persian Empire. Located in western Afghanistan, Herat, with a population of nearly 450,000, is the third-largest city in Afghanistan. The origin and exact dates of the city remain largely unknown. In ancient times this region was referred to as Aria, and was situated strategically along the Central Asian trade routes. As a city, Aria was invaded and conquered countless times throughout history by invading empires. Alexander the Great recognized the strategic importance of this area and erected a large citadel in Aria in the fourth century B.C.E., rebranding the Greek city and naming it Alexandria Arion. The citadel would be destroyed and rebuilt upon throughout future invasions, but Alexander's original foundation still remains standing in Afghanistan. The structure even remained standing after Afghanistan was invaded by one of the most feared conquerors of all time. Implementing widespread fear throughout Afghanistan and neighboring countries, the Mongolian emperor Genghis Khan famously destroyed this region in the early 13th century. Genghis Khan began annihilating the country after one of his sons was held captive and murdered by native rebels. After Genghis Khan slaughtered all the residents and razed the city, the rebuilt sections were destroyed 100 years later by the founder of the Timur dynasty, Tamerlane. After this dual destruction, it would be several centuries before Herat could be reconstructed. Once Herat was rebuilt during the 15th and 16th centuries, it was known as the center for Persian art and architecture.[2] During the Afghan civil war, the city was part of annexation in 1824 and was ruled under one of three independent regions of Afghanistan. However, in 1863 the city was reinstated as part of the country of Afghanistan.

Mazari Sharif is the largest northern city and the fourth-largest populated city in Afghanistan. The literal translation of the city means *holy grave*, and it is known throughout the Islamic world as the site of the Blue Mosque, claimed to be tomb of Hazrat Ali, fourth caliph (religious leader) of Islam and the son-in-law of the prophet Mohammed. The mosque is roughly rectangular in shape, and the center tomb chamber of Ali is one of Afghanistan's greatest treasures with thousands of visitors each year. The Blue Mosque also contains the tombs of various Afghan rulers and religious leaders through the centuries. The city is home to members of the Uzbek tribe, as well as Hazara and Turkmen. The economy of Mazari Sharif depends largely on cotton, silk, melon, and rugs.

Ghazni is the last of the five largest cities in Afghanistan with a population of about 150,000, based on estimates from 2013. Known as Ghazna in ancient times, the city was conquered by the Achaemenid king Cyrus II in the sixth century B.C.E. Located in the central eastern section of the country, the city was a vital part of any empire due to its location between Kabul and Kandahar as a major trade route. Ghazna was the capital of the Ghaznavid Empire in the tenth century, and was another one of Afghanistan's cities razed by the Mongols under Genghis Khan. The city was again destroyed during the Great Game, and also by the Soviet occupation. In 2001 after the collapse of the Taliban, the U.S. forces built a large military base and, in conjunction with the Afghan government, have been trying to rebuild the city and protecting the inhabitants from the Taliban insurgence. Largely a pastoral city now, the primary source of income includes embroidered sheepskin clothing, as well as sheep, wool, and corn.

Natural Environment

Afghanistan has an abundance of natural resources, including natural gas, petroleum, coal, sulfur, and both precious and semiprecious stones. In addition, mineral resources are in great quantity and include chrome, copper, gold, iron, lead, salt, and silver. The northern region is extremely fertile and contains a large amount of the country's minerals and natural gas deposits. The largest export is salt, with nearly 40,000 tons of salt being mined each year.

A land of stark contrasts, Afghanistan experiences extremely cold winters in the northern mountains and endures incredibly hot summer temperatures in the southwestern desert. The dry and arid time of the year is primarily June to September, but even during these hot days, the nights can become very cold. The mountain ranges also face temperature contrasts, as the northern mountain ranges experience frigid artic weather conditions, yet the eastern mountain ranges experience the sultry outcome of neighboring regions. These eastern mountains close to the Pakistan border endure the aftereffects of the Indian monsoons and experience more rainfall and stronger winds than other sections of the country. In these mountainous areas, the climate reaches tropical temperatures, which often includes humidity and windy rains. As a result of this humid climate, the vegetation and plant life is extremely lush and fruitful. In complete opposite, the land of the southwestern desert region is extremely dry and barren, and strong winds contribute to frequent sandstorms. As such, vegetation and plant life is present but only as desolate freckles on the face of this sandy desert. Not surprisingly, annual rainfall is scarce in Afghanistan, with region totals varying from approximately 3 inches in the barren city of Farah to up to 50 inches per year in the mountains. Records show the greatest extent of precipitation recorded is 53 inches of rain in the Salang Pass of the Hindu Kush. The capital city of Kabul, located in the mid-eastern region, experiences relatively normal temperatures, but the climate of Afghanistan is not one of human luxury. In this regard, the climate extremes and the rough terrain further Afghanistan's paradox as a land of desolate differences.

PEOPLE

The most recent figures as of 2016 indicate the population of Afghanistan is projected to be approximately 33 million, with males comprising 52 percent of the population. These figures are rough estimates, as an official census has not been held for over 20 years in Afghanistan.[3]

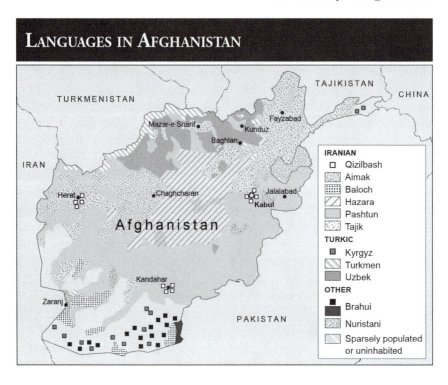

LANGUAGES IN AFGHANISTAN

The people of Afghanistan are comprised of a variety of ethnic groups, a result of the varied cultural generations of the invaders who conquered and populated this land. Of these ethnic groups, the Pashtuns comprise nearly half of the population, and live in the southern and eastern regions of Afghanistan. The other three large ethnic groups are the Tajiks, Hazaras, Uzbeks, and minor ethnic groups comprise the Aimak, Turkmen, and Baloch. These ethnic groups are distinctly unique in their different cultural characteristics, such as family beliefs and languages. Afghanistan has two official languages, Dari (Afghan Persian) and Pashtu. The Pashtuns speak the Afghanistan's principal language of Pashtu, while the Hazaras speak Dari (Persian). Recent U.S. government estimates show that Dari is the predominant language among 50 percent of the population, and roughly 35 percent of the population speaks Pashtu (Pashto). However, it is estimated that as many as 40 different languages are spoken in the country. These include the languages of the ethnic groups in Afghanistan, and include Turkic languages among the Uzbek and Turkmen groups. Other language derivatives include those spoken by the Baluchi, Pashai, and Nuristani people.

The three ethnic regions of Afghanistan are the northern plains, the central highlands, and the southern plains; however, these segments can be further divided into general ethnic sections. The northern region, as divided by the Hindu Kush Mountains, may be separated into two ethic regions. These include the eastern region of the Badakhshan-Vakhan and the western region of the Balkh-Meymaneh. The Tajiks predominantly populate the plateaus and mountains of the eastern region, and these tribal members work as farmers, craftsmen, and artisans. The Uzbeks and the Turkmen inhabit the plains of the western section, and work mostly as farmers and herders in this highly fertile region.

The southern region of the Hindu Kush can further be divided into four regions, named for the principal cities of Kabul, Kandahar, Herat, and Hazarajat. The Kabul region is located in the eastern section of the Hindu Kush, and is the native soil of the Pashtun tribe, which includes both sedentary and nomadic sects. The Tajiks and the Nuristani also are indigenous to the Kabul region. The second region of the southern land of Afghanistan is the Kandahar region, which is populated by the Durrani Pashtun tribes. These tribes live around the city of Kandahar itself, and are most noted for creating the central point of Afghanistan's social and political elite.[4] Additional inhabitants of the Kandahar region include the Balochi and Brahui peoples. The Herat region is the third subdivision and is populated by a combination of Tajiks, Pashtun, and Chahar Aimak peoples. These ethnic groups chiefly reside in the western region of Afghanistan. The fourth section, known as Hazarajat, is a mountainous region in the central highlands of Afghanistan, and the Hazara ethnic group predominantly populates this area. However, due to the scarceness of inhabitable territory, difficulty in communications, and the treacherous mountain terrain, many of the Hazara have moved to other more inhabitable locations. Afghanistan has one of the most poverty-stricken and poorest populations in the world, with the majority of the people living on less than 200 afghanis a day, or approximately the U.S. currency of $2. The afghani is the form of currency used in the country.

The recent civil war in the 1990s, which occurred after the Soviet invasion and the consequential political instability that followed, delayed the much-needed rebuilding of the country and restructuring of the economy. Children as well as adults face starvation and little to no medical care, and as a result, Afghanistan continues to have the highest infant mortality rate in the world.[5] Many sections of the country lack running water and access to medical treatment or education centers. In addition to these often-dismal conditions, young orphans struggle for survival and beg for food and clothes on the streets. Furthermore, due to the overwhelming landmines that litter the land, which exist as a malevolent remnant from constant warfare, many children and adults have lost limbs by uncovering some of the estimated 10 million landmines that remain buried in Afghanistan. During the war with the Soviets, the Russian government and the Communist Party in Afghanistan planted an estimated 30 million landmines throughout Afghanistan. To this day, the majority of these mines remain unmarked and active.[6] As an even further injustice, oftentimes those wounded are unable to receive the proper medical care due to lacking medical facilities.

Government Structure

Until the middle of the 20th century, the people of Afghanistan lived under the absolute power of the king. After enduring three Anglo-Afghan wars, Afghanistan won its independence from British control on August 19, 1919, which is commemorated as Afghan Independence Day. The Constitutions of 1923 and 1931 upheld the previous rule by monarchy; however, the Constitution of 1964 established the new government as a constitutional monarchy with an elected parliament. This differed from the previous rule of an absolute monarch, and the new structure was similar to the U.S. government and included the legislative, the executive, and the judicial branch. This democratic rule was ended by a military coup in 1973, which abolished the 1964 Constitution and established the government as the Republic of Afghanistan. However, political coups and transformations would continue throughout the following decades, including through the period of the Russian invasion and also the Taliban seizure of the Islamic State of Afghanistan, which upon doing so in 1996, the Taliban renamed the country the Islamic Emirate of Afghanistan. The Taliban regime crumbled under the coalition led by the United States after the September 11 attacks. Through another episode of political turmoil, the country was returned to a democratic state. In December 2001, political leaders gathered in Germany to agree on new leadership structures in Afghanistan. Under the Bonn Agreement signed on December 5, 2001, these nations formed an interim administration and named Hamid Karzai the chairman of a 29-member governing committee. Karzai was sworn in as leader on December 22, and in the *loya jirga* (grand assembly) on June 13, 2002, Karzai was appointed as interim president of the Afghan Transitional Administration. Afghanistan's recent political and democratic structure has been one of disorder, but has shown some stabilization under the new and current Islamic republic government, which notably arose after the defeat of the Taliban in November 2001. The first democratically held elections occurred in October 2004, and the people elected the country's current president, Hamid Karzai. The national assembly elections were held in 2005, and the assembly was inaugurated in December 2005. President Karzai was reelected in 2009 to serve another four-year term, his last as outlined under the Afghan Constitution. In 2014, newly elected president Ashraf Ghani assumed control under the country's first democratic transition of power. As it began under President Karzai, the newly elected president Ghani and the Afghani government hope that stability and optimism will return to the Afghani people.

While some progress was made during the Karzai administration from 2001 to 2014 to bring stability to the country, Afghanistan still has great strides to make in order to become a truly stable nation. The region has been ravaged, plundered, and devastated for centuries by social unrest and civil warfare. As the country progresses toward rebuilding its infrastructure, the Afghani people still face many challenges and threats. These hardened people placed their hopes in President Karzai and the new Islamic republic of Afghanistan to lead them to new beginnings. After the contested 2014 elections, which despite widespread corruption ultimately resulted in Ghani's election, threats from the Taliban insurgence continue to challenge the new Afghan government. The world remains hopeful with Afghanistan that the country will finally be able to achieve stability. With such a diverse ethnic backbone, challenges remain unresolved which would allow country to be solidified and seen as a fundamental country in the world. Afghanistan will one day be seen as a country of progress, but in order to do so, great strides must be made to allow for healing and restoration.

Economy

From an economical perspective, Afghanistan is considered to be one of the poorest and least developed countries in the world. Categorized as a Third World country, Afghanistan's economic status ranks as one of the lowest worldwide as the economy continues to recover from decades of conflict. However, the economy has improved significantly since the fall of the Taliban regime in 2001. This is largely due to the infusion of international assistance, as more companies are willing to invest in the country since the Taliban is no longer in control. Further, the recovery of the agricultural sector as Afghanistan continues to eradicate the growing of opium has helped the economy somewhat, though revenue from opium and heroin continues to thrive. Despite the financial and economic progress over the last few years, Afghanistan remains a landlocked nation that is highly dependent on foreign aid. Afghanistan's growth rate slowed markedly in 2013, and has continued to decline in the last few years.

Since Afghanistan is a landlocked country without direct access to seaports, the country must rely on economic partnerships with such countries as Pakistan, the United States, and India for imports and exports.[7] This crippling of the country's financial market clearly began with the Soviet invasion in 1979, and continued under the Soviet's 10-year occupational struggle for the control of Afghanistan. During this fierce rivalry and incursion, Afghanistan's economy was severely devastated, and the successive economic impacts of the Taliban and mujahideen governments forced the economy into a rigid state of collapse. The severe turmoil which has occurred over the past 35 years has not been particularly beneficial for Afghanistan's economy. The economy still has yet to recover fully from years of devastation and disintegration from the Soviet occupation.

Yet for many countries, Afghanistan is regarded as the key to social and economic developments, stability, and growth for this region of the world. Surrounding countries such as China, Pakistan, Iran, and Russia look toward Afghanistan for future economic developments, as these countries have all at one point played a guiding role in the trade and political structure of Afghanistan.[8] Other countries interested in the political, economic, and social developments of Afghanistan include India, Uzbekistan, Tajikistan, Saudi Arabia, and Turkey. As a further impediment, chemical weapons used during the Afghan war with the Soviets caused severe damage to the country's environment and ecosystem.[9] The drought from 1998 to 2001 further hindered the struggling economy and added to the nation's rapidly expanding problems. Yet since the fall of the Taliban in December 2001, the economy of Afghanistan has improved. However, this financial growth is not advancing quickly enough, and regrettably any economic progress for the country is slow moving.[10]

Opium Cultivation

For decades, the country's largest revenue source was a result of illegal drug smuggling, most notably from opium, as the country's source of opium ranks the highest in the world. During the 1980s,

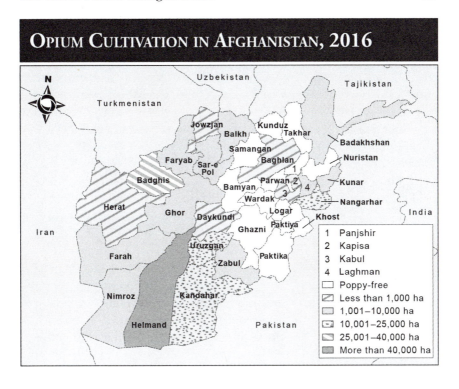

OPIUM CULTIVATION IN AFGHANISTAN, 2016

opium was the country's most valuable crop, and it was estimated that over 80 percent of the world's opium came from Afghanistan. The two areas of Jalalabad and Helmand are acknowledged regions for opium production, and it is estimated Helmand supplies one-fourth of the world's opium.[11] Afghanistan continues to remain the worlds' leading opiate producer, and the high drug sales indicate the opium poppy is undoubtedly Afghanistan's most profitable crop. Opium is harvested from the poppies grown in the fertile northern mountain region. During the 1990s, the profitable market for producing and smuggling illegal drugs was more alluring than the traditional pastoral efforts. For the one-eighth of land in Afghanistan which once grew such crops as wheat, corn, and rice, the farmers now cultivate the soil with poppies for opium and heroin production. Ironically, the Taliban regime was largely successful in eliminating these illegal substances being grown by farmers, who received little profit from the sale of poppy cultivation. After the Taliban's collapse, the provisional government continued to eliminate the illegal drug trade that was mostly continued through the large opium reserves in the country. Corruption and bribery still allow the trade to continue.

The Taliban and other antigovernment groups continue to partici-pate in and profit from the opiate trade, which is a key source of rev-enue for the Taliban inside Afghanistan. Since the fall of the Taliban in 2001, opium production continued to rise steadily as the country's most valuable crop. Between 2002 and 2003, the sale of opium-related narcotics doubled, with 3,600 tons of opium cultivated in Afghanistan in 2003. By 2008, these numbers again doubled to almost 8,000 tons a year. In addition to these substantial crop yields, over half-a-million farmers are estimated to support this profession. While the poppy cultivation somewhat decreased in 2013, with estimates declining to 5,600 tons per year, record-breaking opium totals were reported in November 2016. These numbers indicate the continued reliance on this resource, and may also indicate a major potential funding source for the Taliban.

While opium cultivation is still evident in 2016 and at a 10 percent increase than numbers from 2015, nearly all of the opium poppy culti-vation has been confined to nine regions in southwest Afghanistan.[12] Yet despite this geographical confinement, the country continues to remain the world's largest producer of opium. Eradicating illegal poppy cultivation has been a difficult situation for the Afghan gov-ernment, as funding from the drug trade provides financial support for some of the major obstacles in Afghanistan's economy, including warlords, existing members of the Taliban, and corrupted government officials. Of the over $4 billion in revenue from the sale of drugs in Afghanistan, the farmers receive only roughly 20 percent, with the rest going to corrupt officials and payment for other means of protection.[13] However, for the struggling farmers, producing opium can yield up to 200 times more income than cultivating wheat, rice, and corn. While trying to eliminate the drug trade, many argue that eradicating this source of income for the farmers without providing a substitute income and benefit will further impact the economy and the poverty in Afghanistan.[14] Furthermore, the United Nations estimates that over 250,000 farming households are dependent on this income from opium production.[15] As a method to supplement this income loss, var-ious programs have been developed to help reduce the opium totals, which has been wrought with challenges. Perhaps even more chal-lenging to the Afghan government was the unsuccessful worldwide sponsored program to pay farmers to destroy their opium fields. The funding intended to supplement the farmers for the loss of the opium sales unfortunately resulted in the monetary payments going to the warlords and warlord supporters rather than to the farmers.[16] Addi-tional programs and measures must be put in place; otherwise opium and heroin production will continue to thrive as a lucrative business in Afghanistan. Sustained prevalent corruption and economic instability are not the only aspects that impede the Afghan governments' ability to counter drug eradication efforts. Most of the heroin consumed in Europe and Eurasia is derived from Afghan opium.[17] Afghanistan also struggles to respond to a burgeoning domestic opiate addiction problem, vulnerable to drug money laundering through informal financial networks, and as a regional source of hashish.[18]

Open Markets

Afghanistan has a fairly high tariff rate with a 6.4 percent average tariff rate. In addition, Afghanistan often imposes barriers to trade that include customs delays in order to deter imports. The use of tariffs makes the purchase of overseas goods more expensive, and gives Afghans an incentive to buy domestically produced goods that seem competitively priced or less expensive by comparison. However, the use of tariffs to help provide economic stability can make domestic industries less efficient, since these industries are not part of global competition. Tariffs can also lead to trade wars as exporting countries reciprocate with their own tariffs on imported goods. Further in Afghanistan, the foreign ownership of land is prohibited. Since becoming an Islamic republic government, Afghanistan has faced numerous challenges to economic development. The new Afghan government is trying to overcome this economic transition by regulating institutional development, as well as strategic investments in agricultural reconstruction, establishment of telecommunications infrastructure, and health and education reforms. This neophyte economy continues to struggle with the formation of a new government as many foreign investors are reluctant to invest in a country with poorly regulated banking laws. Reform measures implemented under the Karzai administration have not been sustained, which further undermines future economic reconstruction efforts.

ISLAM

In A.D. 642 during the Battle of Nahavand, Islamic warriors overpowered the Sassanian Empire in Afghanistan. Often referred to by Muslim followers as "the victory of victories," the Arabian Empire had driven out any remaining Byzantine or Parthianian influence in Afghanistan. By A.D. 652, the Islamic faith began to emerge in Afghanistan, and over the next 50 years, the majority of the population converted to Islam.[19]

As the culture and influence of Islam spread, Afghanistan emerged as the center of several predominant Islamic rulers.

The vast majority of the people of Afghanistan and surrounding countries believe in the Islamic religion. Islam has a foundational belief that all in life is related to God and a fundamental belief in the Arabic Qu'ran as the holy book. The *Five Pillars of Islam* are five basic acts in Islam that are considered mandatory by believers. The Five Pillars are considered the principles of Islam, and are the basis of Muslim life. The pillars are summarized in the famous hadith of Gabriel and relate to Muslim life, prayer, concern for the needy, self-purification, and the pilgrimage.

Even with such an expansive cultural diversity comprised of a multitude of ethnic groups, this melting pot of cultures has not hindered the Afghans' ability to unite as a country and defend themselves against foreign invaders. This is a characteristic that has proven to be true in a 5,000-year history of constant invasion and warfare in this conflict-tattered land, for not only are the Afghans shepherds, farmers, and nomads, but they are also intense fighters and fierce warriors. The differing ethnic backgrounds and languages still share a common religious belief in Islam, and it is this religious conviction that serves as the backbone for the population to aggressively resist foreign governments from trying to occupy their land. Throughout history, ownership and control of this region has proven to be only a temporary victory, not only due to the harsh terrain and difficult climate, but also due to the combatant, resistant, and unbreakable population of Afghanistan. The belief in Islam is a principal theme in the culture of the Afghans, as the Muslim faith can be found in every facet of life. The predominant religion of Afghanistan is overwhelmingly Sunni Muslim, comprising more than 80 percent of the population. Shi'a Muslim accounts for nearly all of the remaining population, which includes the Hazara and the Kizilbash peoples. Previously, a small Jewish minority existed in the country prior to the Soviet invasion in 1979, but this population was forced out of Afghanistan. Throughout the 1980s, almost one-third of the Afghanistan people were forced into exile as refugees.[20] The majority of these refugees settled in Pakistan and Iran, and of those who actually remained in Afghanistan as internal refugees, this population resettled in the safety of the capital city of Kabul. Of only the handful of the Jewish population that remains to this day, the majority of this small populace that fled as refugees have yet to return to Afghanistan.[21] After the Soviets pulled all forces out of Afghanistan in 1989, many of the nearly six million refugees repatriated to Afghanistan, only to face more instability and turmoil under such facets as the Taliban regime, economic disparity, food shortages, inflation, and severe drought throughout the coming years. Since Afghanistan is primarily agricultural and rural based, many of those Afghanis raised in refugee camps lack the essential farming expertise needed to survive.[22]

Fact Sheet about Afghanistan

Conventional Country Name	Islamic Republic of Afghanistan
Government Type	Islamic republic
Capital	Kabul
Date of Independence	August 19, 1919 (from British control over Afghan foreign affairs)
Population	31,822,848
Ethnic Groups	Pashtun 42%, Tajik 27%, Hazara 9%, Uzbek 9%, Aimak 4%, Turkmen 3%, Baloch 2%, others 4%
Languages	Afghan Persian or Dari (official) 50%, Pashto (official) 35%, Turkic languages 11%, other languages 4%
Religion	Sunni Muslim 80%, Shi'a Muslim 19%, others 1%
Labor Force	7.512 million (2012 est.)
Unemployment Rate	35% (2008 est.)
Population below poverty line	36% (2009 est.)
Land Area	652,230 sq. km
Climate	Arid to semiarid; cold winters and hot summers
Terrain	Mostly rugged mountains; plains in north and southwest
Geography	Landlocked; the Hindu Kush Mountains that run northeast to southwest divide the northern provinces from the rest of the country
Border Countries	China 76 km, Iran 936 km, Pakistan 2,430 km, Tajikistan 1,206 km, Turkmenistan 744 km, Uzbekistan 137 km

(Continued)

(Continued)

Gross Domestic Product (GDP)	$45.3 billion (2013 estimate of purchasing power parity)
Exports	Opium, fruits and nuts, handwoven carpets, wool, cotton, hides and pelts, precious and semi-precious gems
Imports—commodities	Machinery and other capital goods, food, textiles, petroleum products
Agriculture	Opium, wheat, fruits, nuts; wool, mutton, sheepskins, lambskins
Industries	Small-scale production of bricks, textiles, soap, furniture, shoes, fertilizer, apparel, food products, non-alcoholic beverages, mineral water, cement; handwoven carpets; natural gas, coal, copper
Natural Resources	Natural gas, petroleum, coal, copper, chromite, talc, barites, sulfur, lead, zinc, iron ore, salt, precious, and semiprecious stones
Natural Hazards	Damaging earthquakes occur in the Hindu Kush Mountains; flooding; droughts
Environmental Issues	Limited natural freshwater resources; inadequate supplies of potable water; soil degradation; overgrazing; deforestation (much of the remaining forest is being cut down for fuel and building materials); desertification; air and water pollution

Source: *CIA World Factbook* 2016.

NOTES

1. Sources include the *World Gazetteer* "Afghanistan: Largest Cities and Towns and Statistics of Their Population," www.world-gazetteer .com, and World Urbanization Prospects, 2015. Other sources include Population Division of the Department of Economic and Social Affairs of the United Nations Secretariat, *World Population Prospects: The 2004 Revision* and *World Urbanization Prospects: The 2005 Revision*, http:// esa.un.org/unup.

2. As referenced in the *CIA World Factbook*, 2016.

3. United Nations Statistics Division, "Afghanistan," 2017, http://data.un.org/CountryProfile.aspx.

4. Hafizullah Emadi, *Cultures and Customs of Afghanistan (Cultures and Customs of the World)* (Westport, CT: Greenwood Press, 2005), 111–134.

5. John Woodward, ed. *Afghanistan (Opposing Viewpoints)* (Farmington Hills, MI: Greenhaven, 2006), 3–66.

6. Robert D. Kaplan, "Afghanistan Postmortem," *Atlantic Monthly*, April 1989, Volume 263, No. 4; pages 26–29.

7. Martin Ewans, *Afghanistan: A Short History of Its People and Politics* (New York: HarperCollins, 2002), 2–14.

8. Goodson, *Afghanistan's Endless War*, 167–188.

9. Ewans, *Afghanistan: A Short History of Its People and Politics*, 206–237.

10. Ibid.

11. Peter Marsden, *The Taliban: War, Religion, and New Order in Afghanistan* (London: Zed Books, 1998), 2–18.

12. The Associated Press, "Report Shows Increase in Afghanistan Opium Poppy Cultivation," *The New York Times*, October 23, 2016.

13. Fahiba Nawa, *Opium Nation: Child Brides, Drug Lords, and One Woman's Journey through Afghanistan* (New York: Harper Perennial, 2011), 167.

14. Ibid., 150–167.

15. Ibid., 167.

16. Malcolm B. Russell, *The Middle East and South Asia* (Lanham, MD: Rowman & Littlefield, 2015), 207–217. Reference Public Broadcasting Service (PBS) Frontline on: http://www.pbs.org/wgbh/pages/frontline/shows/heroin/etc/history.html.

17. *CIA World Factbook*, https://www.cia.gov/library/publications/the-world-factbook/geos/af.html.

18. Ibid.

19. Bernard Lewis, *The Middle East: A Brief History of the Last 2,000 Years* (New York: Touchtone, 1995), 57.

20. Goodson, *Afghanistan's Endless War*, 3–4.

21. N.C. Aizenman, "Afghan Jew Becomes Country's One and Only," *The Washington Post*, January 27, 2005.

22. Goodson, *Afghanistan's Endless War*, 91–132.

2

Prehistory: The Emergence of Civilization in Ancient Afghanistan

Modern Afghanistan may be evaluated in the context of how initial inhabitants interacted with the culture, environment, and trade of neighboring regions. When exploring the history of Afghanistan, the regions of the Middle East and Central Asia are used as a reference point for determining the origins of the country. In this regard, the prehistory of the Middle East includes the modern countries of Iraq, Iran, and Afghanistan.[1] During the prehistoric period, the term *Mesopotamia* refers to the overall current region of Iraq, while the reference to Persia encompassed the region of present-day Iran. While the nomadic families advanced and early settlements began to emerge in Afghanistan, the expansion of civilizations in neighboring regions forced the need to trade and exchange goods with these other societies. In examining the origins of the Afghani culture, the region of Afghanistan must therefore be evaluated in relation to early trade and interaction with the regions of Mesopotamia and Persia.

The lifestyle of the nomad left little time for documentation and written history—the passing down of traditions, history, and values was often oral in nature. Not only are the chronology and documentation of the major events in the dawn of Afghanistan's early history highly intermittent during these ancient civilization periods, but the constant world domination of this area has also destroyed many archeological artifacts. The majority of archaeological finds in Afghanistan occurred between the 1950s to the 1970s. During the Soviet occupation beginning in 1979, many archaeological digs and studies were canceled.[2] The vast majority of these efforts have yet to be resumed in a country that has been ravaged by war and conflict over the last 40 years. To date, many unearthed artifacts and historical discoveries have been damaged by the war with the Soviets, Taliban bombs, or simply from exposure to the elements. As a result, the prospect of uncovering precious new archaeological finds is quite unfeasible. To this extent, the damage from war in Afghanistan suggests that extraordinary excavations are regrettably left to the remote chance of future archaeologists and anthropologists discovering unearthed prehistoric artifacts. As a result, those early artifacts that have been discovered are fiercely protected, even to the extent that the historical treasures located in the History Museum in Kabul were hidden during the Taliban regime so they would not be destroyed.[3]

PALEOLITHIC ERA: 2,500,000–10,000 B.C.E.

Often referred to as the Old Stone Age, the Paleolithic era refers to the initial development of human evolution and the advancement of civilizations. The Paleolithic era is considered to be the most extensive segment of mankind's history, and covers a span of approximately 2,500,000 years. On the geological timescale, this period in history is regarded as part of the Pleistocene epoch, approximately 1,800,000 to 11,500 B.C.E. The name *Pleistocene* is derived from the Greek words *pleistos* "most" and *kainos* "new." In archaeology, the end of the Pleistocene epoch occurs in conformity with the end of the Paleolithic age.

The Paleolithic era notices the emergence of the first human development and settlements around the world. During this dawn of life in early Afghanistan, humans lived in caves or settled on the steppe plains. In the crudest element, the living conditions of these early Afghan cultures depended on both the capability to hunt and the ability to gather edible plants from the surrounding environment. This era was in the premature stage for humans to build sophisticated weapons and tools, and northern Afghanistan was a prime area for modern

Homo sapiens to develop and mature physically. As these early humans developed and progressed, they also contributed to the improvement and advancement of Stone Age tools.

LOWER PALEOLITHIC PERIOD: 2,500,000 TO 120,000 B.C.E.

The Paleolithic period is divided into three consecutive divisions, referred to as the Lower, Middle, and Upper Paleolithic period. The Lower Paleolithic period is the earliest division of this age in history, and the longest as it covers the time span of slightly over two million years. The primary distinguishable characteristic of the Paleolithic period, and continually the most controversial, depicts the process of the evolution of the human species. As part of the evolution process, the period began with the introduction of the first stone tools by such hominids as *Homo habilis.* These early humans came into existence around two million years ago and lasted until the introduction of agriculture approximately 10,000 years ago.

During the Lower Paleolithic period, the agricultural and farming lifestyle began in the Middle East, and thus lessened the need for the traditional hunting and gathering of food, although these methods were still important. Continual evolution and development occurred over thousands of years, which allowed humans to advance from a common ancestor to the modern version of *Homo sapiens.* Archaeological finds indicate early man in Afghanistan lived in caves or near riverbanks, as stone tools and implements indicating such settlements existed have been discovered.[4] The Lower period and the first partition of the Paleolithic era is regarded as "the age of stone tools," as these ancestors of modern humans made ancient stone tools such as simple axes or chopping types of tools. These most primitive tools were constructed from eoliths, fragments and pieces of chipped flint and crude stones. Early man needed these tools not only for cutting and hunting, but also as a defense against animals or other nomads forging for food or shelter. The early hunters and food gatherers commonly used the stone tools as handheld axes, which were created by chipping the stone to form a cutting edge, or assembled from fragments struck off a stone. Archeologists currently debate whether eoliths were man-made or the result of natural processes of stone. Discoveries and evidence of such early tools may indicate human habitation of ancient areas before the oldest known fossils. As the era progressed in time, the sophistication and design of these tools advanced as well.

Discoveries indicating the Paleolithic people's use of wood, clay, and animal parts were vital in the advancement of their civilization. Some of these tools found in excavation sites date back to more than 100,000 years ago, and these types of implements are the first Lower Paleolithic stone tools to be discovered in Afghanistan.[5] These extraordinary findings indicate how Afghanistan played a major role in the formation and development of the early societies in the world. Paleolithic cultures are determined by the type and assortment of tools dated to their respective time period. These tools have evident characteristics and are able to provide the basis for a system of classification, and usually are based on both the type of materials used and the tool-making techniques themselves. In general, the people of the Lower Paleolithic period were primarily known as hunters and food gatherers. The tool kits of these early natives were extensive and included such objects as knives, scrapers, needles, and spears. These discovered artifacts represent the engineering and technological skills of these Paleolithic people, which reveal how these tools were made from chipped stone and flint.

MIDDLE PALEOLITHIC PERIOD: 100,000–30,000 B.C.E.

The time frame applied to delineate the Lower Paleolithic period from the Middle era is not definitive, and the genesis of the Middle Paleolithic period varies between 300,000 to 100,000 B.C.E. However, the principal distinction is the Middle Paleolithic Period encompasses many *Mousterian* discoveries, which suggest humans lived between 100,000 and 40,000 years ago known as the Neanderthal man. *Mousterian* is a term used by archaeologists to indicate a style of predominantly flint tools which are associated with early humans from the Middle Paleolithic period. In this regard, some archaeological finds of this nature indicate that early civilization might have occurred in the Hindu Kush Mountain region as early as 50,000 B.C.E.[6] A discovery like this would indicate that northern Afghanistan was among one of the earliest locations to domesticate plants and animals.

During the Middle Paleolithic period, *Neanderthal man* was a species that predominately inhabited Europe and parts of western Asia. As part of the evolution of the human species, this controversial subject suggests that the Neanderthal man evolved from *Homo erectus*. Neanderthal remains are often found in caves, and many of these discoveries indicate these early humans were advanced enough in intelligence to use fire. Furthermore, Neanderthals were known as hunters of prehistoric mammals and enlisted the aid of primitive stone tools. These stone tools were made as part of the "flake" tradition, which indicate the Neanderthal man had the ability for recognition and cognizant thought to cut stones to create a sharper point. Additionally, bone fragments were carved into implements such as needles, which indicate that crudely sewn furs and skins were assembled and used as body coverings.

While it is quite feasible that Paleolithic humans roamed Afghanistan as much as 100,000 years ago, credence must be given to actual historical findings, which thus far it has been difficult to make significant discoveries in Afghanistan. The cave areas of the country are extensive, and the narrow passageways and taverns into these mountainous areas are seemingly infinite. Up to 50,000 earthquakes occur in Afghanistan each year, which makes excavations and discoveries increasingly complicated and any additional archaeological finds are nearly impossible.

UPPER PALEOLITHIC PERIOD: 40,000–11,000 B.C.E.

The first true findings of life in Afghanistan are the settlements which existed during the Upper Paleolithic period. During the Upper Paleolithic period, the Neanderthal man faded away to be interchanged by a variety of *Homo sapiens* such as *Cro-Magnon man* and *Grimaldi man*. During the Upper Paleolithic period, this time is seen as the most enriching and elevating epoch of the Paleolithic period. As part of this era, an amazing number of human cultures, such as the Aurignacian, Gravettian, Perigordian, Solutrean, and Magdalenian, arose and developed in the Old World.[7] This final era of the Paleolithic age marks the beginning of communal hunting and extensive fishing for prehistoric man. The first man-made shelters and primitive dwellings were built, and this also saw the continued emergence of sewn clothing for warmth and protection. Tools were finely crafted and of great variety, including flint, obsidian blades, and projectile points. In Afghanistan in 1954, the cave of Kara Kamar was the first Stone Age site to be excavated. This is the earliest indication of human occupation in Afghanistan based on excavations, and discoveries have uncovered the remains of a human skull, which scientists date to be from roughly 30,000 years ago. These skull fragments were found in a cave in the Badakshan area, which is in the northeastern part of the central highlands, and findings from this archaeological discovery dated tools to approximately 30,000 years ago.[8] Furthermore, these early inhabitants also used such objects as bone, horn, and lapis to make necklaces and other personal ornaments for decoration.

As time moved forward, the Solutrean people of the Upper Paleolithic era migrated to Europe from the east and ousted many of their Aurignacian predecessors. During the Solutrean industry, this period saw advancement in flint tool-making from around 22,000 to 17,000 B.C.E. The Solutrean industry first appeared in what is now Spain, and disappears from the archaeological record around 17,000 B.C.E. Several Solutrean findings have been made in the caves of Les Eyzies and Laugerie Haute, and in the Creswell Crags in Derbyshire, England.

The Solutrean hunters fashioned extremely fine spearheads and hunted wild horses as their primary game. The Solutrean is often noted as a transitory stage between the flint implements of the Mousterian epoch and the bone implements of the Magdalenian epochs. Once the Solutrean and remaining Aurignacian cultures were replaced by the Magdalenian, this culture existed during the final and possibly the most remarkable phase of the Paleolithic period. Throughout this period, unearthed artifacts and dwelling remnants reflect a society made up of whole communities and larger societies of hunters and gatherers. Discoveries of Magdalenian tools denote superior skills and hunting techniques, which include the sophisticated engineering of an array of items that range from small microliths to hunting spears of great length and refinement.

While it is significant that these weapons were highly developed and varied, the crowning achievement of the Magdalenian era were the cave paintings and murals that have endured throughout several millennia as the culmination of Paleolithic art. Toward the end of the Paleolithic Age, humans produced primitive art by painting cave walls with depictions of everyday life. These scenes typically portray such subjects as the hunt of wild animals, and these cave wall images also illustrate human interaction and fertility paintings. While no such discovery has yet been made in the mountains and caves of the Hindu Kush, archaeologists and anthropologists still hope to one day unveil these still-hidden treasures of Afghanistan.

MESOLITHIC PERIOD: 10,000–3000 B.C.E.

The Mesolithic period, also known as the Middle Stone Age, is an interim period in human development that existed between the end of the Paleolithic period and the beginning of the Neolithic period. The end of the last glacial period over 10,000 years ago incorporated both the gradual domestication of plants and animals and the development of settled communities. While Mesolithic cultures would continue in Europe until almost 3000 B.C.E., Neolithic communities developed in the Middle East and Persia between 9000 and 6000 B.C.E. In Afghanistan, archaeological finds reveal early settlers cultivated such products as wheat and barley between 9,000 to 11,000 years ago.[9]

Evidence of Mesolithic cultures indicates a wide variety of hunting, fishing, and food-gathering techniques. Distinctive humanistic traits of the period are indicated in the hunting and fishing settlements along rivers, where both fish and much-needed fresh water were abundant. Microliths, the typical stone implements of the Mesolithic period, are smaller and more delicate than those of the eoliths of the late Paleolithic period. Additionally during this time, cultures and settlements show advancements in pottery, and the use of the bow emerged as a tool for hunting.

The Mesolithic period demonstrates a continual transition from food hunting and collecting to a food-harvesting type culture. Specifically in the Middle East and the region of Afghanistan, the Natufian culture was an Epipaleoithic culture that existed from 13,000 to 9,800 B.C. and was predominant during the Mesolithic period. The Natufian communities are believed to be the ancestors of the first Neolithic settlements of the regions near present-day Afghanistan. Other cultures include the Badarian and Gerzean in Egypt, and the Caspian people in North Africa. The Natufian culture provides the earliest evidence of an evolution from a Mesolithic to a Neolithic way of life.

NEOLITHIC PERIOD: 8000–2500 B.C.E.

In archaeology, the term *Neolithic* designates a stage of cultural evolution or technological progress distinguished by the use of stone tools, the existence of settled villages reliant on domesticated plants and animals, and the presence of crafts, such as pottery and weaving. The term *Neolithic* has also been used in anthropology to indicate contemporaneous cultures which reveal independent farming communities. The domestication of plants and animals usually distinguishes Neolithic culture from the previous Paleolithic or Mesolithic hunting, fishing, and food-gathering cultures. Historians support the belief that pastoralism and farming existed in Afghanistan, and thus harvesting settlements existed as many as 10,000 years ago. Historical evidence widely supports the region of Afghanistan was inhabited during the Neolithic era, whereas existence during earlier time periods is widely believed but not yet validated.

The Neolithic period is also referred to as the New Stone Age, and the completion of the Neolithic period is manifested by such modernization as the rise of urban civilization, the introduction of metal tools, and the first stages of writing. Archeologists and anthropologists have identified the earliest known development of Neolithic culture, which occurred in Southwest Asia between 8000 and 6000 B.C.E. Here, the domestication of plants and animals was most likely begun by the Mesolithic Natufian peoples, leading to the establishment of settled villages based on the cultivation of wheat and grain, and the rearing of such livestock as cattle, sheep, and goats. Around 6000 B.C.E, lapis lazuli was being mined in the Badakshan region of Afghanistan and traded with India with the use of stone tools.

Between 6000 and 2000 B.C.E., Neolithic culture spread throughout the globe, including into Europe, the Nile valley in Egypt, the Indus valley in India, and the Huang He valley located in northern China. In the fertile Tigris and Euphrates river valleys, the Neolithic culture of the Middle East developed into the urban civilizations of the Bronze Age by 3500 B.C.E. With settlements and civilizations blossoming all over the globe, the first true urban dwellings in Afghanistan were established between 3000 and 2000 B.C.E. Prior to this time frame, there is an overall lack of written accounts by these early cultures, which has resulted in hardly any understanding of the language and ethnicity in these settlement areas. However, by the end of the Bronze Age, the area of Afghanistan would be overcome with Indo-Iranian languages as nomadic groups continued to invade and settle in Afghanistan.

NOTES

1. Bernard Lewis, *The Middle East: A Brief History of the Last 2,000 Years* (New York: Touchtone, 1995), 50–65; Peter Marsden, *The Taliban: War, Religion, and New Order in Afghanistan* (London: Zed Books, 1998), 2–18.

2. Frederick Talmage Heibert, *Origins of the Bronze Age Oasis Civilizations in Central Asia* (Cambridge, MA: Harvard University Press, 1994), 5–28.

3. Alisa Tang, "1,423 Secured Afghan Artifacts Are Returned to Kabul Museum," *Union Tribune San Diego,* March 18, 2007, http://www.signonsandiego.com/uniontrib/20070318/news_1n18afghan.html (Accessed 2015–01–12).

4. Reference www.Afghan.net/Afghanistan/prehistory for additional information on the early humans of Afghanistan.

5. Louis Dupree, *Shamshir Glass: Historic Cave Site in Kandahar Province, Afghanistan,* Anthropological Papers of the American Museum of Natural History, Volume 46, No. 2, 1958. Also reference www.Afghan .net/Afghanistan/prehistory.

6. For additional information on these prehistoric archaeological finds in the early history of Afghanistan, reference: http://www .afghan-web.com/history/chron/index.html.

7. Michael W. Pitts and Mark Roberts, *Fairweather Eden: Life Half a Million Years Ago as Revealed by the Excavations at Boxgrove.* 1st ed. (New York: Fromm International, 1998), 6–17.

8. In 1954, anthropologist Carlton Coon is credited with excavating the cave of Kara Kamar (near Haibak Afghanistan). Nancy Dupree, "An Historical Guide to Afghanistan." Afghan Tourist Organization. 1970. Referenced online at http://www.zharov.com/dupree/chap ter23.html.

9. Marsden, *The Taliban,* 2–18.

3

Early Civilization and the Nomadic People of Afghanistan

While the exact emergence of civilization in Afghanistan is not definitive, the majority of research indicates the flux of domestication in the ancient land of the Afghans arose around 2500–2000 B.C.E. Historians theorize that it was during this time period when the Aryan tribes of Central Asia began to migrate into the region now known as Afghanistan. The Aryans were a faction of the Indo-European speaking tribes and are believed to have split the Iranian, Nuristani, and Afghan sects throughout this early civilization period. As the tribes began populating the region, Kabul and other major settlements developed and became established as cities.

ARYAN CIVILIZATION (2500 B.C.E.–551 B.C.E.)

The term *nomad* is commonly used to describe the characteristics of the civilizations that established the first settlements in Afghanistan. In its loosest form, *nomad* generally translates as "wanderer." These early nomadic settlements were born out of a purposeful drive to leave one settlement for another as a survival tool on the steppe plains of Afghanistan. As an illustration, a settlement in one area might be acceptable during the summer months, but this same area would be inhabitable in the harsh winters. Additionally, the pastoral nomad who herds his flock of sheep, goats, or cows must also periodically move to new regions to provide unexploited fodder for the livestock. As difficult as it might have been, these early Afghan nomads purposely traveled to establish new homes in uncharted territory. In some cases, these nomads sought out to inhabit the existing homes of family tribes. To live a cyclical life of settling and resettling was unfalteringly harsh, which the nomads endured in their ritualistic travel and constant movement. This cyclic relocation system created a disturbing environment, and without question this lifestyle placed a weary burden on these early settlers. Yet this livelihood for survival and endurance led to an aptitude of a harsh, unfaltering, and warrior-like mentality.[1] This fiercely combatant culture, developed in the early dawn of mankind, is still ingrained in the livelihood of Afghans to this day.

The early humans who settled in the region of Afghanistan seem to be relatively minor in comparison to the other vast settlements that existed during this time period. The Indus valley civilization is the earliest known "city" way of life, and this Aryan tribe was predominately located on the Indian subcontinent of Pakistan. Consequently, civilization ruins are widespread across the continent, factually supporting the scope and extent of the traveling settlements and civilizations which were established. Due to the wide and expansive settlement of this ancient society, the Indus valley culture is regarded as the most extensive of the world's three earliest civilizations. Other early civilizations include the settlements located in Mesopotamia and Egypt, which both preceded the Indus civilization but were not nearly as sizeable. During their expansive settlement, the Indus civilization established two large cities, Harappa and Mohenjo-daro (both in Pakistan), and also established a multitude of other locations and dwellings as towns and villages. These two cities were quite advanced and substantial in size, with dimension estimates as large as one square mile in breadth and population estimates of approximately 40,000 people.

The Indus civilization likely developed from previous villages by the establishment and implementation of a sophisticated method of irrigating the soil. This method, developed by Mesopotamian predecessors, transformed the region and allowed the Indus civilization to achieve the most efficient agricultural benefit of the fertile Indus River valley, even in times of destructive floods. The crucial characteristic in the formation of these early civilizations was to develop a harvestable and productive food crop to feed and nurture the colony, and in turn the abundance of food increased the population totals. As this society settled in the region and learned how to harvest the earth, this flourishing agricultural civilization would inevitably expand its borders along with the growing amount of inhabitants. In doing so, as the tribe worked to increase the size and the number of the villages, in turn the Indus people propagated in size and scope.

Trade with neighboring regions was also pivotal for the Indus civilization, and included exchange with the nomadic pioneers in Afghanistan. The Indus people primarily cultivated grain products such as wheat and barley, but historical findings indicate the fields also include the earliest discoveries of cotton, which would have been a valuable product in the Indus civilizations' trade-dependent economy. Civilizations bartering for exchanges with Afghanistan, a land rich in minerals and natural resources, trade with the nomads of the steppe primarily included barter of such elements as gold, silver, and copper. Lapis lazuli, a stone-like gem that dates back to as far as 6000 B.C.E., was one of Afghanistan's most valuable natural treasures for trade. This decorative blue-colored stone was highly valued by royalty, including the pharaohs of Egypt. Lapis lazuli remains a highly prized gem from Afghanistan, and to this day the finest lapis still is mined in the northeastern Badakshan region.

Eventually, the Indus civilization entered a state of decline quite possibly due to such characteristics as climate and environment changes. The continuous environmental fluctuation caused the Indus people to abandon their settlements in search of another more stable atmosphere. However, some historians have speculated it is also quite plausible this civilization, which once flourished so well along the riverbanks of the Indus River valley, ceased to exist for another reason. Some historians speculate the Indus valley civilization was attacked and destroyed by invaders who virtually eliminated the culture. With the experience of almost total abolition, perhaps those few who survived merged into other settlements. Little is known about the migration of the Indus people, and other factors might have led to the demise of the Indus civilization. However, the environmental difficulties such as harsh flooding, the abundance of improper housing construction, and the increasing population all negatively impacted the civilization in preparation for defense from attacks. In approximately eighth century B.C.E., the Assyrians were the first Middle Easterners to conquer Afghanistan. This incident appears to be congruent with other episodes, such as the earlier Aryan attacks upon the Indus region. As with the Indus civilization, the early nomadic settlers in Afghanistan faced similar hardships and constraints from the environment in addition to staving off attacks from invaders.

THE MEDES EMPIRE IN AFGHANISTAN
(APPROXIMATELY 700–550 B.C.E.)

Because the country is situated along the vital trade routes with the East and South Asia, Afghanistan's geographical position was a prime location for assaults and land battles. With this strategic advantage position in mind, a western Iranian people known as the Medes migrated into the region of Afghanistan around 700 B.C.E., conquered these feeble Assyrian settlements, and dominated the land.

The Medes are widely considered to have created the first empire in this region, thus marking the beginning of many empires that would toil to overtake the land of the Afghans. The reign of the Medes dynasty endured for over 180 years, and began with Deioces as the first Aryan king of the Medes Empire. Deioces played a significant role in the history of the Medes when he united seven of the Median tribes. Deioces ruled from 701 B.C.E. through 665 B.C.E. The Medes were fierce rivals with the Persians and were later overthrown by this society. The Medes were also associated with another steppe tribe known as the Scythians, a dominant ethnic group that eventually overthrew the remaining Medes Empire.

This period also saw the emergence of religion in Afghanistan. The Medes and the early ancestors of the Pashtun tribe, which originated near the modern city of Kandahar, are believed to have adopted the followings of Zoroaster. These ancestors were primarily pagan, but are believed to have adopted Buddhist and Zoroastrian traditions due to other cultural influences. Zoroastrianism was a prominent religious belief in Afghanistan for centuries until the time of the Arab conquest in A.D 652, when the followings and teachings of Zoroastrianism were nearly eliminated. Today there is a very small following of the Zoroastrianism religion (most notably in India), and in modern times they refer to themselves as the Parsis. It is interesting to note that the Parsis trace their ancestral heritage to the Order of the Magi, the same Magi who are referred to in the Nativity story as the three wise men who present the newborn baby Jesus with frankincense, gold, and myrrh. Although referenced with uncertain dates in regards to the Magi's descent from the Zoroastrians, the origins of the religion commenced approximately during the beginning of the Persian Empire with Cyrus the Great. While the religion itself was for the most part lost, Zoroastrianism gave many influences and beliefs to Judaism and Christianity.

Zoroastrianism is a Middle Eastern religion created by the Iranian prophet Zoroaster, who preached widely in present-day Afghanistan. The teachings of Zoroastrianism spread along with the early pagan beliefs and then later Buddhism. Scholars recognize the prophet as a notable historical figure, but his date of origin remains highly unclear. The debate over the beginning of his life is normally dated between 660 to 630 B.C.E. However, some scholars believe Zoroaster's influence started as early as 1200 B.C.E. If this were the case, it would make Zoroastrianism one of the earliest religions founded. Despite the debate over the exact date of the prophet's birth, the time of Zoroastrianism was the most influential during the sixth to fifth century B.C.E. As the legend unfolds, Zoroaster was renamed Zarathustra after experiencing a blinding vision in the desert. He began preaching throughout the region, but arguably the most pivotal point in Zarathustra's preaching was when he converted King Vishtaspa. King Vishtaspa widely supported Zoroaster and his teachings. The Avestra is the sacred text of the religion, which is divided into five main books and describes the life of Zoroaster, his preachings, and the beliefs of the religion. Those who debate the origin of Zarathustra's birth also speculate the converted King Vishtaspa was not the legendary father of Darius I, but rather an earlier ruler of the same name. The earlier King Vishtaspa ruled in present-day eastern Iran and in Bactria of modern Afghanistan. Zarathustra won over the king and subsequently became the court prophet. While the motives for conversion remain speculation, some legends tell the story that King Vishtapa accepted Zarathustra's (Zoroaster) ideas about one god, which were revolutionary in that time. As the tale is told, Zoroaster healed the king's favorite horse, and the king and his court were so impressed they made Zoroaster the religious council, and thus his teachings began to flourish throughout the kingdom. After the conversion of King Vishtaspa, the religion quickly spread and the beliefs of Zoroaster proliferated.

THE RISE OF THE PERSIAN EMPIRE

In 553 B.C.E., the king of Persia, known as Cyrus the Great, rebelled against his grandfather Astyages, the king of the Medes, and Cyrus finally defeated his grandfather in 550 B.C.E. After Astyages was captured by his own disgruntled nobles and promptly handed over to the jubilant Cyrus, the Medes were now subjugated to their close kin, the Persians. In the new Persian Empire they retained a prominent position, and many noble Medes were often employed as officials, governors (known as satraps), and generals.

The beginning of the Persian Empire in 550 B.C.E. plays an important role in the history of the world. The advancements of the Persians were closely studied and recorded by the Greeks, and these detailed accounts built a solid foundation for outlining the history of Afghanistan. By the time of the Persian conquest in 550 B.C.E., Afghanistan already existed as a culture and society with settlements that were several thousand years old. Current maps of Afghanistan and neighboring territories are vastly different from the maps when Afghanistan was under the control of Persia. Beginning with the rule of Cyrus the Great, the reign of the Persians continued for over 200 years until the defeat of Darius III as the final ruler of the Persian Empire. In one of the greatest anecdotes in the chronicles of history, Darius III and his army were conquered by Alexander the Great in 331 B.C.E., which marked the end of the Persian power in Afghanistan and the rise of the Macedonian rule.

By the rise of the Persian Empire, Afghanistan encompassed several provinces of the Achaemenid Empire. Also referred to as Cyrus II, Cyrus the Great ruled the empire from 590 to 530 B.C.E. Regarded as the founder of the Persian Empire, Cyrus the Great conquered the Medes civilization, united the two Iranian kingdoms, and became the king of Persia in 559 B.C.E. Cyrus worked to constantly expand the borders of his kingdom, successfully gaining advancement into Central Asia, Southern Asia, and parts of the Indian border. The first Persian ruler reigned until his death in a battle in August 530 B.C.E., when his son Cambyses II succeeded him to the throne. Little is recorded about Cambyses II, but most notably during his reign, Cambyses was successful in conquering Egypt in 525 B.C.E., a feat Cyrus himself wanted but never was able to achieve before his death. Very little has been written about Cambyses II, save for historians noting his penchant for drunkenness and corruption. The lack of information can possibly be due to his short eight-year reign as ruler of the Persian Empire. Quite possibly as well, he is overshadowed by two of the greatest rulers in time, sandwiched between Cyrus the Great (his father) and his predecessor Darius the Great, who ruled the Persian Empire when it was at its most extensive.[2]

THE RULE OF THE ACHAEMENID DYNASTY (550 B.C.E.–331 B.C.E.)

Following the death of Cambyses in 521 B.C.E., a new leader emerged to become king. Darius the Great (also as Darius I) ruled much of

Central Asia, including all of present-day Afghanistan. However, in an interesting tale, Darius I inherited the throne in a scandalous manner. As described by two renowned Greek historians of fifth century B.C.E., Herodotus and Ctesias, these chronological descriptions of the Persian Empire record the detailed historical account of Darius's ascension to the throne. However, another derivative of the story exists from Darius's own description of his life story, which is interwoven with legends and tales of his magnificent rule. Some aspects of the story are questionable and contradictory to other accounts by the Greek historians Herodotus and Ctesias.[3] The story as relayed by Darius I in the Bisitun inscription in Iran, a tri-language script carved into a mountain, describes the conquests and inherited lands of Darius I. These lands included Bactria in northern Afghanistan, Ariana in west, Arachosia in the south, and Ghandara in eastern Afghanistan. The most significant aspect of the Bisitun inscription is Darius's description of how he ascended the throne, for he was not of the royal bloodline and was an unlikely successor to the throne. Darius was born as the son of Hystaspes, the satrap of Parthia. Even during his youth when Cyrus the Great ruled, Darius was suspected of plotting to overtake the throne from the Persian king. After Cyrus's death, Darius served as a member of the royal bodyguard with King Cambyses II.

As the story begins and according to the accounts of Darius, Cambyses died by his own hand in March 521 B.C.E. In an elaborate tale, Darius declared that Cambyses and his brother Smerdis (also referred to as Bardia), who were both the sons of Cyrus the Great, were involved in a brotherly battle over the throne and the resulting kingship of Persia. Allegedly on his deathbed, Cyrus the Great promised Smerdis his fair entitlement to a portion of the kingdom, which was Smerdis's birth right to claim the eastern provinces of the Persian Empire. Yet Cambyses II could not allow his brother to attain control of a portion of the kingdom, which would lessen his share and weaken his authority in the empire. As Darius alleges, before Cambyses set off to conquer Egypt, he secretly ordered his brother Smerdis to be murdered. Cambyses feared that in his absence and quest for new territory, his brother would lead a rebellion and overtake his throne. To squelch the chance for an insurgence, he issued the order to murder his brother. Shortly thereafter Cambyses departed for Egypt under the relief his brother was no longer a predicament, and therefore his throne was safe from usurpation.

However, an unfathomable situation waited for Cambyses upon his arrival home. When Cambyses returned from his triumphant clash against the Egyptians, he received the news that his brother Smerdis, the same one he secretly ordered to be killed, was indeed still alive. However, Darius alleged that an imposter assumed the name Smerdis, and this charlatan was a Magian named Gaumata. Hence Gaumata, under the guise of Smerdis, declared himself the king in 522 B.C.E. and seized the kingdom. The interloper Smerdis was recognized throughout Asia, and Cambyses set out to fight against him to win back his kingdom. According to Darius, Cambyses realized his plan was hopeless and killed himself, but not before confessing to Darius about the murder of his brother and elucidating the entire fraudulent story. Under the identity of the brother Smerdis, the imposter Gaumata was therefore next in line for the throne and ruled the as the Persian king over the empire for seven months. As the legend states, no one other than Darius had the courage to oppose the new king. Darius, acting in the belief he was removing the imposter and fraudulent heir to the throne, marched to the kingdom's capital in October 521 B.C.E. At this castle stronghold in Media, Darius and his men seized the faux heir Gaumata, took him as prisoner, and killed him. The story of Cambyses and the imposter Gaumata is mostly recorded by Darius the Great, and his defeat and killing of the false Smerdis was annually celebrated in Persia by a feast called *Magiophani*, which means "the killing of the magian." As inscribed in the Bisitun inscription, Darius defended his killing of Gaumata, and his own ascension as king, that he was restoring the empire to the rightful Achaemenid house. His reign as Darius I lasted from 521 to 486 B.C.E., and through his rule he led the Persian Empire when it was at its most extensive. Since the accounts of Cambyses and his brother Smerdis are told through the hands of Darius, and there are few other recorded historical testaments, many scholars dispute this account. Historians relate to a more realistic account and believe Darius invented this tale of the imposter Gaumata, and the murdered king in Media was undeniably the true son of Cyrus. Further, as both his father and grandfather were alive at the time of Darius's overtaking of the throne, it would be unlikely that Darius was indeed the next in line for the kingship. No matter what the real story may be regarding the tale of Darius as king and the defeat of Smerdis in Media, Darius the Great ascended the throne and governed as the king of Persia.[4] His role in Afghanistan was of paramount importance to the country, as he enabled several critical infrastructures that helped Afghanistan emerge into the civilized world. Under the reign of Darius I, Persian writing emerged for the first time. He also implemented a taxation system and communication network, which was based on his division of the empire into manageable districts led by regional satraps.

Despite the revolts and questionable methods in which Darius I ascended to the title of king of Persia, he is considered to be one of the greatest rulers of the Achaemenid dynasty. The Bisitun inscriptions account for 19 battles, and describe how Darius I defeated nine rebel leaders, all of whom were vying for his crown. In the midst of rebellions and citizen uprisings over various claims to the throne, Darius's army easily suppressed these uncoordinated and impulsive eruptions. Darius I was well known for his genius in battle as well as his ability to implement the construction of great buildings. Further, by 519 B.C.E., Darius I had established his authority in the east and restored internal order to the empire. As was the sovereign code of behavior, rulers needed to constantly strengthen the frontiers of the empire in order to expand territorial boundaries. Additionally, adding more citizens to the army allowed for greater supremacy in battle. The battles waged by Darius I included his successful attack of the European Scythians, and he also conquered the civilizations in the Indus valley.

In 513 B.C.E. after attempting to finally subdue the European Scythians, Darius I decided to push forth and attempted to fight the Scythians of Asia, an effort that even his brother warned him against. As part of this battle endeavor, Darius I constructed an engineering achievement in his design to build a bridge over the Bosporus Strait in order to advance through Thrace into Scythia. The Bosporus, also known as the Istanbul Strait, forms the boundary between the European Turkey and Asian Turkey. Darius I wanted to attack the nomadic warriors of the steppe and thus secure the empire's foothold in the northern plains. However, Darius I made an incorrect geographical assumption that the Hindu Kush Mountains of Afghanistan were near the Black Sea. In his lack of knowledge of the region, the expedition was doomed for failure. Furthermore, the Scythians proved to be too warrior-like and astute for Darius I. As part of the legendary battle techniques of the Scythians, they would draw an enemy into their territory and falsely retreat. In this manner the Scythians continued this artificial dance to draw Darius I further and further west while exhausting his troops and his supplies. After his army advanced for some weeks into the plains of Ukraine, the army ran out of supplies and Darius was forced to return to his empire without a victory or territorial advancement. Darius was clearly unsuited to try and oppose the Scythians, nomads who were extremely skilled adversaries and steppe warriors.[5] However, regardless of his inability to subdue the Scythians, Darius I was successful in expanding the borders created by his predecessors and added new territories to Afghanistan.

In addition to enlarging the territory of the kingdom, Darius I was a great statesman, and by far his most effective contribution to the Persian Empire was his ability to rule as an administrator. Through his ideas and institutions of administrative law, he brought to fruition the idea initiated by Cyrus the Great to organize the empire into satraps, organizing his empire into 20 provinces. These provinces were led by a governor and royal inspector. Increasing the lines of communication among the provinces, Darius I also implemented a form of taxes to be paid each province, and trade and commerce were increased as land and sea routes were developed. Darius also instigated the use of coins in the kingdom, while also establishing a standardized form of weights and measurements. Darius I was by far the greatest engineer of the Achaemenid dynasty, and he notably instituted a unique style of Persian architecture. At his capital of Susa, he constructed an *apadana*, a great audience hall and residential palace. The palace inscriptions and carvings depict how Darius I brought artisans, materials, and skilled craftsmen from all sections of the empire to build the *apadana*, and this architectural accomplishment is considered to be one of his signature achievements during his reign.

While Darius I achieved success in uniting the realms of his empire, he was also respectful of the religious beliefs and followings of his citizens. He recognized the benefit of acknowledging diverse religions, and continued the practice of religious tolerance initiated by Cyrus and Cambyses. As outlined in Darius's personal inscriptions and accounts of his life, these historical accounts seem to indicate that his religious beliefs show the continuous influence of the teachings of Zoroaster.

The Bactriana Province and the capital at Bactria were supposedly the home of Zoroaster. This area, located in northern Afghanistan, eventually became Balkh. The Persians were found to be tolerable of the Zoroastrianism religion and beliefs, with the underlying policy that it was acceptable as long as the followers remained loyal to the empire by paying taxes and sending their sons to fight in the Persian army.

After the death of Darius I in 486 B.C.E., the Persian Achaemenid dynasty experienced a period of several kings in a short timeframe. Control in Afghanistan was governed under Xerxes I, who completed many of the great buildings and kingdom projects initiated by his predecessor. Xerxes ruled for 20 years until 465 B.C.E., when Xerxes I was succeeded by Artaxerxes I, who moved the capital of the empire from Persepolis to Babylon. As king of the empire from 465 to 424 B.C.E., Artaxerxes I established the Persian vernacular as the official language of the government. After his death, his eldest son, Xerxes II, succeeded him to the throne. Xerxes II served the shortest reign as king of the Persians, as his brother assassinated him a mere seven weeks later. However, the satrap of Hyrcania and the illegitimate brother Ochus rebelled against the murdering king and killed him. Ochus assumed the throne as Darius II, and he ruled as the emperor of Persia from 423 to 404 B.C.E. Little is recorded of his reign in the empire, except that he was quite dependent upon his wife Parysatis, who was also his half-sister. After his death, his eldest son Artaxeres II was granted the sole title to the throne and not the younger son Cyrus, despite the pleadings of Parysatis. Even after being named satrap of Lydia, Cyrus continued to fight his brother for the throne for several years and he began to build a rebellion throughout the empire. Cyrus and Artaxerxes met in the Battle of Cunaxa in 401 B.C.E, where Cyrus was killed. After his enthronement, Artaxerxes II was the longest reigning of the Achaemenid kings, and it was during his 45-year peaceful reign that most of the monuments in Afghanistan were constructed.

Conversely, the death of Artaxerxes II marked the beginning of violent rule among the sequential heirs beginning with Artaxerxes III, which includes many stories of betrayal, poisoning, and ascension to the throne by bloody means. In 338 B.C.E., the same year that Philip of Macedon united the Greek states and paved the way for Alexander the Great, Artaxerxes III died and was succeeded by Artaxerxes IV. After quickly attaining the throne, Artaxerxes IV was poisoned by Bagoas, a trusted social advisor and eunuch. Bagoas is said to have killed all remaining children and heirs to the throne, except for the youngest son Arses, whom he made king but then poisoned two years later.

With few options, Bagoas placed Darius III on the throne in 336 B.C.E. When Darius III attempted to become independent of the powerful vizier, Bagoas realized it was time to newly appoint another inexperienced king again through the use of poison. Bagoas tried to murder Darius III as well, but by chance Darius was warned of the plot beforehand. In a turn of events, and in consequence he forced Bagoas to drink the poison himself. Darius III continued to reign, yet instability plagued and threatened the Persian Empire.

GRECO-BACTRIAN RULE IN AFGHANISTAN (330 B.C.E.–150 B.C.E.)

Throughout the mid-fourth century B.C.E., the Persian Empire was beginning to disintegrate, and the control of the outlying regions was in complete disarray. The internal storm which had been brewing for some time finally erupted, and the unstable empire was not prepared for the decisive Battle of Gaugamela in 330 B.C.E. At this crucial battle in history, the Persian Empire fell to none other than Alexander the Great. After the Battle of Gaugamela, the Macedonian ruler Alexander the Great conquered the remaining Persian provinces and began to capture the region of Afghanistan. Alexander ruled as king of Macedonia from 336 to 323 B.C.E., and during his short but impressive reign he achieved such feats as overthrowing the Persian Empire, carrying Macedonian arms to India, and laying the foundation for territorial kingdoms. Alexander the Great would be regarded throughout history as a hero, a military genius, and also a man of myth. To have served alongside Alexander was enough to propel anyone to greatness and in a metaphorical sense, to walk with the gods.

ALEXANDER THE GREAT AND THE RULE OF THE MACEDONIANS

In 356 B.C.E., Alexander was born in Macedonia to Philip II and Olympias, who was the daughter of King Neoptolemus of Epirus. From the ages of 13 to 16, Alexander learned from the philosopher Aristotle, who inspired him with an interest in philosophy, medicine, and scientific investigation. A decisive moment in Alexander's life came in 340 B.C.E. when his father Phillip II attacked Byzantium and left young Alexander in charge of Macedonia. These successful strategic battles for Alexander, including his defeat of the Thracian people (known as the Maedi), his command of the left wing at the Battle of Chaeronea, and his courage in breaking the Sacred Band of Thebes would lay a solid foundation for his military career. However, his father's divorce from his mother Olympias caused severe strain on family relations, and after an argument at his father's wedding feast to his new bride, Alexander and his mother angrily fled to Epirus. Phillip and Alexander would one day reunite, but the argument had threatened Alexander's stance as the heir to Phillip's kingdom.

Philip's assassination in 336 B.C.E. was allegedly by the prince in the royal house of Lyncestis, a small kingdom in the valley of the Crna that had been included in Macedonia by King Philip. Alexander, who was much admired and highly praised by the army, succeeded the throne without disagreement. No one could have imagined Alexander would far surpass the legacy built by his father. He immediately executed the conspirators of his father's murder, along with all possible rivals and those who were opposed to him. From the first moment of his accession to the throne, Alexander was intent on expanding the boundaries of the Macedonian Empire to the ends of the earth, which he thought was just beyond Afghanistan in what is present-day India.

In 334 B.C.E. and after visiting Ilium (known as Troy), Alexander encountered his first enemy force, coming face to face with the Persian army at the Granicus River, located near the Sea of Marmara. The strategy of the Persian military was to attract Alexander across the river to annihilate the young king and his Macedonian troops. From a military history perspective, the style of fighting employed at the time was quite unique. The front line of troops were followed behind by another row of troops, thus as the solider at the front of the line fell, and another solider moved up from behind to replace those who fell in death or were severely wounded and could no longer fight. Once the Persian and Macedonian armies began to clash, Alexander's army continued to thrash the Persians and cut through the military procession. Finally, the Persian line broke and Alexander's army attained victory by pushing through the broken chain and driving the Persian forces into retreat. The majority of the Greek mercenaries under the rule of Darius III fell into carnage, but 2,000 survivors were sent back to Macedonia in slavery.

In the winter between 334 to 333 B.C.E., Alexander conquered western Asia and exposed the region to the rule of the Macedonians. Alexander

Mosaic depicting Macedonian king Alexander the Great's victory over Persian king Darius III at Issus in 333 B.C.E. This defeat led to the capture of Tyre in 332 B.C.E, and his victory was considered to be one of Alexander's greatest military achievements. Alexander's defeat of Darius III and the Persian army marked the beginning of Macedonian rule of Afghanistan. (Jupiterimages)

overpowered the hill tribes of Lycia and Pisidia, and while Alexander was a great military leader, some of his victories were sometimes due to a stroke of luck. Alexander gained a significant advantage following the sudden death of Memnon, the skilled Greek commander of the Persian fleet. This severely hindered the Persian army, as Darius III had advanced northward on the eastern side of Mt. Amanus. While expertise and guidance on both sides were erroneous, Alexander found Darius III drawn up along the Pinarus River. In the battle that followed, Alexander won a decisive victory as the struggle turned into a Persian riot. Darius III fled the battlefield, ultimately abandoning his own family into the hands of Alexander.

Alexander marched south into Syria and Phoenicia intending to isolate the Persian fleet from its bases and weakening the fighting forces. Alexander continued to capture city after city, and in the conquest he acquired Darius's highly valued war chest, containing valuables as well as documents regarding his strategy. Darius III wrote a letter to Alexander offering peace, but Alexander's response required Darius's unconditional surrender to him as the new Lord of Asia. While the seven-month battle of Tyre was in progress, Darius III proposed a new offer to Alexander. In his letter, Darius offered to pay a ransom of 10,000 talents for his family and in addition, Darius III agreed to cede all of his lands west of the Euphrates. In a legendary exchange, Alexander's trusted advisor Parmenio urged his king, "I would accept, were I Alexander." Knowing the offer was inferior and unacceptable, the Macedonian general famously responded, "I would too, were I Parmenio."[6]

The capturing of Tyre in 332 B.C.E. is considered one of Alexander's greatest military achievements. The victory resulted in great bloodshed, and the surviving women and children were sold into slavery. After conquering Egypt, which completed his control of the eastern Mediterranean coast, Alexander the Great returned to Tyre in the spring of 331 B.C.E. As part of his administrative duties, Alexander appointed a Macedonian satrap for Syria and prepared for his advancement into Mesopotamia. In a clever military maneuver, Alexander crossed northern Mesopotamia toward the Tigris River rather than taking the direct route down the river to Babylon. Despite Alexander's cautious efforts, however, Darius III was informed of this maneuver from an advancing force, and Darius III marched up the Tigris to oppose him. In the decisive Battle of Gaugamela, Alexander pursued the defeated Persian forces for 35 miles to Arbela. In arguably the most important military maneuver of Alexander's career, Alexander realized how he could defeat the Persian troops. As part of Alexander's military maneuver, the Companion cavalry was Alexander's elite cavalry and guard, and the cavalry worked as the main offensive support of his army. This "hammer and anvil" metaphor was used to describe the style of Greek combat of the time, as the Companion cavalry was used as the hammer while Alexander's phalanx-based infantry served as the anvil. The phalanx unit worked to confine the enemy in place, as the Companion cavalry moved in from behind or from the side to attack the enemy. With his Companion cavarly command, he was able to break through the Persian line and made charge straight for Darius's chariot. The implementation of this military maneuver gave Alexander the victory at Gaugamela, which finally resulted in his defeat of Persia and thus opened the gates for his control of Asia.

While it is not clear whether Alexander the Great and Darius III met and faced each other on the battlefield, it is certain that once Darius III realized his enemy was close, Darius III retreated to evade the clutches of Alexander. Not afraid of the pursuit, and with the taste of victory tantalizingly within his grasp, Alexander continued to chase Darius III as he fled the battlefield. Alexander had long sought after Darius III, and he knew the importance of capturing the king alive so Darius III could remain as a figurehead for the conquered Persians which would help Alexander control those captured and keep order in the empire. However, when Alexander's military council was informed of troubling news occurring with Parmenio and the Greek army, his military council urged Alexander to return to the battlefield. As difficult as it was to cease the chase of his enemy, Alexander reluctantly ended the pursuit of Darius III and acknowledged the importance of returning to his troops engaged in combat. Darius III narrowly escaped Alexander's clutches, and he exiled himself into Media with his Bactrian cavalry and Greek mercenaries.

The Battle of Gaugamela can legitimately be regarded as the greatest military achievement for Alexander, and the victory allowed Alexander to subjugate the city of Babylon. While not capturing Darius III physically, the defeat of the Persian army propelled Alexander to assume his desired title as the Lord of Asia. As an even more astounding feat, historical records indicate that of Alexander's forces, approximately only one hundred men and one hundred horses were killed in the battle or consequentially died from exhaustion. Yet for the Persian army, more than 300,000 were slain in the battle, and even more than this amount were taken as prisoners.

Alexander had previously captured Darius's wife and children, not to mention his battle spear and war chest of money. Alexander gentlemanly agreed to let Darius's family live unharmed at the capital.

Continuing to march across the continent, Alexander ceremonially burned down the legendary palace of Xerxes at Persepolis, convinced this was a symbolic gesture which stated the Panhellenic war of revenge was at an end. Historians contend, however, the burning of the palace brought shame to Alexander the next morning when he realized what he had done. The following spring, Alexander marched north into Media and occupied its capital Ecbatana. The Thessalians and Greek allies were sent home, and Alexander continued his personal war against Darius III. Alexander simply would not relent, as he viewed his final defeat of the Persians would be marked by his successful capture of Darius III. Furthermore, Alexander feared additional delay would give imposters the opportunity to assume the identity of Darius III, as it was quite common for imposters to pretend they were the genuine ruler, which would hinder Alexanders' defeat of the true Darius III if he wasted time chasing after charlatans. In his continuation of his quest for Darius III, who had retreated into Bactria, by the midsummer Alexander set out at high speed for the eastern provinces. At the same time, Bessus, reigning as the satrap of Bactria and companion to the fleeing Darius III, grew frustrated and was tired of Darius's inability to fight. Bessus believed since Darius III was unable to remain in control of the throne, Darius should no longer serve as ruler of the Persian Empire. Bessus was consumed with resentment for the current predicament, and he initiated a revolt. During the uprising, Bessus and his cohorts killed Darius, and chained his dead body to a wagon on the side of the road. In addition to Bessus, Darius's murderers include Satibarzanes, the satrap of Aria, and Barsaentes, the satrap of Arachosia. After killing Darius, Bessus assumed the title of Artaxerxes as the Great King, and Alexander welcomed the rivalry of the newly titled great ruler in order to defeat him for killing Darius III. Turning his anger onto a new enemy, Alexander now vowed to defeat Bessus for robbing him of the pleasure to capture Darius alive.[7] In a recognition of respect amid their long-standing rivalry, Alexander ordered Darius's body to be buried with due honors in the royal tombs at Persepolis.

MACEDONIAN SUPREMACY IN AFGHANISTAN

The death and unofficial defeat of Darius III in 330 B.C.E. was significant in the formation of Afghanistan as it was the last obstacle to Alexander's self-desired title as the great king, and soon after Alexander's Asian coinage included his title as the Lord of Asia. Alexander continued his advancements to the Caspian Sea, and in Aria he agreed to let the ruling satraps remain in place. In the location now known as modern Herat of Afghanistan, he established the city of Alexandria of the Arians. During the winter of 330 to 329 B.C.E., Alexander advanced further into Afghanistan. Alexander and his army marched up the Afghan valley of the Helmand River and over the mountains past modern Kabul. Here in the country of the Paropamisadae, the great Macedon founded Alexandria by the Caucasus. In continuing the quest for Bessus, the army crossed the mountains of the Hindu Kush and proceeded northward over the Khawak Pass. Despite the tired army, the food shortages, and the harsh terrain of the Hindu Kush Mountains, Alexander brought his army to Drapsaca in pursuit of Bessus and what remained of the Persian army. As Bessus worked to escape Alexander by moving beyond modern Amu Darya, Alexander marched his army toward the region of Bactria-Zariaspa, known as modern Balkh in Afghanistan. Bessus was counting on allegiance with the satrapies in the regions of Afghanistan along with other principalities to join him in the resistance against Macedonian control. After passing over the Oxus River, Alexander sent his general Ptolemy to track down Bessus, who at this point was removed from power by the Sogdian Spitamenes. Bessus was captured, flogged, and sent to Bactria to accept his fate for his crimes, in which the Persian method of punishment at the time was to cut off the nose and ears of the offender. After Bessus received this Persian punishment, he was publicly executed at Ecbatana.

With Bessus now captured, punished, and executed, Alexander continued his quest to defeat the remaining Persian Empire, and accordingly he turned his forces to concentrate on the defeat of Oxyartes, the companion of Bessus and reigning satrap of Bactria. In 327 B.C.E., Alexander still had one province of the Persian Empire to defeat, located in Balkh of Bactria in Afghanistan. In fear of the wrath of Alexander, Oxyartes secured his wife and his daughter Roxana in the fortress of Sogdian Rock, a fortress that allegedly could be captured only by "men with wings." Alexander arrived at the fortress and requested the surrender of Oxyartes and consequentially the remaining Persian Empire. With no response from the king, Alexander scoured his troops for volunteers to climb the steep walls of the fortress. Upon his capture of the fortress of Sogdian Rock, Alexander gazed upon Roxana for the first time, a woman whose legendary beauty overwhelmed him. Completely taken with her, Alexander made Roxana his bride, and the marriage was also an attempt to subdue the Bactrian satrap's rule to Alexander. After the wedding, Alexander moved forward with conquering India, then known as the far end of the world.

In 327 B.C.E., Alexander left Bactria with a revitalized army and marched forward into the world's end. Alexander's dream of completing his empire could not happen fast enough as he sought to march his army to the last corner of India. After again crossing the treacherous terrain of the Hindu Kush Mountains, Alexander thought it best to divide his forces. In what Alexander devised as a maneuvering advantage, the great general sent a portion of his army through the Khyber Pass in Afghanistan. Alexander led the remaining troops through the hills to the north. Alexander did not have much knowledge of India's vastness beyond the Hyphasis, but the young Macedon was fervent to discover the extent of his soon-to-be-completed empire. After the tiring and exhausting march to the Hyphasis the army faced many difficulties, and eventually the troops were weak from hunger and exhaustion. These fatigued souls simply refused to go any farther. Alexander was overcome with anger, but his troops pleaded with him to return home. Finding the army adamant in their stance, in tandem with the exhaustion and death tolls rising, Alexander agreed to cease the exploration and turn back into Afghanistan. While returning through the Mulla Pass, Quetta, and Kandahar into the Helmand valley of Afghanistan, the extensive attempt at advancement into India took a severe toll on the army. Alexander's march to the far end of the world proved disastrous. The barren desert, lack of water, and shortage of food caused great distress to his troops, and as a result many of Alexander's troops perished.

Despite not achieving much victory in India, Alexander continued to battle and to expand his empire. After conquering region after region, all the while subjugating different races along the way, Alexander believed that unification of the races would be necessary to successfully unite the empire. Alexander began his plans for racial fusion after conquering Susa in 324 B.C.E. Alexander celebrated the seizure of the Persian Empire by instituting his custom of combining the Macedonians and Persians into one master race. Alexander believed that uniting the races would make the Persians on equal terms, not only in the Greek army but also as satraps of the provinces. In supporting this challenging endeavor, Alexander encouraged his Macedonian officers to take Persian wives, referencing how he himself had married the Persian Roxana. Of those who were already married, some 10,000 of Alexander's soldiers with native wives were given generous dowries as compensation. This policy was harshly begrudged by the Greeks, and in consequence brought increasing friction to Alexander's relations with his Macedonians. His determination to incorporate Persians on equal terms with the Macedonians in both the army and the administration of the provinces was severely resented. Macedonians interpreted this as a threat to their own privileged position, especially after a large amount of Persian youths received a Macedonian military training. To add further insult to the Macedonian warriors, Persian nobles had been accepted into the royal cavalry bodyguard.

At this time in his reign, Alexander was widely respected for his military advances and skill. Many historians regard him as the greatest military general of all time. Alexander's energetic personality, strong determination, and ability to push for excellence with both himself and his army earned him respect and admiration. Alexander successfully maintained loyalty throughout his reign, and it was only his unsuccessful attempt to conquer India that Alexander failed to preserve unfaltering allegiance. However, Alexander's plans for racial synthesis were a complete failure. The Macedonians rejected the concept of cultural synthesis, and the customs of the Greeks would remain dominant. In the summer of 323 B.C.E. in Babylon, Alexander was quite suddenly taken ill after a banquet. Historians debate whether Alexander was poisoned or simply died of a natural illness. Alexander clung to life for 10 days and on June 13, he died at the age of 33. Alexander the Great had reigned for over 12 years, and his body was eventually placed in a golden coffin in Alexandria. In spite of Alexander's short reign, he had a profound impact and long-lasting influence in the history of Europe, Asia, and the Middle East. In Afghanistan, Alexander created many cities, established a new political structure, and inserted a great deal of Greek influence to the region. Alexander's short-lived empire further ascertains to the incomparable warrior-like mentality of the early Afghans, for not even the Great Alexander was able to fully conquer and control their land.

NOTES

1. Erik Hildinger, *Warriors of the Steppe: A Military History of Central Asia, 500 B.C. to 1700 A.D.* (New York: Sarpedon, 1997), 5–14.

2. Lewis, *The Middle East*, 21–32.

3. Hildinger, *Warriors of the Steppe*, 33–34.

4. Ibid., 36.

5. Ibid., 36, 39.

6. Stephen Tanner, *Afghanistan: A Military History from Alexander the Great to the Fall of the Taliban* (New York: Da Capo Press, 2002), 17–52.

7. Ibid., 17–52.

4

Afghanistan from Hellenistic Culture to the Introduction of Islam

Alexander the Great had conquered much of the known world, but in his rush to do so, he failed to secure an adult heir to rule the empire he left behind. While Alexander lay dying in his deathbed, his military generals asked him, "To whom shall you leave your vast empire?" Alexander simply replied, "To the strongest." After the death of Alexander the Great in 323 B.C.E., the demise of the great conqueror is regarded as the genesis of the Hellenistic period in Afghanistan. The term *Hellenistic* is a cultural description that is determined by the spread of Greek influence over non-Greek cultures. The death of the great king left the Macedonian empire in political disarray and resulted in remarkable conflict among the Diadochi, the name of the trusted and high-powered generals of Alexander's army. The period immediately after Alexander's death is eloquently branded as the Wars of the Diadochi, and indeed it was a time of war. The Macedonian generals argued and engaged in a bitter struggle to determine the successor to Alexander's throne. Unable to agree on one ruler, the generals established the Partition of Babylon in which the territories were ultimately divided among the Diadochi shortly after Alexander's death. These territories would then be under the oversight of one of Alexander's greatest and well-regarded generals, Perdiccas.[1]

THE DIVISION OF THE MACEDONIAN EMPIRE (323 B.C.E. TO 310 B.C.E.)

As the struggle for the throne continued, Perdiccas assumed the role of regent of the empire. Through his role as regent, Perdiccas handled the administrative duties since the appointed successive ruler did not officially serve on the throne. In most cases this was because the appointed ruler was still quite young, absent from the throne, or incapacitated and could not serve. Perdiccas recognized the empire was far too extensive, and accordingly should be divided among Alexander's generals. At the Partition of Babylon in 323 B.C.E., Perdiccas championed for an agreement between the Diachodi, and appointed Alexander's remaining generals to become the satraps of the various provinces. Also in accordance with this agreement, the Diachodi appointed two kings to share in the overall rule of the provinces. The Diachodi appointed the first king based on general family relation to Alexander. Philip II of Macedon fathered an illegitimate son named Philip Arrhidaeus, and therefore as Alexander's illegitimate brother, he was the closest heir to the throne. Philip Arrhidaeus would become Phillip III of Macedon and was appointed as heir to Alexander's kingdom along with Alexander's then unborn son Alexander IV. Roxana gave birth to the second king several months after Alexander's death.

Even with this agreement in place, Perdiccas continued to act as regent of the empire. For years, the Diadochi fought for supremacy over Alexander's vast empire and eventually challenged the rule of Perdiccas. Ptolemy, the satrap of Egypt, was keenly aware that some of the other governors were thirsty for more power. Armed with this knowledge, Ptolemy led the rebellion to oppose the Perdiccas as regent. Perdiccas fought the rebellion for over a year but was eventually assassinated by his officers in 321 B.C.E. Ptolemy's revolt and usurpation of Perdiccas led to a new division of the empire known as the Partition of Triparadisus. With the continuing struggle for the throne and no regent to protect it, the kings as appointed under the Partition of Babylon agreement were ultimately murdered. Phillip Arrhidaeus was the greater threat as the older king and was the first to be assassinated in 317 B.C.E. Alexander's mother Olympias was also vulnerable to attack, as her role had become champion and defender of the young grandson Alexander IV as the one true king, and she was ultimately murdered in 316 B.C.E. After living for several years under almost complete collapse of Alexander's empire, Roxana and her son Alexander IV were both assassinated around 310 B.C.E.

AFGHANISTAN DIVIDED UNDER SELEUCID AND MAURYAN RULE (310 B.C.E.–180 B.C.E.)

The death of the young king Alexander IV marked the beginning of a fascinating aspect in the country's history, as this initiated the period in time when Afghanistan was ruled under two completely different civilizations. During the regent rebellion with Ptolemy, Alexander's cavalry commander Seleucus I Nicator participated in the insurgence against Perdiccas. After the assassination, Seleucus seized control of Alexander's empire in the east and established himself in Babylon in 312 B.C.E. Thus commenced the Seleucid dynasty, and Seleucus successfully extended his authority through the Bactria Province in northern Afghanistan. As it was throughout Alexander's rule, the Greek soldiers and colonists would remain in the Hindu Kush region. The dream of racial infusion as originated with Alexander the Great continued throughout the Seleucid Empire and became part of Hellenistic culture. Seleucus's sovereignty was extensive throughout the region, and he was ruthless in his approach to extend the domain of the realm.

The division of Alexander's empire further continued until 306 B.C.E. when the provinces were broken apart into independent kingdoms. In an effort to gain more power and influence over the region, Seleucus pushed the boundaries of his empire as far as the Indus River in India, and it was here in 305 B.C.E. when the Mauryan dynasty of India engaged in a crucial conflict with the Seleucids. After facing a completely devastating battle and almost utter defeat, Seleucus reached an agreement with Chandragupta Maurya, the king of the Mauryan tribe in India. The Indian Mauryan Empire had settled and laid claim to the northern region of the Indian subcontinent, which also included efforts for the colonization of the southern regions in Afghanistan. As part of the battle negotiations and in exchange for land, Seleucus's power would cease beyond the Hindu Kush Mountains. As a result, southern Afghanistan would in turn be allocated as a part of the Mauryan quest for territorial expansion from India. The Mauryan Empire hence would continue into the area south of the Hindu Kush Mountains, stretching from Kabul to the southern Kandahar region. As part of the settlement for the southern area of Afghanistan, the Mauryans agreed to the demands of the Seleucid dynasty. In exchange for the land west of the Indus River, Seleucus demanded a substantial force of 500 elephants to strengthen his army. At the time, this large army of elephants was regarded as a significant military asset. However, the agreement included the Seleucid Empire ceding vast amounts of land, not just the southern part of Afghanistan but also considerable sections of Persia. Seleculus's agreement to cede vast amounts of land is something that historians continue to debate. Even though he relinquished control of these lands, Seleculus's victory at Ipsus was solely due to the elephant brigade he acquired under this treaty. Nevertheless, historians still debate if the exchange of land for elephants was the best choice for the Seleucid Empire. The treaty also included a matrimonial agreement, known as *Epigamia* in ancient times, although historical records are not particularly clear on the exact specifications of the marriage arrangement. This conjugal treaty could imply either a dynastic alliance between a Seleucid princess and the Mauryan dynasty, or the marriage could refer to a symbolical unity between the Greeks of the Seleucid Empire and the Indians of the Mauryan dynasty. Despite these other treaty stipulations, Seleucus was easily swayed since he knew the strategic value of gaining a large force of elephants as part of his military fleet. This aspect of the treaty would play a decisive role in the Battle of Ipsus in 301 B.C.E., where Seleucus took control over Anatolia and northern Syria and would continue his expansion efforts for 20 years. However, for Chandragupta Maurya, the payment of 500 elephants would have little impact to his army, which included a force of over 9,000 elephants.

Regardless of the loss of the vast quantity of land to the Mauryan dynasty, the Seleucid Empire expanded from the Aegean Sea to Afghanistan and brought together a multitude of races and cultural influences. After trying to expand his empire into Europe, Seleucid was assassinated in 281 B.C.E. by Ptolemy Ceraunus. Following Seleucus's assassination, his son Antiochus I Soter would rule from 281 to 261 B.C.E. As his successor, Antiochus would ultimately fail at expanding the empire, which was already undeniably quite vast. The struggle and tearing apart of Alexander's empire during the Wars of the Diochadi ended nearly 40 years after his death with the division of the empire into four territories. The empire was divided among the Ptolemaic dynasty in Egypt based at Alexandria, the Seleucid dynasty in Syria and Mesopotamia based at Antioch, the Antigonid dynasty in Macedon and central Greece, and the Attalid dynasty in Anatolia based at Pergamum. Both Antiochus I and his son Antiochus II, who governed from 261 to 246 B.C.E., were plagued with major challenges in the west, including repeated wars with Ptolemy II and Celtic invasions of Asia Minor. At the end of the reign of Antiochus II, several provinces would rebel and assert their independence from the ruler, which contributed to the rise of the Greco-Bactrian secession in 250 B.C.E.

THE RULE OF THE MAURYAN DYNASTY IN SOUTHERN AFGHANISTAN (305 B.C.E.–185 B.C.E.)

In 262 B.C.E., a figure that would have a pivotal role in shaping the religious beliefs of Afghanistan emerged. As the last major emperor in the Mauryan dynasty of India, Asoka conquered all of India and much of Afghanistan. As his most influential imprint on Afghanistan, Asoka was a vigorous supporter of Buddhism. During his reign (dates vary but the reign of Asoka was approximately 262 to 238 B.C.E.), Asoka promoted the beliefs and teachings of Buddhism throughout India and into Afghanistan. This belief in Buddhism began early in his reign. After leading a successful but rather bloody conquest at the Kalinga country on the eastern coast in approximately 255 B.C.E., Asoka renounced armed battle and embraced what he referred to as the guiding principles of life. As described by Asoka, the suffering and pain the war caused on the defeated Kalinga people consumed him with remorse, and he vowed to abandon the life of the sword. After turning to the influence of Buddhism beliefs and principles, Asoka was determined to live his life according to the dharma principle to value all forms of life. The dharma principle is based on personal behaviors to value and respect life. It is based on ideas found in Indian-based religions such as Hinduism and Buddhism. Forsaking his years as a soldier, Asoka toiled for the remainder of his life with the philosophy to work for and serve all of humankind.

As part of his influence, he developed a deep understanding of the humanity of all people, and Asoka also developed a policy of respect and acceptance toward all other religious sects. Asoka granted non-Buddhist believers the full freedom to live in accordance with their own religious beliefs and principles, but he consistently strove to request they also work to increase their own inner worth. While supporting their religious expression and beliefs, he still felt obliged to encourage three guiding principles: a livelihood of respecting others' religious values, to acknowledge the good deeds and acts of people, and also to withhold criticism of the differing viewpoints of others. In this manner, Asoka's goal was to lead people to follow along his lifeline path of dharma through reasoning with people, rather than issuing commands to follow his beliefs.

The pillar of Asoka at Vaishali, India. Asoka was the last emperor of the Mauyran dynasty. His most significant influence on Afghanistan was promoting the beliefs of Buddhism. His teachings were carved on rocks and pillars throughout India and Afghanistan. Asoka's inscription on the pillar at Vaishali shows his passion for charity, compassion, and serving humanity. (Sudalim/iStockphoto.com)

To make his message known, Asoka held public oral proclamations for his teachings and his work. His teachings on the principles and beliefs of his religion were also engraved on rocks and pillars sites. These bilingual inscriptions are known as the rock edicts and pillar edicts, and contain proclamations regarding Asoka's personal thoughts, actions, and life teachings. Two of these rock edicts are located in the southern area of Kandahar and also in Laghman, located on the eastern side of Afghanistan. Significantly, scholars note the tone of sincerity in these principles and statements of Asoka, as these writings appear to be his genuine beliefs. Thus it is with positive assertion that Asoka governed his attitude and lifestyle by the dharma values of humanity. Asoka's writings as inscribed on the pillars and rock edicts display his authentic passion for charity, compassion, and serving humanity. Furthermore, the Kandahar edicts are the farthest Western Buddhist edicts to be found outside of India, and these edicts in Afghanistan are the only ones to have used the Greek language. The edicts serve as a remarkable illustration of Afghanistan's role in uniting Eastern and Western empires, and are a perfect representation of the Greek and Indian influence in Afghanistan.

As a result of Asoka's patronage and encouragement to a belief in Buddhism, the religion spread quickly throughout the Mauryan Empire from India to Afghanistan. When Asoka reached his state of enlightenment after the violent and horrific battle at Kalinga, Buddhism transitioned from being a small religious sect that was once confined to a few locations in India to one that had widespread and popular beliefs throughout the empire. Clearly it was his influence during his reign that helped the religion spread throughout India and subsequently into southern Afghanistan. For the early Afghans who lived south of the Hindu Kush, this period in history was a time of compassion, tranquility, and humanitarianism.

The occupation of the Mauryan dynasty in southern Afghanistan was significant in the early years of Afghanistan, and it is impressive these beliefs still remain in spite of the short rule of the empire outside of India. While the Mauryan rule might be considered one of the briefest occupations in the overall history of Afghanistan, the most influential aspect of the dynasty was the religious inspiration it brought to the country, especially in such a short time span. Under the guiding tutelage of Asoka, the Mauryans successfully introduced Buddhism to the region during their occupation in southern Afghanistan, and it became a religion almost as prominent and influential as Zoroastrianism.

The rule of the Mauryans would decline after Asoka's death, as his death was followed by the rule of several ineffective kings. By the time of the reign of the last Mauryan ruler Brhadrata, the dynasty and the kingdom had shrunk considerably in size from Asoka's rule. During the Sunga coup of 185 B.C.E., the leader Pusyamitra Sunga assassinated Brhadrata and established the Sunga Empire. By overthrowing the dynasty, the Sunga Empire instated the beliefs of Hinduism and virtually eliminated the followings of Buddhism, even to the point of threatening Buddhists with persecution. Although historians debate if the Sunga coup eliminated Buddhism in Afghanistan, the Sunga Empire encouraged the beliefs of Hinduism and as a result it became the prominent religion in Afghanistan.[2]

INDEPENDENT RULE IN AFGHANISTAN: GRECO-BACTRIAN AND PARTHIAN SECESSION FROM THE SELEUCID EMPIRE (250 B.C.E.–125 B.C.E.)

The Hellenistic successor states of the Seleucids and Greco-Bactrian were a society composed of both Greek and Near-Eastern cultures. During this short period in the history of Afghanistan, an independent Hellenistic state was declared in the Bactria region. In the year 250 B.C.E., while Asoka was simultaneously spreading his Buddhist beliefs across southern Afghanistan, Diodotus ascertained independence from the Seleucid Empire and assumed control of the Bactria Province of Afghanistan. After asserting independence, Diodotus formed the Greco-Bactrian Kingdom and over the next 10 years he eventually overthrew the Seleucids and Mauryans in both western and southern Afghanistan. In addition to the Greco-Bactrian revolt for independence, the Iranian rule of the Parthians declared independence from the Seleucids as well. The Parthians established control over the Sistan border region located between eastern Iran and southern Afghanistan. Furthermore, the Parthians also assumed the control of the Kandahar region in southern Afghanistan.

The far northern region of Afghanistan was still under the rule of the remaining Seleucid Empire. The region prospered but was not nearly as peaceful as the southern region under the influence of Asoka. In the northern terrain of Afghanistan, Antiochus III (also known as Antiochus the Great) was the Seleucid king of the Hellenistic Syrian Empire from 223 to 187 B.C.E. During his reign, Antiochus III rebuilt the empire in the East, but failed to overpower the Roman superiority in Europe and in Asia Minor. Additionally during his reign, Antiochus III transformed the empire by reducing the size of the provinces and administratively reducing the power of the governing satraps. As part of his reformation, Antiochus III also believed in the custom of enhancing interaction with neighboring regions by marrying off his daughters to the princes of nearby empires.

From 212 to 205 B.C.E., Antiochus III pursued his eastward expansion campaign and sought to advance the empire into India. Antiochus III achieved victory in the northern region of Bactria and defeated the ruler Euthydemus in 208 B.C.E. As part of the defeat, Antiochus decided to allow Euthydemus to continue his reign in title, thus allowing him to serve as a political figurehead. This method is also in accordance with the code of Alexander the Great, as Alexander wanted to capture Darius III alive because he recognized the political significance of retaining the ruler to serve as a figurehead, which would stifle a rebellion from the conquered empire. Continuing his eastern campaign, in 206 B.C.E., Antiochus marched toward Kabul by crossing the steep hills and valleys of the Hindu Kush Mountains. Once his eastern campaign was completed, Antiochus III believed his triumphs entitled him to a higher designation, and thus he assumed the title of the Great King. By taking this name, Antiochus was in one manner paying tribute to the ancient Archamenid title, but also encouraging the Greek comparison to Alexander the Great. Antiochus changed his appellation, and accordingly he became known as Antiochus the Great. Antiochus III title of "the Great" was briefly assumed after his eastern campaign and appears in historical accounts through 202 B.C.E. After his victory at Koile Syria, Antiochus assumed the Greek title *Basileus Megas*, Greek for "Great King." However, Antiochus would not be honored with this title for very long.

The Seleucid Empire suffered a threefold loss to the Roman Republic at the Battle of Thermopylae in 191 B.C.E., the Battle of Magnesia in 190 B.C.E., and also the sequential defeat of the Seleucid navy. At the Treaty of Apamea in 188 B.C.E., Antiochus the Great agreed to relinquish his control of all of his empire in Europe and his land holdings in Asia Minor. Also as part of the massive settlement, Antiochus was forced to submit to the Roman Empire in multiple forms. This included such stipulations as the payment of reparations for the war, which included approximately 15,000 talents, paid out over 12 years to recover the costs of the war, and also the surrender of his massive military fleet, including the elephants previously granted to him in exchange for these lands. As further insult, the peace treaty required Antiochus to provide persons selected by the Roman Empire to serve as prisoners for a period of three years, which included his son Antiochus IV. In the comprehensive treaty, the terms of the hostages were very clearly stipulated. This entailed the selection of 20 hostages by the Roman council, and these hostages would be traded out every three years. The treaty greatly reduced the size of his kingdom to the areas of Syria, Mesopotamia, and western Iran. In return, the Senate granted him a Roman agreement of peace and friendship. However, the agreement masked with these embarrassing stipulations did not result in amicability between the empires. Nearly three years later, Antiochus the Great was murdered in a temple near Susa, a city located in present-day Iran. After seizing control, the Greco-Bactrian rule spread quickly over multiple territories, and by 170 B.C.E. reached from northeastern Iran in the west to the Ganges River in India in the east. However, internal disputes between the Greek and Hellenized rulers inundated the empire, and weakened the strength of the kingdom. Further, the exceedingly ambitious attempts to conquer and extend the boundaries of the empire further east in India contributed to the demise of the dynasty.

Simultaneously in southern Afghanistan, the Mauryan Empire fell into decline after the death of Asoka. This creates an interesting timestamp in the history of Afghanistan, as all future aspiring leaders never fully conquered Afghanistan to the north of the Hindu Kush. By 180 B.C.E., Demetrius I of Bactria invaded India and formed the Greco-Indian Kingdom, which in consequence ended the Mauryan dynasty. Under Demetrius I, the Greco-Indian kingdom ruled in Afghanistan's Bactria region until 125 B.C.E. when the empire was invaded and overthrown by nomadic tribes from the north. The empire was overrun by two groups of northern nomadic invaders from Central Asia, believed to be the Parthians of eastern Iran and the Sakas. Historical accounts also allege that the invading nomadic tribes possibly included the Scythians. In approximately 135 B.C.E., a loose confederation of five Central Asian nomadic tribes united together under the one Kushan tribe, and this newly unified tribe banded together to fight and conquered the Afghan area. Historical evidence and excavations in Ai Khanoum indicate the invasion by nomadic cultures. Located in the Kunduz region of northeastern Afghanistan, the site was excavated between 1964 and 1978, but was abandoned at the beginning of Afghanistan's war with the Soviets. Afterward, very little original archeological evidence remained due to damage from the war or from thieves raiding the site. During these conquests, these nomadic invaders established control over Sistan (the border region between Iran and Afghanistan) and Kandahar in the south, previously controlled by the Parthians.

THE KUSHAN EMPIRE (150 B.C.E.–224 C.E.)

The Yuezhi confederation of China conquered Bactria in the second century B.C.E. and divided the country into five chiefdoms, one of which would become the Kushan Empire. Recognizing the importance of unification, these five tribes combined under the one dominant

Kushan tribe, and the primary rulers descended from the Yuezhi. The Kushan overtook southern Afghanistan from the Bactrian Greeks and ruled over most of the northern Indian subcontinent, Afghanistan, and parts of Central Asia. The rule of the Kushan Empire endured for nearly four centuries and crossed over into the Christian era of history. The domain of the empire spread from the Kabul river valley in the Hindu Kush into Asia as far as the central Indian plateau. Under King Kanishka I, who reigned from 78 to 144 c.e., the Kushan kingdom was recognized along with China, Rome, and Parthia as one of the four great Eurasian powers of the time. King Kanishka was by far the most powerful ruler of the Kushan Empire, and during his reign the empire reached its greatest coverage, stretching from Afghanistan into Asia and included the locations of Kashmir and Tibet.

As patrons of religion, the Kushan Empire was instrumental in spreading Buddhism throughout Central Asia and China, and King Kanishka particularly encouraged Asoka's beliefs of Mauryan Buddhism. As part of the Kushan Empire's penchant for religion and art, the world's largest Buddha figures were carved into a cliff in the Bamian (Bamyan) Mountains of Afghanistan. The two statues each measured approximately 175 feet and 120 feet tall, and these statues were an iconic tribute to the religious beliefs of the enlightened one. Commonly referred to as the Buddhas at Bamiyan, the statues were located along the Silk Road, the ancient trade route in the Bamyan valley that linked China, India, and Europe, located approximately 143 miles northwest of Kabul. The majestic Buddhas at Bamiyan were destroyed by the Taliban in 2001, and several countries such as Japan and Switzerland have pledged support for the artistic rebuilding of the statues. The statues were widely regarded as a perfect representation of Greco-Buddhist art and influence to the region of Afghanistan.

Under King Kanishka, the Kushan Empire became affluent through trade particularly with the Roman Empire; however, in addition to trade with the Romans, the Kushan carried luxury goods and traded with vast empires such as India and China via the Silk Road at Balkh in Afghanistan. As part of their successful ability and affinity for trade, the Kushan gold coins exhibit the figures of Greek, Roman, Iranian, Hindu, and Buddhist deities, and furthermore display Greek letters and inscriptions. These images and inscriptions on the coins demonstrate the influence and magnitude of the various forms of religion and art that prevailed in the Kushan Empire. Despite achieving this zenith of religious and cultural acceptance, the Kushan dynasty would never be as powerful as it was under King Kanishka. In the third century c.e., the empire was segmented into several smaller kingdoms. While several Kushan princes governed in various kingdoms throughout the empire, this weakened the Kushan Empire and thus left the kingdoms extremely vulnerable to attack. After the Kushan Empire separated into multiple kingdoms, the trade interaction with China and Rome simultaneously decreased, and in consequence this severely impacted Kushan prosperity. Without unity in the kingdom and no income to assist in the kingdom's defense, the Sassanian Empire of Persia easily overtook the control of Afghanistan from the Kushan Empire. After the rise of the Sassanian dynasty in Iran and local powers of the Gupta dynasty in northern India, the Kushan rule sharply declined and ultimately ceased. As a result, the Sassanian kingdom established the control over parts of Afghanistan in approximately 241 C.E.

CONTINUOUS CONQUEST: THE SASSANIAN DYNASTY AND WHITE HUN INVASION (241–565 C.E.)

The Sassanian dynasty ruled in Afghanistan for over a century, even though the dynasty was unsuccessful in uniting and fully conquering the region. As a result, northern nomadic invaders easily defeated the Sassanian dynasty in 400 C.E. Afghanistan was yet again invaded by another group of conquerors, this time known as the fierce Hepthalites of Central Asia. Also referred to as the White Huns, the Hepthalites were ferocious attackers who swept into Bactria and into southern Afghanistan, obliterating any remaining Kushan and Sassanian kingdoms along the way. The White Huns also engaged in continuous conflict with the western Sassanian. The rule of the White Huns lasted for nearly 200 years in Afghanistan, and during this time the country was ravaged and destroyed by these Indo-European nomadic invaders. The White Huns were also well known for their ruthless destruction of Buddhist shrines in Afghanistan.

The Western Turks would eventually overthrow the Hepthalites in the mid-sixth century C.E. The Western Turks were also nomads of Central Asia, and in the conquest in 565 C.E., the Hepthalites lost control of the territories north of the Amu Darya River. The concurrent resurrection of Sassanian control forced the Hepthalites to also relinquish domination of the lands south of the Amu Darya. Afghanistan was subsequently ruled under several small kingdoms, the majority of which were ultimately under Sassanian rule led by either Kushan or Hepthalite monarchs.

Impressive archaeological findings of this time period indicate humans lived in the caves of the Hindu Kush Mountains. Historians speculate that these humans sought refuge in these caves while the Hepthalites and the Sassanians battled for supremacy in Afghanistan.[3] Due to the severe impact of the Hepthalites, some historians believe, the name *Afghanistan* is derived from Faganish, the fierce Hepthalite ruler in this region who was defeated by the Sassanians.

Along with the Sassanian rule also came the renewed influence of Hinduism in Afghanistan. The exact date of the emergence of Hinduism is shrouded in obscurity, but civilizations in the mid-seventh century Afghanistan constructed Hindu kingdoms in the areas of Kabul, Gardez, and Ghazni. Historical findings of marble statues of Hindu deities, including the elephant god Ganesh, have been discovered in the cities Ghazni and Koh Daman. These remarkable findings have led scholars to conclude that the Hindu god Ganesh actually originated in Afghanistan. Other remnants discovered include the carvings of the Hindu god Shiva and her consort Durga. The exciting discovery of these figures is a remarkable facet in Afghanistan's history, and these statues currently reside at the country's national museum in Kabul.

THE RULE OF ISLAMIC EMPIRES IN AFGHANISTAN

During the pre-Islamic period in Afghanistan, the cultural religious beliefs predominately functioned under the threefold influence of Hellenistic, Buddhist, and Hindu cultures. China and Rome also had influence on the region as indicated in the artesian artifacts found in Afghanistan. The year 642 marked the beginning of the Arab conquest of the Middle East. In this year at the Battle of Nahavand, Islamic warriors overpowered the Sassanian Empire. For 10 years the Arabian Empire defeated and overthrew the remaining Parthinian and Byzantine empires. By 652, the Arabs had invaded Afghanistan and thus began the emergence of the Islamic faith in Afghanistan. While the conquest of Afghanistan and the emergence of Islam occurred in tandem, it was not the intent of the Arabs to introduce Islam by force. The Arab Empire conquered the remainder of Afghanistan from 706 to 709, and over time the majority of the population converted to Islam.[4] As the culture and influence of Islam spread, Afghanistan emerged as the center of several predominant Islamic rulers.

THE FIVE PILLARS OF ISLAM

The *Five Pillars of Islam* are five basic acts in Islam which are considered mandatory by believers. In addition to the belief in the Arabic Qu'ran as the holy book, the Five Pillars are the principles of Islam that are the foundation of Muslim life. The pillars are summarized in the famous hadith of Gabriel and relate to Muslim life, prayer, concern for the needy, self-purification, and the pilgrimage. The Five Pillars are:

1. *Shahadah or Creed*: The creed for Muslims to declare there is no god except Allah, and Mohammed is God's Messenger (*la ilaha illa allah, Muhammada rasul Allah*).
2. *Namaz or Prayer*: Muslims are required to perform a ritual prayer five times a day—in the morning before sunrise, at noon, in the afternoon, in the evening, and at night before going to bed. If for any reason the Muslim is not able to perform the prayer at the dedicated time during the day, the Muslim shall make up the prayer during the evening prayer time. Prayer is *fard* (obligatory) for all Muslims except those who are disabled, prepubescent, very sick, pregnant, frail and elderly or traveling on a long journey.
3. *Sawm or Fasting*: During the blessed month of Ramadan, Muslims must fast between sunrise and sunset. It is a time of self-control for reflection, and no food, drink, smoking, or sexual activity may occur. Children, very sick, and travelers are not required to fast.
4. *Zakat or Charity*: Those who have the financial means must give a percentage of their income to the poor and needy.
5. *Hajj or Pilgrimage*: Those who are capable must make the pilgrimage to Mecca at least once in a lifetime if they are able to do so. The prophet Mohammed declared that any Muslim who made the trip and performed the *hajj* ceremony will be freed of all sins. Once this is completed, the Muslim is referred to as *Hajji*.

The remaining centuries resulted in Afghanistan being the focal point of many distinguished empires, most notably the Ghaznavid Empire from 962 to 1151. Certainly of unique origins, the Ghaznavid Empire began when a slave guard of the Turkish Empire, referred to as a *malmuk*, revolted against the ruling Samanids. Alptigin was a Turkish malmuk from Ghazni, and he established the Ghaznavid Empire by usurping the throne of the weakened Samanid Empire. As has often been the case throughout history, the rights to the throne lay in the usurper's personal strength and determination to overthrow those in power. Alptigin crossed the Hindu Kush Mountains from Balkh with this intention, and sequestered Ghanzi from the declining Samanid Empire. Predominately a Sunni Muslim establishment located on the eastern side of Afghanistan, the fort was located advantageously on the Silk Road between Kabul and Kandahar. After seizing control of the Fort of Ghanzi in 962, the once-insignificant settlement was transformed into one of the most dazzling capitals of the Islamic world.

The center of the Ghanzi Empire was the pinnacle of prestige, enjoying artisans, poets, musicians, and philosophers amid the backdrop of opulent palaces, gold-encrusted mosques, and lavish gardens that spread to India. Throughout the reign of the empire, many iconoclastic movements were unleashed into India, and the empire spread from Afghanistan into India, Persia, and Central Asia. After the Battle of Dandanaqan in 1039 with the Seljuks, who were another Muslim dynasty of Turkish descent, the Ghaznavid Empire lost control of the western territories, including the western part of Afghanistan. The Ghaznavids were forced to rule while being presided over by the Seljuks of Iran, and the empire never returned to the same opulence and splendor.

Historically, the Ghaznavid Empire is significant because it was the first considerable Islamic empire that spread across Asia. At the empire's greatest extent, the domain of the Ghaznavid Empire was vast and encompassed much of modern Iran, Afghanistan, India, and Pakistan. Of further historical magnitude, the Ghaznavids are believed to have spread Islam into India, a land that was dominated by Hinduism. For the next century, the Ghaznavids' diminished rule was still extensive, until the Ghorid Empire would overthrow the remaining territories in 1151.

The last Ghaznavid king of the empire, known as Sultan Bahram Shah, engaged in antagonism and opposition with the Ghori Empire. Founded by Muhammad Ghori, his descendants ruled over a diminishing empire consumed with bitter struggles and competition. In trying to quench his anger over the death of his brother and as revenge, King Ala'uddin Ghori conquered Ghazni in 1151 and set the city ablaze for seven days. The Ghori Empire would reign in Afghanistan from 1151 to 1219, and would continue the lavishness which began under Ghanzi rule. At the height of the empire, the boundaries extended from modern Iraq through Afghanistan, and as far to the east as India. The region flourished with wealth and opulence, speckled with lavish palaces surrounded by magnificent gardens. In this land of the Afghans, the soil thrived from the remarkably engineered irrigation systems that led water to fields and gardens of splendor. Alas, in 1219, the empire and the land of Afghanistan would be ransacked and overthrown by a ferocious warrior the likes of whom the world had never seen. When Genghis Khan and his Mongol cavalry invaded Afghanistan in 1219, the ruthless Mongols destroyed the country and forever changed the landscape of Afghanistan.

NOTES

1. Tanner, *Afghanistan*, 53–80.
2. Romila Thapar, *Asoka and the Decline of the Mauryas* (London: Oxford University Press, 2012).
3. Dupree, *Shamshir Glass*.
4. Lewis, *The Middle East*, 51–101.

5

The Mongolian Invasion of Afghanistan through the Shah Dynasty

The astonishing expansion of the Mongols as they conquered Central Asia can only be accredited to the military genius of one man, Temujin. The very name *Mongols* literally translates as "the invincible ones," which certainly describes the attitude of these ruthless invaders in the 13th century. In 1206, the revered Mongol warrior Temujin united his warrior tribe with the other prominent tribes, forging an alliance that created one of the most powerful armies the world has ever known. As the Mongols grew in numbers, the original tribe blurring with others, the Mongols evolved into the overall collection of the tribes that marched across Central Asia and resulted in the all-encompassing Mongol Empire.

The consequences of the Mongol invasion over 800 years ago carried across nearly all facets of present-day Afghan life, from the people to the topography. Descendants of the Mongols exist to this day in Afghanistan, and include the ethnic groups of the Mongol, Hazara, and Aimak people. Moreover, the siege warfare methods of the

Mongols left an everlasting imprint on Afghanistan, as the Mongols were famous for diverting rivers and water sources from towns to starve the villagers out and force surrender. Over time these tactics dried up many rivers and streams across the country. As a result, a majority of Afghanistan's barren and desolated desert landscape is historically accredited to the Mongols. Yet before leaving an imprint on the country, which has lasted for centuries, how did Temujin unite these unbalanced tribes into an unyielding force like the Mongolian army, and become one of the greatest conquerors the world has ever known?

THE RISE OF TEMUJIN AND MONGOL EXPANSION

Mongolia is located on a high plateau, east of the Altai Mountains, and this location itself fostered the need for nomadic movement across the far-reaching pastures. In the late 12th century, many disparate warrior tribes, including the Tatars, Naimans, Merkits, and Keraits, lived across Central Asia. One of the more well-known competing tribes was the Mongols, comprised mainly of Turk descendants living along the open grasslands of the Eurasian steppes, which stretched along the coast of Europe to Manchuria.[1] The Mongols were similar to the other tribes in the quest for overpowering sedentary neighbors, but their vast expansion is credited to the military genius of a man named Temujin.

Not quite Mongol nobility, yet born to a Mongol minor chieftain, the story of Temujin's birth depicts a gallant prophecy for his life as a Mongol warrior. The Mongols are cabal believers in spirits and the afterworld, often believing the souls of the deceased will live on in a sacred relic after death. The birth of Temujn was presided over by a shaman, whom the Mongols revere as a person who can communicate with the dead and has influence over benevolent and malevolent spirits. Temujin was born with a blood clot on his right hand, which the shaman saw as a sign of his destiny to be a great leader for the Mongols. As the mysterious shaman forecasted, Temujin entered the world with enormous strength in his hands, and proclaimed one day Temujin would become a significant force in the world. As was customary at the time, a shaman examined the newborn for the sign of an omen. Given the birth name Temujin, the shaman declared the birthmark on his right hand was a symbol of strength. The date of birth for Temujin is not certain, but is believed to be approximately somewhere between 1155 and 1162.[2] Though not truly a part of the khan structure or nobility, Temujin began life well, but these early fruitful years did not last for long. Temujin's fortunate life ended abruptly at the age of nine when a competing Tatar tribe poisoned Temujin's father. His family was forced into exile, and this swift fall from grace forced Temujin and his family to survive by seeking refuge in the nearby mountains and forests. Throughout many years of refuge, Temujin and his family lived in banishment among the forest trees. Instead of a life filled with servants and reverence, young Temujin experienced a cold and bitter world as a child. Subsistence and nourishment was found only from harvesting plants and berries, and in some instances the family was fortunate to capture small woodland creatures and trapped marmots and rats for food.

Temujin's mother played a pivotal role in his life during this time not only by teaching him how to survive in such a harsh landscape but also in her emphasis on the need to forge alliances against opponents. She most likely learned these skills from her husband, as historians speculate the chief of a tribe understood and fostered the need for tribal coalitions in order to survive in such difficult terrain. The harsh environment in the Eurasion steppe meant that many tribes needed to sacrifice independence in order to ensure continued existence. The survival by numbers approach in these alliances, though resulting in a lapse in independence, ultimately assisted in being mated with a stronger tribe which offered protection and sustenance.[3] Through these learning experiences as navigated by his mother, Temujin learned valuable skills which assisted him in his military career later in life, and developed his incontrovertible genius approach to solidify Mongolian endurance.

Another critical event that shaped Temujin's outlook occurred when he was 13 years old. Temujin killed his own brother Bekhter after an argument over stealing fish and hiding it from the family. Temujin had three brothers, two of whom were half-brothers to Temujin, Bekhter and Belgutei. The two had gone hunting together, and returned unwilling to share any food they caught. Because it was customary in Mongolian culture for family members to share their hunting spoils, upon their return they hid the fish instead, which led to Temujin confronting Bekhtar and Belgutei. However, it is apparent that more than just fish was a factor in the sibling rivalry. It is believed Bekhtar was older than Temujin, and therefore he would have been a threat to Temujin's family leadership and desire to rise to power in Mongolian society.[4] While historical accounts make it clear there was a family rift with an alliance among the two branches of the family, the confrontation over the fish ultimately resulted in Temujin killing Bekhtar assisted by his younger brother, Jochi-Kasar.

Before his death however, Bekhtar asked that Belgutei be spared, which he was if he assisted with the killing of Bekhtar. This incident arguably had the most significant impact on Temujin, and he is accredited saying later in life of the incident, "It is to Belgutei's strength and Kasar's prowess that I owe the conquest of the World Empire." Temujin's relationship with his mother was obviously strained after the fratricide. Overwhelmed in her grief she branded her children as destroyers. This is why it is largely surmised that Temujin really killed his brother in order to rise to a level of leadership in his family.[5]

The overall experience of falling from grace and into exile, as well as the fratricide, hardened Temujin and toughened his mind and body to the harsh surrounding world. Adding to these experiences which influenced and shaped him, Temujin was captured by a rival Tayichi'ut tribe and enslaved. It was not uncommon in those times for a family member to be captured and held hostage for ransom or some other form of payment, but the event altered his perception of the world and forced him to never want to be in such a compromising situation again.[6] After his capture, Temujin married his first wife Borte around the age of 16 and merged back into tribal society. Shortly thereafter both Temujin and his bride were captured by a rival Merkit tribe. Temujin was imprisoned and managed to escape, and returned back for his wife, assisting her escape under the cover of darkness. During her capture, Borte was supposedly forced into marriage with a Merkit chieftain. After her escape, nine months later Borte gave birth to her first child. The issue of paternity plagued Temujin throughout his life, and these doubts played an eventual role in determining how to divide up his kingdom upon his death. However, these situations of being captured likely influenced Temujin's approaches in battle, which was to conquer completely because surrender would never be an option again.

PREPARATION FOR WORLD DOMINATION

The four major events that shaped Temujin and prepared him for his role in conquering the world include the murder of his father and his family's subsequent banishment into exile, the fratricide of his brother, his own kidnapping and enslavement, and the abduction and supposed rape of his wife. Using these early life lessons and experiences, Temujin quickly conquered disparate tribes and rose to power among the Mongols and as a fierce warrior. Eventually, Temujin cleverly ascertained the magnitude of merging the tribe of the Central Asian confederations under one inclusive tribe, the result of which would fuse the Mongols into a more resilient force. Part of his reason for the unification was due to Temujin's desire to enact revenge upon the Jurchen, a neighboring tribe that had often instilled conflict between the different Central Asian tribes. The Jurchen were also known for seemingly unjustly executing the Mongolian people, and Temujin had grown tired of tolerating such excessive oppression.

At the turn of the 13th century, Temujin had amassed a reputation for bravery as well as breaking with traditional steppe methods and implementing cunning military maneuvers. Known for rewarding courage and honesty, he chose individuals who exhibited these characteristics to serve in his top military positions. In one such instance, Temujin's favorite horse was shot with an arrow and killed in battle. Once Temujin defeated the confederation, he gathered the soldiers and demanded to know who dared to kill his noble, "yellow war horse with the white mouth."[7] One man stepped forward, acknowledging what he had done despite facing almost certain execution or punishment. Temujin stated since the man was brave enough to acknowledge what he did, when most others would have cowered in fear and remained silent, he chose him as one of his top commanders. He renamed the man Jebe, which means "arrowhead," and Jebe became one of his highest leaders. Jebe further achieved great prominence as one of Temujin's four "Dogs of War" generals. The others were Jelme, Qubilai, and Subotai.[8] Temujin had secured his position of prestige and power in the Mongolian Empire and developed a reputation as a just leader with a shrewd ability in battle and an unyielding discipline. Temujin looked to dominate other world empires and bring his birth prophecy to life.

On a dark night in 1206, in a dimly lit sanctuary set aglow by burning candles and smoldering cinders, the Mongolian assembly of tribal chiefs known as the *quriltai* declared Temujin the "universal ruler" of the Mongols. The *quriltai* is a revered assembly of Mongolian nobles and khans.[9] Temujin began his new role as the supreme leader, and assumed his new title of Genghis Khan. The unification of the tribes distressed local empires, since some of the critical trade routes were now part of the "invincible ones" territory. As rightfully feared, these empires were concerned the much-needed items for commerce would be confiscated along the trade route and placed under the control of the Mongols. By the time Temujin assumed his title of Genghis Khan and unified the Mongolian tribes, he was already nearly 60 years old.

As a result, the Mongol alliance was a severe threat to the neighboring regions, and clearly not without justification based on the legacy of trepidation embodied by Genghis Khan.

THE RISE TO MONGOL RULE IN AFGHANISTAN (1206–1332)

After overcoming some initial difficulties, Genghis Khan mercilessly defeated and conquered the well-protected cities of neighboring empires. By 1209, the dreaded Genghis Khan was acknowledged by the Tangut Emperor as the reigning lord of the region. Genghis Khan continued to annihilate the various dynasties until these empires were under his domain. Less than 10 years later, by 1218 the Mongol Empire was extensive and spread from the Caspian Sea to the Persian Gulf.[10] Included in this region was the land known today as Afghanistan, and Genghis Khan worked to unite his power with neighboring empires. He sent communication to the Khwarizm Empire in Afghanistan, in which he conveyed in his message that he was the sovereign ruler of these lands. As such he presented an amicable letter of friendship, and in accordance requested the Khwarizm ruler to accept this declaration of Mongolian supremacy. The letter was accompanied with treasures and vast wealth, including such riches as gold, silver, silk, furs, and a gaggle of 500 camels. The caravan never reached the shah, and instead was seized by the overly greedy border commander who was overcome with the prospect of all the wealth and fortune in the caravan. The border commander killed all of the convoy members save one. A camel boy escaped unnoticed and returned to Genghis Khan to tell him of the incident. Furious at the insult against his generous offer, Genghis Khan dispatched a messenger party to the shah and ordered him to immediately agree to the previously delineated terms, concede to the Mongolian army, and to deliver the commander for punishment. The overly confident shah naively refused such a declamation, and as further insult, he killed the Muslim messenger and sent the other Mongol couriers with shaved beards back to Genghis Khan, which was seen as the ultimate insult.[11] This offense might have stifled any other potential invader, but the act was too insulting to Genghis Khan. Whether or not he intended to destroy the empire prior to his gesture of amity, the Mongol ruler unleashed over 200,000 Mongolian soldiers into Afghanistan, crippling cities such as Herat, Balkh, Ghazni, and Bamiyan and slaughtering every man, woman, and child along the way.

The Mongols conquered and destroyed the Khwarizm Empire between the years of 1219 to 1221, and afterwards Genghis Khan divided the army into two separate forces. Genghis Khan led his army on a forceful storm across Afghanistan, Pakistan, and India, continuing to destroy the region as punishment for the shah's insulting actions. His other military force, led by his two top generals Jebe and Subotai, marched their soldiers through Russia and Caucasus. For the most part, the campaign was not to conquer more territories but rather to subdue those in these lands by pillaging settlements and forcing those inhabitants to recognize Genghis Khan as the only universal ruler of the world. After several years of adding more territories to the empire, which included Persia, the once-divided forces united again in Mongolia in 1225. Genghis Khan was callous in his defeat of these lands, and historical records describe accounts of vast fields filled with the bones of slain enemies and slaughtered horse carcasses scattered among the bodies on the battlefield. The stories of the Mongols' method of conquest were extremely terrifying, for once the army entered the city, bodies and blood filled the streets. Genghis Khan was brutal in his methods, and in one such instance, he poured molten hot silver into the eyes and ears of his enemy as retribution for a previous insult. This references the execution of Inalchuq (Inalchuk), Genghis Khan's enemy that he pursued endlessly for months. The capture of Inalchuk was a dramatic experience that resulted in his imprisonment and brutal public execution.[12] The legend of these malicious methods caused many shahs to tremble in fear of the Mongol army. Understandably, once this fear was instilled in a man's heart, it was hard to find the courage to fight such savage warriors. The Mongols' ruthless mission was for the most part a simple instruction from Genghis Khan: slay the men, rape the women, and enslave the children.

Despite his legacy of ruthless savagery, Genghis Khan was remarkably intelligent and a skilled leader. He instilled advanced military disciplines to his army, including such concepts as psychological warfare, military intelligence, and advanced mobility tactics that encouraged combat on horseback, fighting often with multiple horses on the battlefield. The Mongols were highly skilled and unrivaled equestrian riders, learning to ride horses as early as the age of three. As a magnificent illustration of the Mongols' equestrian dexterity and control, the rider traveled with three horses and the rider was skillful enough to jump from his fatigued horse to a fresh steed in the midst of combat, while still being able to continue firing arrows at the enemy. This ability granted the Mongols a significant advantage over their less-equestrian-knowledgeable adversaries, and even presented a deceptive impression of the Mongols having more soldiers than originally

A Mongolian rider firing arrows in battle. The Mongols were highly advanced equestrians, and training began as early as age three. In battle, Mongolian soldiers often traveled with three horses, and in the midst of combat, the rider was skillful enough to jump from a fatigued horse to a fresh one while continuing to fire arrows at the enemy. (Pictures from History/Bridgeman Images)

estimated on the battlefield. The Mongolian horse was a prized aspect of the Mongol army, and the rider's swift ability often made the army fight as if they were double or triple in numbers. Those horses that served and died in battle with exceptional swiftness and agility would be skinned and preserved as honored vestiges.[13] Genghis Khan organized an extremely efficient army composed of strict discipline, tremendous loyalty, and remarkable adeptness. The Mongol army was thus an intense military force that was the most feared and ruthless power to enter the battlefield. By using their highly developed skills in military techniques of surprise ambush maneuvers and extreme equestrian mobility, the Mongols were able to defeat and conquer enemy armies with swift vengeance and merciless punishment. While these shocking actions may be regarded as the acts of menial and inferior savages, the Mongols were anything but inferior in intellect.

In addition to his military genius on the battlefield, Genghis Khan developed an ingenious communication system in order to effectively relay orders to his men with quick speed. He used supply routes to create multiple communication stations throughout the Mongolian empire, known as the *yam* and the *barid* network, which worked to gather and quickly disseminate communication intelligence. While it was not the first messenger system in history, as earlier systems had been in effect under the Persian and Roman empires, the Mongolian *yam* network was unprecedented in size and efficiency.[14] Each rider had an engraved metal pendant, usually circular or rectangular, known as a *paiza*. The pendant was the token that authenticated the rider as a messenger of Genghis Khan. The *paiza* was a revered token, as these riders often covered up to 300 kilometers per day and were well respected by the Mongol people. The *yam* network was an ingenious invention, as this system revolutionized and greatly increased the speed of communication and the ability to relay military intelligence throughout the Mongol Empire. The *yam* network was specifically designed for the Mongolian messengers who often covered great distances of nearly 200 kilometers over one or two days. These messengers arrived at relays stations along the route for food, water, and spare horses.[15] Genghis Khan's desire to understand and defeat his enemy may be considered passionate to the point of being fanatical, and as a result his extensive spy network was unrivaled.

As demonstrated by the Mongols' ability to quickly subdue enemies, the conquering Mongol army was keenly adept at learning the strategies and techniques of the defeated empires. In the Mongols' desire to learn the methods of defeated opponents, the Mongols spared only those with certain skills from death, such as engineers and architects. If these skilled opponents agreed to live as slaves to the Mongol Empire, highly skilled engineers and architects were captured and instructed to teach the Mongols their skill in order to enhance Mongolian war expertise. As a result of this strategy, the most significant contribution came from the Chinese engineers who taught the Mongols how to strike and defeat walled cities. Those few enemy soldiers who acknowledged Genghis Khan as the one universal ruler were spared death and were instead ordered to fight as part of the Mongol army. Not only did this technique expand the army, but this also gave the Mongols the advantage of learning new military techniques and skills to use against other enemy forces. As a result of the innovative war techniques led by Genghis Khan, the Mongol Empire grew not just in domain but also in intellect as the army continued to pillage and devour other empires, learning and employing their secrets along the way.

The Mongols were one of the most ethnically and culturally diverse empires in history, composed of mainly nomadic inhabitants from all regions. Keenly aware of the cultural differences of his empire, Genghis Khan was supportive of the various religions in the empire as long as they did not challenge his rule. Genghis Khan was supportive of all religious beliefs, but executed those that resisted the Mongol rule, such as the Ismaili Muslims. As a further testament to the strength of the army, he refused to divide his troops into different ethnic sects. Since he recognized this would be a weakness as it could segregate his army, Genghis Khan believed in supporting a sense of unity and loyalty among the conquered tribes through the integration of all individuals throughout the army despite their cultural differences. Thus the Mongolian army would fight as a force of one unified people composed of multiple ethnicities, rather than as divided units of smaller clans based on religious, tribal, and ethnic backgrounds. Of course, despite the resistance or disagreement, discipline was strictly enforced and included severe punishment for those who tried to oppose his policy.

Genghis Khan imposed a revolutionary concept to the Mongol army by basing his military on the Asian decimal system. The army was divided into units, the most basic of which was composed of 10 men, known as an *arban*. In this regard, each man was assigned to his *arban* for life and it was forbidden under any circumstance, whether religious, cultural, ethnic, or just plain dislike of his other members, to leave and join another group. The leader of the *arban* then reported to the leader of the *jagun*, the next highest unit composed of 100 soldiers. The remaining units included the *mingghan* (1,000 men) and *tumen* (10,000 men). Both units employed the title of *noyan* for the leader, which indicated a form of respect as a military commander, but yet *noyan* was not a military rank. To further the seriousness of the strict regime of the army, it was a grave insult and disgrace if a solider chose to abandon his *arban,* and thus as punishment the entire *arban* would be executed for this treason. If all 10 men of the *arban* deserted, then the entire *jagun* would be executed. The leaders of the *tumen* were regarded as Mongol nobility. The title *Khagan* (Great Khan) designated the leader of 10 *tumens* and was reserved for Genghis Khan himself. In the Mongol Empire, there were only five true *Khagans*, Genghis Kahn and his direct descendants, including Ogedei, Kublai, Mongke, and Guyuk Khan. The title of *Khaghan* is thus reserved for the emperor of imperial rank, and in translation means khan of khans, similar to king of kings. Other rulers are referred to as khans, despite the large amount of rulers that claimed the title *Khaghan*.[16]

As was the typical terrain and climate of Afghanistan, the Mongol warriors were accustomed to the extreme weather conditions.

Interestingly, the Mongols preferred to travel during the winter months in order to better navigate across rivers. Further, these hardened nomads were used to traveling great distances in little time. The Mongols often traveled without much difficulty, seeing as they were accustomed to these conditions as part of their nomadic lifestyle. Despite working under these harsh circumstances, the Mongols were exceptionally skilled at siege warfare. Such military methods included the diversion of water sources to a city by blocking the rivers and tributaries to the town in order to weaken the opponent's defenses. Additionally, the Mongolian army would often take enemy prisoners and force them to march in front of the army as a shield when engaging in combat with other enemy forces. By far the most devastating practice, and arguably the most favored technique by the Mongols, was to simulate retreat and feign escape from the battlefield. Once the enemy army was lured into a faux victory, the pursuit of the seemingly retreating Mongols instead divided the enemy army into smaller sections. Now disjointed from larger army forces, the Mongols had skillfully lured the army into an ambush. Genghis Khan was blessed with a cadre of extremely gifted generals who were exceptionally skilled in such novel ideas and unprecedented tactics. In having such an elite force in his *tumen* commanders, their keenness for military maneuvers allowed Genghis Khan and the Mongols to excel and crush opponents. As further support to the mystical alignment of the forces, other examples in history include Alexander the Great's generals of Parmenio, Hephaestion, Craterus, Perdiccas; Napolean Bonaparte's marshalls of Massena, Davour, Ney, and Murat; and also Robert Lee's army of Jackson, Longstreet, Stuart, and A.P. Hill. These leaders, much like Genghis Khan, were successful due to the rare happenstance of the exceptionally talented leaders who surrounded them. [17]

After a conquest, the Mongol army would plunder the villages, and the valuables stolen after such defeats were basically the only payment the soldiers received. In the case of those who resisted the invasion or rule under the Mongols, the Mongolian army operated by leaving none alive. The massacre totals in the region of Afghanistan are particularly startling in Herat, Nishapur, and Samarkand. In one legendary tale of the Mongols fierceness, an Afghan woman was captured and cleverly tried to beg for her life by arguing she had swallowed a pearl, and thus per her desperate words, it would be wise not to kill her with the precious treasure in her belly. Swiftly, without hesitation, and while she was still breathing, her stomach was sliced open as the soldier rummaged through her entrails for the tiny orb. Upon hearing the account, Genghis Khan instructed the soldiers to search all bodies in the same manner, and each inhabitant was turned inside out so their bowels could be searched for other concealed treasures.

In the early days of August 1227, the great khan was plotting to overthrow the Hsi-Hsia (Xi Xia) dynasty near the Liupan Mountains, and he was suddenly struck ill. Fearing his death was imminent, he ordered his closest commanders to secretly carry him to the nearby forest in a covered cart. In this manner he could continue to outline the final defeat of the Hsi-Hsia dynasty in seclusion from spying eyes. Genghis Khan knew the Hsi-Hsia army would have a momentous advantage if they realized he was dying or dead, and thus he was carried away in secret so the severity of the illness would not be leaked. His closest advisors carried him off with the grim hope that the healing plants of the forest would help him recover. Alas, on August 18, 1227, Genghis Khan succumbed to the mysterious illness.

There are several famous legends regarding the secret death and burial of Genghis Khan. These stories include instructions from the great khan which were given in secret. These orders include the gravesite was to be trampled with horses, or perhaps also even to bury Genghis Khan and then divert a river over his grave so none of his enemies would know he was dead. As legend has it, the burial party was to be killed by another party, and so forth and so forth so the gravesite could never be discovered.[18] The death of Genghis Khan is entirely omitted from *The Secret History of the Mongols*, the staple reference text of the Mongols written in the 13th century, and the text has no reference to the burial of their greatest Mongolian leader. However, some historians argue it was Mongol tradition to be buried without a monument, as the soul would live in the revered Mongolian "spirit banner," similar to a flag fabricated from horse or yak hair. In Mongolian culture, warriors used the spirit banner as an extension of their identity and to stand as a perpetual guardian outside their tents. As the Mongols worshipped the powers that existed in nature, a warrior's personal spirit banner always remained outside under the open sky while the hair captured the power of the wind, sky, and sun. The spirit banner harnessed this energy for the warrior, and these captured powers from nature helped the warrior find his destiny, perhaps to help him fight on the battlefield, explore new opportunities, and create his own fate. The spirit banner represented such a strong union between the warrior and nature, and upon his death, his soul would be symbolized as living on through his spirit banner. Genghis Khan's spirit banner was used throughout battle until 1647, when it was finally interned and displayed.

History has often presented Genghis Khan in a negative view, with the majority of observers citing his destructive and cruel nature. The Mongolians regard Genghis Khan as a cherished and revered ruler and believe historical records are inaccurately harsh and embellished.[19] Embracing the positive attributes of Genghis Khan, he instituted valuable practices gained from his knowledge and ability to master others' tradecrafts. Genghis Khan instituted several unique practices, such as tax exemption for religious leaders, doctors, and some teachers. He introduced many liberal regimes while embracing artistic and cultural growth. His extensive *yam* communication and spy checkpoint network was unparalleled in his time, and his efforts at increasing communication resulted in his development of a written language for the Mongols. By leading the Mongols in capturing the Silk Road, he brought control to the trade regions and allowed increased communications between the Middle East and Central Asia. His enforcement of traditional Mongolian beliefs and traditions provided stability to the Mongol empire, and for these reasons, he is celebrated as a hero in Mongolia.

Yet despite these values, Genghis Khan is widely known for the destruction he brought to many countries. In Afghanistan, he is remembered as a detrimental and genocidal ruler who ransacked and pillaged the land. His purposeful drive to destroy the irrigation systems in Afghanistan left the region an unfertile desert of sand, with the ramifications of his actions still felt to this day. Due to his spitefulness for revenge and penchant for burning vast amounts of land, Genghis Khan is blamed for the barren and unfertile soil in Afghanistan. Through his conquering and invading army, Genghis destroyed the cities of Herat, Balkh, and Ghazni, plundered the once-fertile agricultural soil, and slaughtered countless Afghan civilizations.

At the time of his death in 1227, Genghis Khan's Mongolian Empire was vast but not as extensive as it would become after his death. Genghis Khan designated that his empire would be shared among his four sons, Ogedei, Chagadai, Tolui, and Jochi. Prior to his death, Genghis Khan contemplated the difficult decision of which son would inherit his empire, and he eventually discussed the situation publicly with all four of his children. The young Temujin had toiled endlessly to regain his wife Borte when they were both captured by the Merkid. After he dramatically rescued her, the young couple returned home and Borte delivered a son that Temujin named Jorchi (which translates to "visitor" or "guest"). The origins of Jorchi would haunt Temujin and the royal empire throughout his rule as Genghis Khan. As it plagued him throughout his reign, if Jochi might have been fathered by a Merkit when Jochi's mother Borte was held captive, then he was not able to inherit the kingdom. With this in mind, at the statement that Genghis Khan would leave his empire to the oldest, his second son Chagadai exclaimed he would not be subjugated to live under the rule of a bastard child. Chagadai purportedly suggested the empire be bequeathed to the third son, Ogedei, as he was the most deserving. Genghis agreed and the empire was bestowed to Ogedei, but despite his designation as the successive *Khagan*, all four of Genghis's sons would receive a portion of the empire.[20] The empire was divided into Kanates, which were designated as subterritories and their ruling khans were to follow the one great khan Ogedei.

Women were regarded as important in the Mongol Empire, not only in regards for family life, but also to serve in leadership positions. As the men fought on the battlefield, the women were imperative to the success of the empire by remaining on the home front to administer and manage the empire. After Genghis Khan's death, his third son Ogedei ruled the one part of the empire but was never in a coherent state to rule due to his penchant for drunkenness. However, his wife ruled for over 10 years as the administrator of the empire. Her efforts were widely recognized, and her influence as queen was even acknowledged on the seal of the empire.[21] During Ogedei's reign the expansion of the empire was significant, and his nephew Halagu Khan reigned while defeating the Muslim lands to the southwest, including the modern countries of Iran, Iraq, Afghanistan, and Pakistan. The rule of the Mongols would continue under the Ilkhahates and was advanced under the domination of Timur Lang.

RULE OF THE TIMURID EMPIRE (1370–1506)

In the late 14th century, a man by the Turkic name of Timur arose as the new great leader of the Mongols and also as the founder of the Timurid Empire in Central Asia. Prior to his rule, he was regarded as a fugitive and hid in the mountains of Afghanistan for protection. During his time in exile, he engaged in combat with other expelled rebel warriors. It was either during this rebel carousing or in an attempt to steal a sheep in which Timur was injured and the damage changed his name. As a result of this situation, his knee was pierced by an arrow and caused him to limp, earning him the name Timur Lang, or Timur the Lame.

Alleging to be a bloodline descendent of Genghis Khan, in 1369 Timur returned to the center of the Kart Empire at Balkh to claim his kingship. Timur overpowered Amir Husayn, the fellow fugitive turned noble aristocrat who once forged a strong alliance with Timur. After his capture and execution, Timur seized Amir Husayn's vast empire centered in Balkh. Timur was not particularly brilliant in political maneuvers, and rather than assuming the title of shah, he desired to be called the *amir*, the Turkic word for prince or nobility. Until his death 35 years later, Timur would subject the land to endless wars and bloodshed, much like Genghis Khan had during his reign. However, unlike his supposed ancestor Genghis Khan, Timur is credited with rebuilding the cities he destroyed. Timur believed once the city was claimed as his own, despite being razed to the ground, the cities were to be rebuilt to display the glory of the Timurid Empire. After defeating part of the Persian Empire in 1383, Timur marched along the Helmand River toward Herat, destroying all of the irrigation systems along the way. Once he captured the city of Herat, he ruthlessly massacred all inhabitants. In these instances, Herat and Balkh were destroyed and rebuilt by Timur to embrace the artesian culture and atmosphere Timur desired, and in particular, the capital city of Herat would flourish and be adorned with beautiful buildings.[22] This embodiment of annihilation continued for the next 20 years, including the invasion and capture of Baghdad in 1401 that killed over 20,000 residents. Some of Timur's bloody conquests saw the death counts expanding to nearly 70,000, but yet his time of rule in Afghanistan is regarded as one of peace and prosperity.

Upon Timur's death in 1405, the time had come yet again for a familiar story in Afghanistan. The fight began among the Timurids over the throne of the empire, and rival family clans erupted to seize their rightful claim to the throne. After many years and bloodshed, Timur's youngest son Shah Rukh would emerge as the heir to the kingdom, which stretched from China to the Tigris River in Iraq. Shah Rukh governed from the capital of Herat, and much like his father, he was a passionate supporter of the arts and cultures of the region. The kingdom celebrated artisans, philosophers, and poets the likes of which had not been seen since the Kushan rule in the third century. To this day in Herat, many artifacts and designs from the Timurid Empire are still celebrated and embraced for their striking intricacies and inspiration. The hostility for the throne began again in 1447 after Shah Rukh's death, and was further amplified after his wife, Qawhar Shad, was murdered 10 years later. The reign of Sultan Husain Baiqara from 1468 to 1506 would continue the glory of Herat, but unfortunately his kingly duties focused on opulence rather than administration of the empire. He was easily overthrown and removed from the seat of power in Afghanistan, and now at the end of the Timurid Empire, once more the battle for the throne began in Afghanistan.

MOGHUL AND SAFAVID RULE (1506–1709)

Afghanistan was divided into several sections throughout the 16th, 17th, and 18th centuries. In the early dawn of the 16th century, a figure emerged that would fight feverishly and gallantly for his kingdom, all at the young age of 17. Originally named as Zahiruddin Mohammad, he was renamed Babur and was a descendent of Genghis Khan and Timur Lang. Already the ruler of the Kingdom of Ferghana, Babur was the founder of the Moghul Empire and made the capital at Kabul in 1504. Furthering the empire's expansion efforts, in 1522 he seized the city of Kandahar, and he marched into Delhi in 1526. His achievement and victory in India would be a pivotal point for Afghanistan. At the First Battle of Panipat, Babur defeated the last sultan of the Delhi Empire, Ibrahim Lodi. Having been informed of an internal schism in the Sultan's communication channels, Babur let the attack on India with a force of 12,000 soldiers, and easily overthrew the Sultan's disconcerted army of 100,000. Under Babur, the Muslim armies, composed of Mongol, Turkic, and Afghan warriors, invaded India.

Afghanistan continued to endure countless expansion conquests throughout the 17th century under two primary empires. The Moghuls of India avidly ruled from Kabul, while the Safavids of Persia ruled from Herat. The Safavids of Persia challenged the Moghul Empire, and the Persians overtook the area in the middle of the 17th century. The expansion conquests would continue into the early 18th century and by approximately 1707, had increased Afghanistan's borders from south of the Hindu Kush and the eastern provinces into India. The city of Kandahar was divided among a fierce rivalry between the two most important tribal groups: the Ghilzai and the Abdali tribes, and the Abdali would later be known as the foremost Durrani tribe. Due to the intense hostility between these tribes, the greater part of the Abdali tribe had previously been transferred to Herat. This gave the Ghilzai more power by residing as the majority tribe in Kandahar, and eventually the Abdali's fostered bitter resentment that intensified into hatred and revenge.

Under the Persian rule at Kandahar, the court at Isfahan began to decline and the tribes became more and more impatient. Previously, the court had been tolerant of the differing religions in Afghanistan, as the court was predominantly Shi'ite Islam while the Kandahar tribes were mainly Sunni Muslim. However, a new Sufavid leader named Sultan Husain had decided to put an end to the religious tolerance, and as such he sought to convert all the tribes under one religion. The rivalry between the tribes became overbearing, and the Sultan appointed a Georgian noble named Abdullah Khan to cease these insurgences. Under his rule as the new governor of Kandahar, Abdullah Khan was given the arduous task of forcing all inhabitants to convert to Shi'ism. The new governor was defeated by the Baluchs, and in response to these insurgents, the court sent Gurgin Khan to meet with Mirwais Khan Hotak, the influential leader of the Ghilzai. Gurgin Khan was a Georgian man known for his adamant strictness against rebellion, and upon arrival and without hesitation, he captured and imprisoned the usurpers. Aware that Mirwais was the mastermind behind such rebellions, Gurgin sent him to the court at Isfahan to be treated as a dangerous criminal. Upon arrival at the center of the Persian Empire and the nucleus of domination over the Afghan people, Mirwais observed firsthand of the accounts of decadence and decay at the court, and this solidified the reports that the Persian Safavid Empire was on the brink of collapse. However, due to Mirwais's wealth, diplomacy, and penchant for persuasion, the Persian sultan shielded Mirwais from punishment and he was released as prisoner and returned to Kandahar. With the newfound enlightenment of knowing firsthand how the court had grown weak, Mirwais devised plans for ousting the despot Gurgin. If his plans were successful, these tactics would lead the way for ending the Persian control in Afghanistan.[23]

In 1709, the Pashtun tribesmen under Ghaznavid Khan Nasher revolted against the Persian Safavids. These Afghans moved into power and briefly ruled the region under a sentiment of Afghan independence which was bravely championed by Mirwais Khan. During this heightened sensation of autonomy in Afghanistan, Mirwais seized his chance and assassinated Gurgin. Details of the assassination vary, but according to the Kandarian legend, Mirwais invited Gurgin to a picnic on his country estate outside Kandahar. The guests dined on rich food and strong wine until they were consumed with drunken debauchery. In a coordinated attack launched at the most opportune moment, Mirwais struck and killed Gurgin and his escorts, and Mirwais led the rebellion as they marched to the citadel. The court at Isfahan was in no position to battle, as the empire of the Safavid Persians had weakened considerably in corruption and debauchery while the tribes had become impatient. Mirwais Khan established Kandahar independent of the Safavid Persians through the imprisonment of emissaries and in the defeat of the Persian army. In 1708, the Persian court could do nothing but watch in astonishment as Kandahar was taken from their kingdom. Mirwais knew if they were to remain free, the tribes must be united, and he worked for this until his death in 1715. His brave acts solidified him in history as Afghanistan's first great nationalist, and he was laid to rest in a blue mosque outside Kandahar, near the very orchard where he assassinated Gurgin Khan. After his death, his brother was to assume the throne, but Mirwais's son was thirsty for power. Mir Mahmud killed his uncle and moved to the seat of power, and in 1722 he invaded Persia and occupied the Safavid throne at Isfahan. In 1725 he was mysteriously killed and was succeeded by his cousin Ashraf, who ruled until 1730. By this time, the Afghans began to lose control of Persia, as the unification led by Mirwais never materialized under his successors.

Nadir Shah of Persia pushed back the Afghans in the Battle of Damghan in 1729, and furthermore Nadir Shah marched on Isfahan and defeated Ashraf, removing him from the seat of power. After occupying southwest Afghanistan for two years, in 1738 Nadir Shah conquered the remaining provinces of Afghanistan, seizing Kandahar and occupying Kabul, Ghazni, and Lahore. The assassination of Nadir Shah in 1747 resulted in a *loya jirga* (grand council), in which Ahmad Shah was chosen to be king. After his enthronement in 1747, the Ahmad Shah changed his name to Ahmad Durrani, meaning "pearl of pearls" in Persian. The Durrani Empire became the principal Afghan rulers until the British Invasion in the early 19th century. The Durrani Empire would establish the governmental structure that exists in Afghanistan today, but the country's borders would not be defined until the British in the late 19th century.

NOTES

1. George Lane, *Genghis Khan and Mongol Rule* (Westport, CT: Greenwood Press, 2004), 2–3.

2. Jack Weatherford, *Genghis Khan and the Making of the Modern World* (New York: Crown Publishers, 2004), 3–30.

3. Lane, *Genghis Khan and Mongol Rule,* 5.

4. Ibid., 16–17.

5. T. N. Haning, *Genghis Khan: His Life and Legacy* (Oxford: Blackwell Publishers, 1993), 24.

6. Lane, *Genghis Khan and Mongol Rule,* 13–16.

7. Ibid., 24–25.

8. Ibid., 25–28.

9. Ibid., 30–31.

10. David Morgan, *The Mongols* (Cambridge: Blackwell Publishers, 1986), 23–26.

11. For more information on the story of the Mongol invasion of Afghanistan, reference: www.afghanan.net/afghanistan/mongols.htm.

12. John Man, *Genghis Khan: Life, Death, and Resurrection* (New York: Thomas Dunne Books of St. Martin's Press, 2004), 85.

13. Time-Life Books: *The Mongol Conquests.*

14. Lane, *Genghis Khan and Mongol Rule,* 33–35.

15. Morgan, *The Mongols,* 30–36.

16. *The Secret History of the Mongols* (author unknown and written in 1240 C.E.).

17. Tanner, *Afghanistan,* 81–108.

18. Man, *Genghis Khan,* 217–277.

19. Ibid., 252–277.

20. Weatherford, *Genghis Khan and the Making of the Modern World,* 10–16.

21. Ibid., 160–192.

22. Justin Marozzi, *Tamerlane: Sword of Islam, Conqueror of the World* (Cambridge: De Capo Press, 2004. Originally published: London: HarperCollins, 2004), 108–156.

23. Tanner, *Afghanistan,* 81–108.

6

The Birth of Modern Afghanistan (1747–1826)

Modern-day Afghanistan was founded by Ahmad Shah Durrani, one of the most influential leaders in Afghanistan. At the height of his reign, the Durrani Empire encompassed much more than present-day Afghanistan. The domain and territory of Ahmad Shah Durrani's empire was extensive and stretched from the Amu Darya (Oxis) River in the north to the Arabian Sea, and from Mashad in Iran into Kashmir and Delhi in India. The empire included the regions of Kandahar, Herat, and Sistan. In an act that would help define his legacy, in 1768 he negotiated with the emir of Bukhara, Murad Beg, on how to divide the northern border of the country into the current regions. As a token of appreciation for working the agreement, the emir presented Ahmad Durrani with a *kherqa*, a cloak that is said to have been worn by the prophet Mohammed. Ahmad Shah Durrani so revered the gift that he had a shrine built in his capital city of Kandahar to house the relic. The shrine is widely held as one of the holiest sites in the country, and is often referred to as "the heart of Afghanistan."

A truly inspiring military leader, Ahmad Shah Durrani was not only a clever politician who successfully prevented British control of the country, but he was also a well-renowned Pashto poet. He was very astute in his understanding of the need to not alienate the Pashtun tribes, which helped to join Afghanistan into one country. Ahmad Shah Durrani established his rule as the newly elected leader of the empire at the city of Kandahar in 1747. Under his influential regime, the Durrani Empire would establish the republic governmental structure that exists in Afghanistan today, yet the borders of the country would not be defined until the British in the late 19th century. After the assassination of Nadir Shah, Ahmad Shah was elected king of Afghanistan in a royal intertribal assembly known as a *loya jirga*. Ahmad Shah led the country to unified state through his political advancements as well as his popularity as an inspirational leader. For many Afghan citizens, Ahmad Shah Durrani is the "father of our Nation" because he united Afghanistan under one native rule. However, this took more than a century to fully take hold in the country.

DURRANI EMPIRE (1747–1818)

The beginning of the Durrani Empire is regarded as the beginning of modern Afghanistan. At the time of Ahmad Shah Durrani's election as king, the Pashtun people were composed of a multitude of ethnicities and cultures, not only including the descendants from the Aryan tribes, but also other ethnic clans such as the Turks, the Waziris, the Mahsuds, and the Ghilzai people. Prior to the end of the 16th century, a diverse collection of tribes, including the Shinwaris, Yusufzais, and Mohmand tribes, moved from the upper Kabul River valley into the Peshawar region.[1] For centuries, the chosen habitation of the Afridis was the difficult terrain of the Khyber Pass located in the Hindu Kush. In spite of these contrasting cultural experiences and ethnic backgrounds, the one commonality between these diverging civilizations was the use of the Pashtu language. In an effort to join this melting pot of differing cultures, Ahmad Shah worked throughout his reign to unite the chieftains and provinces into one country.

AHMAD SHAH DURRANI (1747–1772)

Ahmad Shah was younger than the other contenders to the throne, but regardless of this impediment, there were several other factors in his favor. Primarily, not only was Ahmad Shah a Pashtun of the Abdali clan, but he was also a direct descendent of Sado, the patriarch of the Sadozai people and the prominent Pashtun tribe at the time. Furthermore, he was without question a magnetic leader and an experienced warrior who had already established himself as the commander of several thousand cavalrymen. Previously, Ahmad Shah had moved up the ranks to become the elite commander of Nadir Shah's royal Abdali bodyguard, respectfully achieving this feat before turning 25 years old. After Nadir Shah became overly suspicious of those around him, including his own son whom he had blinded for fear of assassination attempts, Nadir tasked the young commander Ahmad to murder all those he once trusted as his closest advisors and guardians. Yet somehow the Afghan council was informed of Shah's murderous intentions, and due to the advance warning they were able to depose of Nadir Shah by having him captured and beheaded. Some historians speculate Ahmad Shah forewarned the council regarding Nadir Shah's execution order, and as a reward for this notification, Ahmad Shah was thrust to the forefront of the potential successors. In spite of the speculations why the young Ahmad Shah was appointed the primary candidate for the throne, a holy man named Mohammad Sabir Khan championed him for the throne. The holy leader argued that Ahmad was already a proven commander, and his tribal affiliation would be beneficial in reducing clan opposition. Nonetheless, as an experienced warrior and one of true Afghan descent, Ahmad Shah still would have been the obvious choice for the throne.[2] A tribal holy man championed for Ahmad Shah and announced Ahmad was the "Durr-i-Durran," meaning the pearl of all pearls (or the pearl of all ages), and henceforth after his appointment to the throne, the Abdali Pashtuns were referred to as the Durrani clan.

One of his most significant acts for the kingdom occurred when the young Ahmad Shah Durrani captured the city of Ghazni from the Ghilzai tribe. After this triumph, he continued to overthrow other rulers, and quickly seized Kabul from the local chieftain without much of a fight. He advanced his campaign amid the crumbling Mogul Empire and rapidly conquered Peshawar. Moving eastward in 1749, Ahmad Shah seized other locations such as Sindh, the Punjab region, and the land west of the Indus River. In a shrewd maneuver, Ahmad Shah informed the reigning Moghul ruler he must relinquish control of these lands in order to save the capital from attack. In fear of losing the center of the empire and also what remained of his power, the Moghul ruler conceded these lands to Ahmad Shah. The result of this decision allowed Ahmad Shah to gain a substantial amount of territory in less than two years on the throne. After swiftly acquiring these lands, Ahmad Shah Durrani returned to Afghanistan to capture Herat from Shah Rukh of Persia, the grandson of Nadir Shah. The conquest of

Herat lasted for nearly a year, the duration of which resulted in much bloodshed and devastation. After finally falling into Ahmad's control, the Afghan king immediately sent an army northward through the Hindu Kush Mountains to subdue the northern areas from revolt. In quick succession, the fierce military subdued the Turkmen, Uzbek, Tajik, and Hazara tribes in northern Afghanistan. The young cavalry commander had proven himself to be a fierce leader and skilled military strategist, and this combination for the monarchy was exactly what Afghanistan needed—a vivacious ruler with the courage and tenacity to subdue and conquer these differing tribes.

Upon his return to the Indian continent, Ahmad defeated what little authority remained of the Moghul Empire. The Moghul force had been steadily declining in power since the death of their celebrated Emperor Aurangzeb in 1707. In several successive onslaughts, Ahmad Durrani finally gained control over the Punjab and Kashmir regions. In 1757, he pillaged the capital at Delhi but in a typical political maneuver, he allowed the reigning leader of the Moghul dynasty to remain in control, but by title only. In doing so, the leader acknowledged Ahmad Shah's reign over the Punjab, Sindh, and Kashmir regions, and as a result the Moghul leader would continue on the throne as a figurehead to restrain and control the inhabitants of the Indian region. Despite the authoritative agreement, Ahmad Shah Durrani appointed his second son Timur Shah to protect the Durrani Empire and ensure order in India while he marched east back into Afghanistan.

However, Ahmad Durrani would not be in Afghanistan for long, as upon returning to Kandahar in 1757, he was informed the Maratha Confederacy in India had swiftly and successfully exiled the court of Timur Shah. Ahmad was forced to return to India and declared a *jihad*, known as an Islamic holy war, against the Marathas. A multitude of tribes heralded the call of the holy war, which included the various Pashtun tribes, the Balochs, the Tajiks, and also the Muslim population residing in India. Led by Ahmad Durrani, the tribes joined the religious quest and returned to India, easily defeating minor skirmishes along the way. In 1760, the army had reached Lahore and moved forward to face the Maratha army. The Marathas had also banded together into one great army, and this Indian defense vastly outnumbered Ahmad Shah and his forces. With both sides vying for control of northern India, the Third Battle of Panipat was fought between Ahmad Shah's Muslim army and the Hindu army of the Marathas in January 1761. After the confrontation was over, the Muslims had clearly defeated the Hindus, and these circumstances were regarded as the high point of Ahmad Shah's power and control. The Third Battle of Panipat positioned the Durrani Empire and Afghanistan to become one of the largest Islamic empires in the world.[3] Ahmad Shah's victories in these prominent battles would thrust him to the center of Afghan power as both a military commander and Islamic leader, and also by his courageous call for jihad. In spite of this triumphant victory, his peaceful control would soon be plagued with other challenges in the kingdom.

The domination and control of the empire began to loosen in 1762 when Ahmad Shah Durrani crossed Afghanistan to subdue the Sikhs, followers of an indigenous monotheistic religion of India founded in the 16th century by the guru Nanak. The Sikhs were a threat to the Durrani Empire because they had gained considerable control in the Punjab region, and in doing so the Sikh's had become a powerful opponent to the empire. Ahmad Shah greatly desired to subdue the Sikhs, and his army attacked and gained control of the Sikh's holy city of Amritsar, where he brutally massacred thousands of Sikh followers. Not only did he viciously demolish the sacred temples and buildings, but he also ordered these holy places to be covered with cow's blood as an insult and desecration of their religion. All of this was in an effort to subjugate the Sikhs permanently, but Ahmad Shah and his successors were not successful in this endeavor. In actuality, Ahmad Shah Durrani tried four separate times in his career to subdue the Sikhs but was never able to do so. Similarly in northern Afghanistan, the Uzbeks rebelled against Ahmad Shah's regime, which led to many consequential revolts in the north. Upon the recognition of his inability to subdue these insurgents, Ahmad Shah reached a compromise with the Uzbek emir of Bujhara, Murad Beg. The agreement stipulated the lands to the north of the Amu Darya would remain under the Uzbek's control, and the lands to the south would belong to the Durrani Empire. In an effort to solidify this agreement between the two leaders, the emir bestowed upon Ahmad Shah Durrani a cloak worn by the Prophet Muhammed. For nearly 250 years the relic was closely protected, and only the leaders of Afghanistan were allowed to view it. The cloak has been publicly displayed several times but only during times of crisis to help provide reassurance. In 1994 when the Taliban seized control of Kandahar, Mohammad Omar famously removed the cloak and wore it while addressing his followers. This highly symbolic act was seen as a pivotal moment for the Taliban and promulgated Omar and his Taliban to the forefront.

After many years of combating the Sikhs, Ahmad Shah's health began to decline and he withdrew to his home in the mountains in 1772. His villa was located to the east of Kandahar, where he would spend the remainder of his life.[4] It is believed Ahmad Shah Durrani health had been failing due to his suffering from skin cancer. By the time of his death several months later, Ahmad Shah had lost all control of the Punjab region to the Sikhs. Upon his death in 1772, he was placed in a mausoleum in Kandahar, one of the highly respected sites in Afghanistan near the sacred mosque he built to house the cloak of Muhammed.

The Sikhs remained in control until being defeated by the British in the First Anglo Sikh War in 1846. Regarding his defeat of the Sikhs and the Uzbeks, Ahmad Shah successfully balanced tribal alliances and unity, his overall goal aimed at diverting rebellion. Although he never achieved a true nation state, Ahmad Shah Durrani is credited with unifying these tribes and forging a nation composed of a multitude of ethnicities and diverging cultures. After his death, the Durrani Empire had been established both west and north of Kandahar. For his efforts in unity and the remarkable role he played in establishing Afghanistan, he is regarded as Ahmad Shah Baba, the "father of Afghanistan."

RULE OF TIMUR SHAH DURRANI (1772–1793)

Historically, it is not unusual to have a strong and charismatic ruler followed by several weaker and less triumphant successors. Unfortunately, history would once again repeat, for after Ahmad Shah's death, the other Durrani rulers would be regarded as incompetent governors of the empire. As a result much of the territory acquired under Afghanistan's beloved father, Ahmad Shah Baba, was lost to neighboring countries. Within 50 years, the Durrani Empire would for the most part no longer exist, and without question the empire certainly never exceeded the zenith once attained by Ahmad Shah. Throughout the duration of the Durrani decline, Afghanistan would be torn apart in multiple Anglo-Afghan civil wars and serve as a territorial tug of war between the prominent European powers of the time.

While he failed to subjugate India in 1757, Timur Shah was named Ahmad Shah's successor. Several historians consider this selection was most likely only because he was the king's son. At the time of his father's death, Timur Shah served as governor of Herat. His older brother, Sulaiman Mirza, at first contested the appointment of Timur to the throne but quickly escaped the country after seeing the support Timur received in Kandahar. However, the Durrani chieftains grudgingly accepted Timur's appointment to the throne, still quite leery of Timur's inadequacies in the menial administration of his father's territories in northern India. Timur's reign would last for over 20 years, from 1772 to 1793, and most of this was spent fighting Afghanistan's civil war and trying to calm other rebellions in the empire. Due to these continuous tribal outbreaks and his inability to control them, Timur was forced to relocate the capital from Kandahar to Kabul in 1775. As a result of these tribal circumstances, his inadequate response to the events during his reign, and in examination of the overall history of Afghanistan, he is regarded as one of the most incompetent and weakest rulers to govern the country. Historians believe it was due to his inability to govern and squelch rebellions, coupled with his overall lack of political savvy and military astuteness, that it was only a matter of time before the Durrani Empire began to unravel under his hands. Perhaps in his most appalling act as the leader of Afghanistan, in 1791 near the end of his reign, he was rescued from an eastern Pashtun insurgence, the result of his continual pro-Persian and pro-Shiite stance. After the uprising, Timur had his leaders tortured to death, which further tarnished his reputation and quite possibly condemned him forever as the worst leader in the history of Afghanistan. On an interesting aspect, Timur had an astounding number of children, estimated to be over 30, of whom 26 were sons. Some accounts simply state "over 20 sons" as it has been historically difficult to determine the exact count.[5] His fifth son would succeed him to the throne upon his death in 1793, but several of his other sons would become the sovereign leaders of various territories in the Durrani Empire throughout the remaining decades.

ZAMAN SHAH DURRANI (1793–1801)

When Timur died in 1793, he had failed to appoint an heir to the throne, which created a brief period of pandemonium called *badshahgardi*, or "ruler turning." At the time of Timur's death, he had not announced a designated heir, and he instead left a multitude of sons vying for the throne that led to disorder and chaos over who would succeed him. While most of his sons desired to be king, his son Zaman Shah Durrani was particularly ambitious and clever in his pursuit of the throne. Zaman Shah Durrani was the fifth son of Timur, and Zaman held the prestigious title as the governor of Kabul; however, two of his brothers who governed Herat and Kandahar were also strong contenders for the throne. While all three served respectful positions as the governors of prestigious cities, Zaman held the upper hand by being the governor of the capital. His ability to vie for the crown was aided by the respectable *wazir* Painda Khan, who had served as the deputy to Ahmad Shah, and was experienced in helping Zaman retain control. Since Zaman happened to be in the capital as the governor, he quickly seized the throne promptly after his father's death. Zaman became shah at the young age of 23, and his reign as king would last from 1793 to 1801. However, his path to the throne was not without animosity, and many of his brothers were imprisoned in the capital for trying to revolt against the kingdom and elect a new Shah. It is said that Zaman Shah had imprisoned all but two of his brothers and forced them into compliance by starvation. Humayan was the oldest of Timur's sons and also the governor of Kandahar, and as such he was the greatest competitor. For these reasons, Zaman ordered Humayan to be blinded for conspiring to assume the throne, and the incident would eliminate him as a threat to new amir.[6] The internal strife among the new leadership and family threw Afghanistan into turmoil, weakening the country internally and thus making the country more susceptible to attack from foreign countries.

Meanwhile, other European powers were continuing to plot their own advancement efforts into Central Asia. As originated under the Russian tsar Peter the Great, Russia continued the campaign for expansion and the establishment of Russian colonial territories in Asia. At the time, Britain was in control of India and Russia was a constant threat on the horizon. In addition to these strong European powers, France also devised plans for the region with a strategic purpose of establishing colonies in these regions. Napoleon Bonaparte of France was intrigued with Persia enough to launch an attack on the British in India, especially after his efforts to do the same from Egypt had failed. In 1800 and with the aid of Russia and Tsar Paul, Napoleon planned to invade India by way of Afghanistan.[7] However, the plan was ultimately thwarted by the assassination of Tsar Paul in 1801. The British forces became aware of the potential Franco-Russian invasion, which would have resulted in a disaster for the British. The enlightenment of this strategy was enough to alarm the British to limit any further potential land threats into India, and this would ultimately intensify their stance with the politics and foreign affairs of Afghanistan. As a result, the prominent theme in the 19th century in Afghanistan would be a call to holy war, or *jihad*, to protect the Islamic foundation in Afghanistan from these Christian infidels. As such, the Islamic call to a jihad would be launched against the Christian forces of the European powers of Russia and Britain. In these Islamic countries, it was deemed the sovereign duty of their respective leader to declare a jihad against the foreign invaders that tried to conquer their lands. The jihad call to arms to defend Islamic rule unified the multitude of tribes and ethnicities. For many, the true potency and valor of a leader is in his willingness to declare a jihad for defense of the country.[8] For the Pashtun tribes, the jihad was a call to support the *Pashtunwali*, the Pashtun Islamic religious code of honor and ethics.

Beginning his reign after his father's own unscrupulous rule, Zaman Shah faced many difficult challenges during his tenure as shah, which included the implementation of one monarch to lead all of the Pashtun tribes amid a severe lack of funding and tax revenue. In addition, he struggled with applying the Pashtuns' desire to rule without intervention and permission of the Pashtun tribal leaders. Alas, these ambitions were never achieved due to constant strife with the Sikhs. The Sikhs were continuously rebelling against the Pashtuns, and in an effort to finally gain control, Zaman Shah made the misguided mistake of appointing a Sikh tribal chief to rule as governor of the Punjab region. Ranjit Singh was a dynamic and vigorous young Sikh chieftain, and the Afghan emir had hoped the appointment of Ranjit Singh would assist the Durrani Empire by ruling with the intention to subdue and to control the Sikhs. However, instead of reigning as a puppet monarch whose purpose was only to mollify the Sikhs from rebellion, this warrior chief used his position to become a fierce opponent to the Pashtun powers of Afghanistan.

Zaman Shah tried exhaustingly and overzealously to enforce his rule over the region, and ultimately his efforts to consolidate power led to his demise as the ruler of Afghanistan. Previously under Ahmad Shah Durrani's sovereignty, he had created a diplomatic equilibrium between the reigning leaders by placing all sects of the Durrani tribes into positions of power, as he did not want a council formed of despotic authority coming from one tribal clan. As such, this balanced system brought a sense of stability to Afghan supremacy and politics by ensuring all tribal clans were equally represented. In his attempt to strengthen his control of the region, and especially the oppression of the Sikhs, Zaman Shah was determined to cease this harmonious council balance. He elected instead to remove the multi-clan leaders and to institute new representatives from his own lineage of the Sadozai tribe. This action prompted the ousted Durrani leaders to conspire against Zaman Shah, led by Painda Khan Barakzai and other ejected Barakzai leaders. However, Zaman Shah thwarted the plan and as a consequence of this insurgence, these newly instituted leaders were put to death. This execution not only included the chiefs of the Nurzai and Alizai Durrani clans, but also the chief of the Qizilbash clan.

Zaman Shah's actions instilled conflict and confusion among the tribes, which led to an utter breakdown of governance and law. After the outbreak of chaos in 1801, Painda Khan's son Fatteh Khan (sometimes stated as Fateh or Fath Khan) fled to Iran to pledge alliance support to a new ruler of Afghanistan, Mahmud Shah. Mahmud was another of Timur's sons and also Zaman's older brother, who previously served as governor of Herat prior to his brother's usurpation to the throne. To avenge their executed leaders, these clans united with the rebelling forces and seized Kandahar from Zaman Shah. Mahmud Shah would begin his first reign for only two years until being ousted by Shuja Shah in 1803 when Shuja marched on the capital and seized Kabul, after failing two years before. In tandem, Shia-Sunni riots in Kabul weakened Mahmud's ability to respond. Recognizing he was outdone and defeated, Mahmud lost control of the city and yielded the capital, and in addition he lost Kandahar due to his inability to control the Sunni revolts. Once more, Fatteh Khan fled the region and waited for the next insurgence opportunity.

SHUJA SHAH DURRANI (1803–1809)

Shuja Shah Durrani ruled for six years amid the severe disorder and civil strife in Afghanistan, and also during the continuous battle between the European powers. Most notably at the end of his reign, Shuja Shah signed a political and commercial treaty with the British in an effort to stop Persian aggression against the British and their territories. Britain desired to control the foreign policies of the country, and constantly strove to maintain Afghanistan as a buffer state to halt aggression between France and Russia into India.[9] The British were constantly seeking to administer and control the political and foreign affairs of Afghanistan. To secure these intentions, the British inserted stipulations in the treaty that Shuja Shah must oppose any other foreign territories from passing though Afghanistan. This stipulation indirectly implied the most significant menaces, of course, both France and Russia, were now banned from occupation of Afghanistan.

The treaty would be the first of many agreements with the European power, but soon after this contractual arrangement, his forerunner Mahmud Shah returned to overthrew Shuja Shah. The British would reinstate Shuja Shah again 30 years later during the First Anglo-Afghan Civil War, and he reigned again from 1839 to 1842 as a puppet monarch for the British. Until then and with the aid of Fatteh Khan once again, Mahmud seized Kandahar and Kabul in 1809. The ultimate defeat of Shuja Shah occurred at the battle at Nimla located between Kabul and Peshawar, and Mahmud Shah was poised once more as the ruler of Afghanistan.

MAHMUD SHAH DURRANI (1809–1818)

As reaction to the deplorable treaty Shuja Shah had agreed to, Mahmud Shah Durrani reclaimed the throne of Afghanistan, reigning this time for nine years until 1818. Most notably during his second reign he separated from the Barakzai tribe, which was instigated when he fell into disagreement with Fatteh Khan. Apparently the two had fallen into unfriendly terms, and the Afghan ruler ordered Fatteh was to be blinded and executed by dismemberment, with no concern of Fatteh's assistance in championing Mahmud's return to the throne. However, despite the lapse in the original treaty between the British and the reinstated Afghan amir, British concern still lingered in relation to Afghanistan's foreign policy. The British wanted to secure their interests by validating with the Afghan ruler that Afghanistan would remain a barrier country for any other European aggression. In 1814, the British returned to Afghanistan to request the shah to consent to another treaty. The terms were similar to the previous agreement under Shuja Shah, but included an additional stipulation that was intended to protect the British control of India. In this regard, the treaty specified the Afghan ruler would not interact with or make any agreements with other countries, specifically those which were enemies of the British. Persia would be granted a yearly subsidy if it would uphold the treaty and not engage in any further wars or aggressions. The subsidy agreement was terminated in 1827 after aggressions escalated between Persia and Russia.[10]

Another son of Timur Shah, Sultan Ali Shah, briefly annexed the throne in 1818 and assumed the name Ali Shah Durrani. He ruled for only one year, since the Sadozai rulers under Ahmad Shah Durrani were not able to control more than the city of Kabul. The Durrani line had lost control of all previously held territories, the result of which separated them from other tribes and with reduced protection they were easily overthrown. However, due to Fatteh Khan's respected intelligence, political savvy, and influential control in Afghanistan, he had previously championed for two of his brothers to gain access into prominent positions as the governors of Peshawar and Kandahar. Another of the younger Barakzai brothers, Dost Mohammad Khan, had worked his way into an influential position in Kabul. In the midst of the weakened empire, by the year the 1826 Dost Mohammad was in the prime stance to take control of the Afghan kingdom.

NOTES

1. Senzil Nawid, *Religious Response to Social Change in Afghanistan, 1919–29: King Aman-Allah and the Afghan Ulama* (Costa Mesa, CA: Mazda Publishers, 1999), 97–108.

2. Tanner, *Afghanistan*, 109–128.

3. Nawid, *Religious Response to Social Change in Afghanistan*, 97–108.

4. Martin Ewans, *Afghanistan: A Short History of Its People and Politics* (New York: HarperCollins, 2002), 29–45.

5. Hafizullah Emadi, *Culture and Customs of Afghanistan (Cultures and Customs of the World)* (Westport, CT: Greenwood Press, 2005), 13–52; Tanner, *Afghanistan*.

6. Ewans, *Afghanistan*, 29–45.

7. Lewis, *The Middle East*, 244–272.

8. Nawid, *Religious Response to Social Change in Afghanistan*, 112.

9. Lewis, *The Middle East*, 244–272.

10. Ibid.

7

European Influence in Afghanistan (1826–1919)

During the 19th century, the confrontation between the expanding British and Russian empires for territory in Central Asia drastically impacted Afghanistan. Primarily, the British were concerned about the growing number of Russian forces encroaching into Central Asian countries, most notably into India and Persia. This increasing aggression and escalating concern resulted in a series of three separate wars in Afghanistan. The political and diplomatic confrontation between these two countries is appropriately referred to as "The Great Game."[1] The British intelligence officer Arthur Conolly is originally credited with coining the term "the Great Game" in a letter he wrote to Sir Henry Rawlinson in 1829. Conolly served in many British reconnaissance missions in Central Asia, and he often traveled in disguise and used the name Khan Ali, a play on his last name. British novelist and poet Rudyard Kipling glamorized the term in his work *Kim* written in 1901, in which the novel is set during the competitive movement in the 19th century for territory between two of the world's supreme powers, Great Britain and Russia. Originally referred to as the Afghan wars, the title was changed to Anglo-Afghan wars in the late 20th century to differentiate these earlier wars from the multiple successive Afghan civil wars that have occurred since the Soviet invasion of 1979.

The heightened rivalry during the Great Game also contributed to the Siege of Herat during 1837–1838 and the Panjdeh Incident in 1885. During the Siege of Herat, the Persians tried to retake Afghanistan and drive out the British and Russian occupation. The city of Herat was severely destroyed during the encounter. During the brief skirmish of the Panjdeh Incident, Russian forces seized territory at Panjdeh in Afghanistan and killed nearly 600 Afghan soldiers. In an effort of British diplomacy, the incident was diverted from a full-scale war by negotiating a settlement with the Russians. However, the event would be significant in the launch of the Second Anglo-Afghan War several years later. As part of the competition between Russia and Great Britain, the launch of the First Anglo-Afghan War in 1838 is regarded as the first major conflict of the Great Game.

DOST MOHAMMAD KHAN (1826–1839 AND 1843–1863)

Dost Mohammed Khan was the younger brother of Fatteh Khan and was well aware that Fatteh Khan had taken an extremely guiding role in assisting Mahmud Khan to achieve the seat of power in 1801 and again in 1809. Dost Mohammad and Fatteh Khan had both marched into Herat in 1817, and Dost Mohammad had been instructed to seize the city. Interestingly enough, somehow Dost Mohammad found his way into the Saddozi harem where he allegedly tore off the jeweled *perjamas* (the pants of pajamas) belt of the prince's wife. For this insult, Dost Mohammad's actions were part of the reason for Fatteh Khan's brutal death, and thus served as inspiration for Dost Mohammad to defeat the Afghani ruler.[2] Dost Mohammad would never forgive Mahmud for his brutal actions to have Fatteh blinded and killed in 1818, literally cutting him into pieces before Fatteh breathed his last. It was this revenge for his brother that fueled Dost Mohammad on his quest to power. After his brother's atrocious death, Dost Mohammad advanced from Kashmir and annexed the fortress of Peshawar and Kabul. After a bloody conflict, Mahmud was forced to abandon all control over his regions except for Herat, and the remaining provinces were divided among Fatteh's brothers. Dost Mohammed Khan was allocated control of Ghazni, and now additionally controlled Kabul and Jalalabad. In 1826 he assumed the title of amir in Kabul and founded the Barakzai (Barakzay) dynasty in Afghanistan, thus bringing an end to the Durrani line. As soon as Dost Mohammad began his rule, he was instantly engaged in conflict with Ranjit Singh, the Sikh ruler of the Punjab as established by Zaman Shah. After several years, in 1834 and under the oversight of Ranjit Singh, the once-dethroned Shuja Shah attempted to reclaim his kingdom. In 1836, Dost Mohammad declared a jihad and defeated Shuja Shah at Kandahar, but the distraction allowed Ranjit Singh to successfully capture and assume control of the fortress of Peshawar, a feat that would prove troublesome for the Afghan amir.

THE FIRST ANGLO-AFGHAN WAR (1838–1842)

The competition for territory in Central Asia began in the early 18th century with the British and the Russians each racing for mastery in these lands. However, in the early 19th century, events would catapult the clash into the British invasion of Afghanistan. As implemented under the reign of Zaman Shah, the main objective of the British imperialists was to dominate and control Afghanistan by keeping the country weak and thus blocking any further development in the country so that it would be dependent on the British government.[3] As was the situation in 1836, Dost Mohammad had removed Shuja Shah from power, thus removing the British figurehead and puppet monarch as established by the treaty in 1809. The British tried to secure a new friendship with Dost Mohammad in an effort to retain the Afghan's amicable favoritism to British occupation in Afghanistan. However, Dost Mohammad was resolute in his stance of Afghan independence from foreign occupation and refused to allow the British to roam at will throughout his state. He no longer agreed with the British treaty signed by Shuja Shah to not allow other countries (namely Russia) to pass through Afghanistan. Gradually, the British began to hear of Dost Mohammad's interaction with the Russians and the Persians, most notably the ruler's endeavor to signify the British treaty would no longer be part of Afghan policy.

However in 1837, Dost Mohammad attempted to form an alliance with Britain in the hopes of capturing Peshawar, and in turn the British captain Alexander Burnes was invited to Kabul. The British were willing to discuss and outline the strategic alliance against Ranjit Shah, but before doing so, Dost Mohammad would have to retract any agreements with other European powers. At the time, Mohammad Shah of Persia had tried to capture Herat, which the British knew was the strategic foothold to gain entrance to India. Burnes arrived as a representative of Lord Auckland, the British governor general of India, and also to represent the British interventionist diplomat Sir William

Macnaghten. As such the British swore to protect Dost Mohammad from Ranjit Shah if he ceased his attempts to recover Peshawar. Burnes would not offer the assurances Dost Mohammad needed, and instead Burnes insisted the Afghan amir should place Afghan policy and control under British guidance. Recognizing the conundrum of his situation, Dost Mohammad rejected the British and quickly sought to form an alliance with Russia. On the cusp of Burnes's failure to subdue Afghanistan, the situation was further intensified upon witnessing the Russian emissary Lieutenant Vitkievitch in Kabul. The British retreated to India, and in 1838 Lord Auckland declared war on Afghanistan.[4]

The First Anglo-Afghan War had officially begun, and in February 1839, the British forces advanced through the Bolan Pass, a mountain pass of the Toba Kakar Range in Pakistan, approximately 120 miles from the Afghanistan border. By late April, the army arrived in Kandahar to find the Afghan princes had abandoned the area. Lord Auckland achieved his preliminary goal and restored the now-quite elderly Shuja Shah to the throne as amir of Afghanistan. Dost Mohammad had previously fled the capital city and was forced to retreat into the Hindu Kush Mountains. Among the harsh terrain and extreme weather, Dost Mohammad and his supporters sought evasion in the caves of the mountains for nearly a year as the British intently pursued him. Finally weary of the advancing forces, Dost Mohammad surrendered to the British on the evening of November 4, 1840, by allegedly riding on horseback up to General Macnaghten and offering his amicable surrender. As prisoner he was held in captivity during the British occupation of Afghanistan, and Dost Mohammed would be released after the recapture of Kabul in the fall of 1842.

By the end of 1841 and after having to endure watching their ruler be ousted and imprisoned by the British forces, the Afghan tribes rallied to support Dost Mohammad's son Mohammad Akbar Khan. Over the following months, the British forces faced numerous revolts and bloody executions, including the murder of Sir Alexander Burnes and his aids by an angry horde in Kabul. After the attack, the British General Macnaghten tried to negotiate with Mohammad Akbar Khan to allow the British to remain in the country, but in a severe act of defiance against the British, Mohammad Akbar ordered Macnaghten to be thrown in prison. Macnaghten never made it to his confinement, for upon his march to the prison he was attacked and dismembered by a livid Afghan crowd. As a gesture of their intolerance of any more British occupation in their country, the mob triumphantly paraded his dead and nearly limbless corpse around the streets of Kabul. The

British forces under attack near the city of Gandamak, Afghanistan, during the First Anglo-Afghan War. As part of the competition between Russia and Great Britain, the launch of the First Anglo-Afghan War in 1838 is regarded as the first major conflict of the Great Game. (DeAgostini/Getty Images)

British recognized the severity of their situation in Afghanistan, and in January 1842 they reached an agreement to provide the immediate retreat of the British forces out of Afghanistan. As the exodus began, the British troops struggled through the snowbound passes and were ambushed by Ghilzai tribesmen. Along the treacherous pass between Kabul and Gandamak, almost 16,000 British soldiers and British supporters were attacked and ruthlessly slaughtered. Only one survivor arrived at the British outpost in Jalalabad to describe the tale, and by that point Dr. William Brydon was barely breathing and slumped over his horse with the faint trace of life left in his body.[5] The horrifying massacre was enough to rejuvenate the British to return later in the year to relieve the British garrison at Jalalabad and rescue any remaining British occupants and prisoners in the country. The loss of life and property in Afghanistan, including the destruction of the marketplace in Kabul, known as the bazaar, resulted in a severe hatred of foreign occupation that is ingrained in the culture of Afghanistan to this day.

Often referred to by the British as "Auckland's Folly" due to Lord Auckland's erroneous judgment and decisions against the Afghan people, the First Anglo-Afghan Civil War from 1839 to 1842 resulted in the destruction of the British army, including the loss of nearly 20,000 soldiers, 50,000 camels, and costs that were upwards of £20 million.[6] In addition to these tangible costs of war instigated by Lord Auckland, as a further embarrassment the British lost substantial respect in India of the war's outcome. Further, the defeat and refusal of British hegemony serves as an accreditation of the Afghans' fierce resistance to foreign invaders attempting to occupy their lands. By the end of the first British invasion and Afghan war, Shah Shuja was presumably assassinated in 1842. After several months of chaos in Kabul, Moham-mad Khan was able to secure control of the city until his father Dost Mohammad was set free at the decision of the British government to abandon the control of internal politics in Afghanistan. On his return from Hindustan, Dost Mohammad was welcomed back to the seat of power in Kabul and in April 1843, Dost Mohammad resumed his title as king. Over the next decade Dost Mohammad would work at resum-ing control of the regions of Mazar-e-Sharif, Konduz, Badakshan, and Kandahar.

Upon his return to power, Dost Mohammad set forth with his plans to implement his authority and control against the British. He once again sought to defeat the Sikhs, who were engaged in combat with the British. In 1848 Dost Mohammad seized the opportunity to take con-trol of Peshawar. However, in February 1849, his army was defeated at Gujarat, and he abandoned his previous intentions to control Pesha-war. After he led troops back into Afghanistan, Dost Mohammad real-ized he would not be successful in his actions to capture Peshawar, and he abandoned any further efforts to do so. By concentrating on other regions, Dost Mohammad conquered Balkh a year later, and furthermore in 1854 he captured Kandahar and successfully assumed control over the southern Afghan tribes.

In retaliation for the humiliation endured in the First Anglo-Afghan War, the British attacked Afghanistan again, but this time the onslaught included a large Indian force. After several battles, new Brit-ish forces relieved the previous Jalalabad garrison and then advanced onward into Kabul, destroying the central bazaar and the large cita-del. By 1854, the British were ready to recommence associations with Afghanistan. In the following year, the British opened up diplomatic relations with Afghanistan in the Treaty of Peshawar. The treaty rec-ognized the authority of each country, and additionally acknowledged each country's territorial boundaries. In doing so the treaty declared henceforth a British-Afghan relationship of amenity in political inter-action and unity in defeating enemies. On March 30, 1855, the Afghan leader agreed to the alliance with the British government, and as a specification of the treaty, the province of Herat was placed in control of the Barakzai sovereignty. The coalition of the Afghans with the British resulted in both forces declaring war on Persia in 1857. During the period of Indian Mutiny in Afghanistan, Dost Mohammad abstained from supporting the uprising rebels, despite the call for jihad in which the Sikhs were supporters of India's movement against British occupation. Two years later in 1857, the treaty was amended so that while the British were fighting with the Iranians, Afghanistan's parliament would allow the British military to maintain a presence at Kandahar. The Iranians had previously attacked Herat in 1856, and as such Dost Mohammad was eager to accept the terms in the addendum.

While America was fighting its own Civil War, Dost Mohammad's final years were troubled with revolts out of Herat and Bokhara. In 1863 he personally led the Afghan army with the British troops at his flank, and they drove the Persian army from Kandahar. Due to the treaty allowance for the British presence, Dost Mohammad was able to seize back Herat from the Iranians only a few months before his death. On May 26, 1863, Dost Mohammad and his Afghan army captured Herat for good, but surprisingly Dost Mohammad died suddenly in the midst of his triumph. During his life he played a pivotal role in shaping Central Asia and Afghanistan, and upon his death his son Sher Ali Khan had been appointed as his heir to the kingdom.

SHER ALI KHAN (1863–1866 AND 1868–1879)

At the time of Sher Ali's enthronement, his older brother Mohammad Afzal was in power at Kabul. Once Sher Ali had taken control of Kabul, the British government yet again viewed Afghanistan as a buffer state. As such the British were willing to support Sher Ali's regime financially and with weapons rather than sending troops to provide the much-needed physical support forces. Sher Ali was not able to succeed in his father's quest and recapture Kabul until 1868. While once joined as a united team, over the next 10 years the relationship between the two governments deteriorated rapidly. Increasingly over the years, the Afghan ruler was leery of the Russians advancement into Afghanistan. In May 1873, led by the Russian general Von Kaufman, the Russians attacked the city of Khiva. By the early 17th century, Khiva was established as the prominent capital of Khanate of Khiva, located in modern-day Uzbekistan. The Russians were now in control of the Khanate and frighteningly close to advancing into Afghanistan. The Afghan ruler called upon his British counterparts to provide support.

THE SECOND ANGLO-AFGHAN WAR (1878–1880)

Unbeknownst to Sher Ali, the British signed an agreement with the Russians the previous year stating the Russians agreed to respect the boundaries of Afghanistan. Upholding the terms of the previously signed treaty, the British did not provide any support to Afghanistan and furthermore would not provide any promises or reassurance to Sher Ali. After the Congress of Berlin in June 1878, Russia sent an uninvited representative to Kabul, which Sher Ali tried to refuse. The Russians worked to persuade the Shah to accept their visit by offering such enticements as troop support against the British, and further offering to build roads and install telegraph lines. No longer able to defer the encounter and with reluctance, Sher Ali finally succumbed and turned to his Russian associates once again. However, once the British verified the existence of a Russian envoy in Kabul, the British demanded the Afghan ruler welcome a British diplomat as well. The British persistence was to counter the Russians instance on visiting Kabul, which through intelligence interception of mail correspondence, the British had known the Russians had been attempting this meeting for a number of years. Again, Sher Ali refused, but the British intently persisted they too needed to visit the Afghanistan amir, and even proceeded with sending the British envoy forward into Kabul. Conversely, the troops were intercepted at the Khyber Pass and instructed not to proceed further or they would be met with a resilient Afghan force. Once the British were refused at the eastern entrance of the Khyber Pass and forced to turn back, this was the unofficial commencement of the Second Anglo-Afghan War.

The rebuke resulted in the British cabinet declaring war on Afghanistan. Sher Ali was given the opportunity to grant a British summit once again, and while allowing the Afghan leader three weeks to make a decision, General Britton moved ahead with his military planning. Lasting for two years, the Second Anglo-Afghan Civil War began when the British marched into Afghanistan in August 1878. The British plan for invasion and political usurpation was to divide the army into three forces and invade Afghanistan at three different locations. Unable to gain support, Sher Ali retreated to Mazar-e-Sharif (Mazari Sharif) and died on February 21, 1879.

YAQUB KHAN (1879)

The British had invaded much of the country when Sher Ali's son Yaqub Khan succeeded him. In return for the provinces of Jalalabad and Kandahar, and with little option, Yaqub signed the Treaty of

Gandamak in May 1879 to prevent the British from conquering the remaining provinces of Afghanistan. Perhaps in fear of the first Afghan War, Yaqub agreed to outlandish stipulations that in essence gave the British control over Afghanistan. Not only did he cede these territories, but Yaqub also ceded the lands of Pishin and Sibi. The treaty also included multiple stipulations, such as that British authority would be physically represented in Kabul and other cities, that British control would include the Khyber Pass and also the Michni pass, and finally that Afghanistan must release certain frontier lands to the British. Once the Afghani people realized the magnitude of the agreement, which included releasing all control in the foreign affairs of Afghanistan to the British, the strong-willed Afghani population rebelled against Yaqub Khan.

In September 1879, the Afghan insurgence killed the British emissary and his escort while they were stationed in Kabul, and in fear Yaqub fled the throne under the guise of British amnesty. British forces marched into central Afghanistan, and simultaneously defeated the Afghan army in October and then restored Yaqub to the throne. By March of the following year, the British realized controlling Afghanistan as a buffer state would require controlling the dissenting Afghani people, and even defeating them did not mean they had overpowered their strong-willed spirits. Knowing full well of the continuous threat of rebellions and uprising, and recognizing the disastrous experiences of their British predecessors in the First Anglo-Afghan War, the British finally realized they could not control Afghanistan.[7] The British implemented the removal of Yaqub Khan and the induction of Amir Abdur Rahman to the throne of Afghanistan, with Britain retaining control of Kabul's foreign policies and interactions.

ABDUR RAHMAN KHAN, "THE IRON AMIR" (1880–1901)

In 1881 the British removed their forces from Afghanistan, but not before offering Abdur Rahman Khan the throne and requiring the new amir to uphold the Treaty of Gandamak. Despite gaining a minor amount of territory and influence in Afghanistan, the British knew the Afghan people would embrace Abdur Rahman Khan since he was the nephew of Sher Ali, and he would also remain loyal to the influence of the British and conduct Afghanistan's foreign policy through the government of India. During Amir Abdur's 20-year reign from 1880 to 1901, the British and the Russians established the official boundaries and territorial lines of present-day Afghanistan.

Also during this timeframe, the British implemented a new method of protecting the territories of Afghanistan. Known as the Khyber Rifles, this group was established during the British invasion of Afghanistan and was one of eight "frontier-corps" that served as auxiliaries for the British Indian army, and was one of the oldest military units of the Northwest Frontier Province. The corps began as an assembly of Afridi tribesmen known as the Khyber Jezailchis in November 1878 led by Captain Gais Ford, and he commanded until 1881 when the regiment was turned over to Mohammad Aslam Khan. The British commanders from Indian regiments were the primary leaders, and the Afridis were established as the second line of command. Under Mohammad Aslam's 16-year reign as commander from 1881 to 1897, the corps changed from the Khyber Jezailchis to the Khyber Rifles and would henceforth support all areas rather than the previous support to only the Khyber Agency. The Khyber Rifles established their command center of operations at Landi Kotal, and the main purpose of the regiment was simply to guard the Khyber Pass. The brigade included three main strongholds of the Khyber Pass, which included the primary location at Landi Kotal located at the western end. The other two major command centers included Fort Maude located on the eastern side and Ali Masjid located in the center of the Khyber Pass.[8] Unification of the corps was vital, and to symbolize their objective, the badge was emblazoned with two crossed Afghan daggers encircled with the name KHYBER RIFLES.

One of the most historically significant events in Afghanistan is the division of Afghanistan and Pakistan known as the Durrand Line, named after the British cartographer Sir Mortimor Durrand. The Durand Line issue began in 1893 and would take over four years to negotiate due to the constant difficulties in the delineation location, and the feelings of resentment the Durand Line created. From the Afghan point of view, the implementation of the Durand Line would mean Afghanistan would remain a landlocked nation and would never have access to a seaport. Abdur Rahman had little choice after four years in the signing of the treaty, and in spite of his hand being forced by the British, the citizens of Afghanistan would never forgive the Iron Amir for signing such an agreement. However, he is widely renowned as a popular figure for creating a unified kingdom that was circumscribed of tribal authority. His reputation was hindered by his resolution of the Durand Line issue, his encouragement of brutal torture and execution methods to force rebellions tribes to submit to the law, and also for his lack of implementing social and economic reforms.

Throughout his reign, Abdur Rahman's goal was to break down these tribal alliances and institute one nation under one rule, and during his reign he endured and crushed more than 40 tribal revolts. By furthering his regime and earning him the title of "The Iron Amir," he enforced the migration of 10,000 Ghilzai families to relocate in an effort to break apart the tribal structure that had formed in the Hindu Kush Mountains. Furthermore, he restricted the movement of migrating tribes by stating the tribes could not relocate without the approval of the Afghan government. By doing so, he further suppressed the Hazara tribes from revolt. While toiling to implement his command for ethnic cleansing and relocation of ethnic tribes, there was little money left in the vaults of the treasury, and he ordered tax collectors to collect the revenue across Afghanistan. These tax payments were difficult for the disenchanted and relocated tribes, and those who revolted against the payment of taxes were brutally punished. By the time of his death in 1901, Abdur Rahman had successfully subdued tribal revolts so he could control the country, and he additionally developed a spy and informant network to assist his monitoring of tribal actions and any planned insurgency, including the use of Afghanistan's first secret police force.[9] Interestingly enough, he was against such technological advancements as the telephone and the railroad, as he believed these advancements would be a way for the British to move troops into Afghanistan.

HABIBOLLAH KHAN (1901–1919)

In quite a unique turn of events upon Abdur Khan's death, Habibollah Khan's ascension to the throne was a peaceful one, mostly because the country was already quite pacified under his father's reign. Upon commencement of his reign, Habibollah's regime would prove to be much different from his father's. In stark contrast, his tenure in office is regarded one of severe neutrality in foreign policy. Though he was supported by only a few tribal chiefs, he gave local tribal chiefs more leniencies, instituting legal reforms even to the point of abolishing his father's spy system on Afghani tribes and foreign countries. Habibollah also allowed many exiles to return to the country, welcoming back one of the most notable exiles, Mahmoud Beg Tarzi. As a nationalist and party advisor, Tarzi was a prominent figure in Afghanistan and was a key proponent of the modernization of the country. Habibollah Khan is regarded as a progressive thinker who sought to establish a modern land with advancements in technology, education, and medicine. Despite his dominating policy of noninvolvement in

World War I, he is credited with opening the technology portal for Afghanistan by introducing such innovations as electricity and the automobile.

Overall the country of Afghanistan remained neutral during World War I, despite the encouragement of the Germans to persuade the Afghans into anti-British sentiment and action. Regardless of the Germans efforts to create a British rebellion in Afghanistan, most notably along the borders of British India, it was the sovereign choice of the king of Afghanistan to remain nonaligned in the war even with the predominate sentiment toward British rule. Habibollah Khan treated the affairs of World War I with indifference, and announced early in the situation that the country of Afghanistan would remain neutral, despite pressures from Turkey and other leaders. Many Afghan citizens were enraged by his continual stance on neutrality as they viewed World War I as a holy war. Even after the overthrow of the czar in 1917 by the Bolsheviks in Russia, many urged this to be the opportunity for Afghanistan to reaffirm its Islamic mission and liberate the country from non-Muslim rule. Habibollah Khan refused to participate and insisted Afghanistan would remain neutral in spite of the world's events. Rather than focusing on outside affairs, Habibollah desired to focus on the internal aspects of the country and sought to modernize and advance Afghanistan. For this reason, Habibollah Khan worked to pacify tribal schisms in Afghanistan, and in support of this regime he instituted tribal state council to monitor tribal affairs. Despite the efforts of Lord Curzon in India to engage the Afghan leader in the war, Habibollah Khan was able to stall the British from a meeting for three years by arguing he could not abandon the throne of Kabul for such a rendezvous. Due to his lack of engagement, Lord Curzon sought permission of the London cabinet to declare war and authorize an invasion of Afghanistan. After the British cabinet overruled this effort, Habibollah continued the neutral stance much to the chagrin of his British counterparts and Afghan council. However, his neutrality would change once Turkey became confrontational toward Afghanistan. In September 1915 a Turko-German mission arrived in Kabul that left Habibollah Khan anxious and unsettled.[10] As justification for his neutral stance, he did not want to risk any further aggression with Russia and Britain. Yet in spite of these foreign pressures and the implicit internal call to jihad, Habibollah Khan continued to insist Afghanistan would remain neutral.

As a result of his penchant for impartiality and a nonaligned status, the country endured a widespread belief that by his actions to remain neutral he was not supporting Afghanistan's ideology of Islamic beliefs. Habibollah Khan failed to conciliate not only the war party, but also the religious, political, and tribal leaders. Habibollah Khan was assassinated in 1919, presumably by his family members who were resistant to British influence and control. Not much was achieved during his reign as he was impacted with a severe limitation in financial capital, but he at least was able to begin the movement of social and economic reforms that would be further implemented and blossom under the hands of his successor Amanullah Khan.

NOTES

1. Peter Hopkirk, *The Great Game: The Struggle for Empire in Central Asia* (New York: Kodansha America, Inc., 1994), 1.

2. Ewans, *Afghanistan*, 45–59.

3. Abdul Ghaffar Farahi, *Afghanistan during Democracy and Republic: 1963–1978* (Kabul: UNO Education Press, 2004).

4. Karl E. Meyer, *The Dust of Empire: The Race for Mastery in the Asian Heartland* (New York: Public Affairs, 2003), 113–138; Ewans, *Afghanistan*, 45–59.

5. Tanner, *Afghanistan*, 129–154.

6. Ewans, *Afghanistan*, 71–98.

7. Ibid.

8. Jules Stewart, *The Khyber Rifles: From the British Raj to Al Qaeda* (Stroud, UK: Sutton Publishing, 2005), Kindle Edition.

9. Ewans, *Afghanistan*, 90–98.

10. Ibid., 110–117.

8

From the Age of Reformation to the War with the Soviets (1919–1979)

As the sentiment of Afghan nationalism began to rise, the assassination of Habibullah Khan in February 1919 may be regarded as the first monumental political step toward the formation of a constitutional government in Afghanistan. Previously under King Habibullah's government, a social group of intellectuals known as "the Young Afghans" supported the contrasting viewpoint of the anti-British occupation movement and the modernization of the country. Throughout Habibullah's reign, the Afghan amir's stance of pro-British occupation primarily contributed to the increased sentiment of aggravation with the Afghan government. This frustration gave birth to the modernization movement in the early 20th century initiated by Mahmud Beg Tarzi, an influential writer and champion of Afghan freedom. Tarzai's independent newspaper, *Siraj-ul-Akhbar* (*Lamp of the News*) promoted pan-Islamism and British imperialism and scoffed at outdated social and religious customs as he believed they slowed progress to reform. King Habibullah practiced some form of modernism and was tolerant of these political articles. He endorsed Tarzai's newspaper, as long as these freedom-laced writings did not create an insurgence. After ruling with this policy of tolerance for a number of years, Habibullah became outraged in 1916 at Tarzi's call to the nation to rise up and defeat the British in defense of Islam. Tarzi's criticism of European dominance in the nation coupled with Afghanistan's stance of neutrality in World War I was well received by the young Prince Amanullah, and his support of the influential writer even resulted in marriage to Tarzi's daughter in 1916.[1] Several members of the Young Afghans were arrested in an attempt to murder King Habibullah with the intention of replacing him with his modern-thinking son. However, the plan was uncovered and the king's own son Amanullah was named among the conspirators. Amanullah escaped severe punishment due to intervention from his uncle Nasrullah, but obviously the incident created a bitter sentiment and he was banished from the king's favor. With their plan defeated, the Young Afghans became more fervent to institute Prince Amanullah since he embodied their beliefs in nationalism and independence from foreign occupation.

SOCIAL REFORMATION IN AFGHANISTAN UNDER AMANULLAH KHAN (1919–1929)

King Habibullah Khan was assassinated while he was on a hunting trip in February 1919. He was presumably killed by his family members due to his refusal to support Turkey against Britain and other Allied forces in World War I. Shortly after the assassination, the king's brother Nasrullah promptly assumed the kingship and both of young Amanullah's older brothers supported this arrangement. However, in Kabul, Prince Amanullah emerged as the new champion and defender of Islamic freedom and independence. While his uncle had already assumed the kingship, within several days, Amanullah was thrust to the forefront by declaring Nasrullah was involved in the assassination of the king. Further, Amanullah declared his brothers had abandoned their rights to the throne by supporting their uncle and his heinous acts, and consequentially Amanullah vowed to seek vengeance for his usurped father. As a result, two political parties championed for the throne, one led by Amanullah and the other by Nasrullah. While both groups were united in the fight against British occupation, Nasrullah supported the orthodoxy political movement, whereas Amanullah supported Afghan nationalism. The result promulgated Amanullah to be in the prime position for the throne, since by discrediting his uncle, he gained the support of Afghan nationalists and the Afghan nobility that were allied with King Habibullah Khan.

THIRD ANGLO-AFGHAN WAR AND AUTONOMY

King Amanullah's primary objective was to complete his father's goal of Afghan independence, and as a result he was resolute in his stance on Afghan autonomy from foreign control. In the past 40 years in Afghanistan since the Second Anglo-Afghan War, the boundaries of the country had been devised by foreign governments and their desire to implement Afghanistan as a buffer state. The various treaties and agreements over the years, some of which Afghanistan was forced to comply with, instilled Amanullah's implementation of a regime to create a nation composed of independent rule. The British imposed Treaty of Gandamak in 1879, and the application of the Durand Line in 1893 helped to ensure British control and influence in Afghanistan. On the opponent side of the Great Game, the Russians imposed the settlement of the lands of the Amu-Darya in 1888 and also the 1895 settlement of Parmir. These frontiers had been established for Afghanistan by foreign governments with no correlation or respect for the ethnic boundaries and the Muslim faith.[2] As perceived by King Amanullah, Afghanistan was a devout Muslim state that was created by the infidels of Britain and Russia.

With the country's independence secured, King Amanullah launched the Third Anglo-Afghan War in May 1919 by attacking India with the intention to finally gain control over Afghanistan's foreign policy. Previously during the Russian Revolution in 1917, Afghanistan served again as the battleground for the Russians and the British who were simultaneously vying for control in the Asian heartland. After growing tired of this repetitive pattern, King Amanullah desired to implement reforms in Afghanistan that could be accomplished only by finally attaining Afghan independence from the British.[3] In this regard, King Amanullah sought to finalize Afghanistan's independence in May 1919 by surprising the British in an attack, and the British retaliated with an aerial assault in which King Amanullah's house was attacked in the bombardment. The incident is the first aerial invasion in Afghanistan's history and forced a truce agreement known as the Treaty of Rawalpindi, and the details of which were so complicated that the final details of the treaty took for nearly two years to complete the negotiations.[4] In the treaty, the British recognized Afghan independence and agreed the British kingdom would not extend beyond the Khyber Pass. Before completion of the treaty in 1921, the Afghanistan ruler had already established foreign relations with most major countries, including Russia, which was outside of British coordination. Without question, the Khyber Pass was of utmost strategic importance during these negotiations and foreign policy agreements. In spite of the excessive duration of time to resolve the document, the Treaty of Rawalpindi symbolizes Afghan independence and the end of the Great Game between the Russian and the British empires. This remarkable day on August 19, 1919, is commemorated as Afghanistan's Independence Day. After nearly 60 years of fighting against British oppression, Afghanistan successfully fought and won freedom from British control and influence. By signing the Treaty of Rawalpindi, the war-weary British relinquished control of Afghanistan, not just territorially but also in any other affairs, internal or foreign. This noteworthy agreement opened the door for King Amanullah to finally begin the age of reformation in Afghanistan. After 10 years as the Afghan ruler, his revolutionary changes in social, economic, and political reforms infiltrated not only Afghanistan's domestic dealings but foreign relations as well and created a period of rebirth for the country.

While both parties agreed on Afghan independence as stipulated in the first treaty, the debate and peace negotiations continued into a second deliberation, since both parties could not agree on the territorial boundaries of the Durand Line. This cartographical delineation represented a division of the British and Afghan control of the Pashtun tribes, and ultimately was designed to act as a British buffer zone for further Russian aggression and encroachment into India. Delineated in 1893 and reluctantly agreed to by Amir Abdur Rahman in 1897, the meandering Durand Line had detached the eastern Pashtun tribes near Pakistan from Afghanistan and created what would be referred to as the Pashtunistan Issue.[5] This sensitive issue refers to the artificially imposed Durrand Line, which resulted in the segregation of the Pashtun tribe between their occupied lands in Pakistan and Afghanistan. As part of the Afghan resentment in devising the Durand Line, Sir Mortimer Durand created the artificial line in such a crooked manner that the line even divided a farmer's house from his field. The ethnographic Durand Line had been a cause for friction among the Anglo-Afghan empires for many years, and the continual debate in 1921 still would not resolve the issue. The British refused to abandon their control, and simultaneously the Afghans were unrelenting on the ethnical unfairness of the agreement. Despite the begrudgingly agreed-upon terms, for many Afghans the compromise in 1921 was regarded as merely an informal agreement on a continually unsettled issue.

The Pashtunistan issue was not the only cause of ethnic friction facing Afghanistan during the Third Anglo-Afghan War in 1919. A well-known section of land between Afghanistan and Pakistan, known as the Khyber Pass, was critical for the Silk Road and regarded as a key strategic military vantage point. A paramilitary unit known as the Khyber Rifles was stationed along the Kyber pass, with the primary mission of protecting British interests in Afghanistan. Since the Khyber Rifles were a band of Afridi tribe members from the northwest Afghanistan and Pakistan, led by British commanders, ethnic frictions continued to escalate in Afghanistan. Many of the Khyber Rifles simply deserted the effort, which included nearly 12,000 sepoys.[6] As a result of the desertion, the Khyber Rifles Regiment was disbanded for being unreliable and capricious, and was not reinstated until World War II.

While the British and the Afghans were struggling to finalize their independence agreement, the Russians moved forward with establishing amicable relations with Afghanistan. Prior to these advancements in Afghanistan, the Bolshevik Revolution of 1917 led to dramatic changes in the Russian government, and also in the pacification efforts of their Muslim inhabitants. The Soviet government sought to establish amiable relationships with neighboring Islamic countries to mollify any uprisings from the Muslim population in Russia. In this regard, the Russians were eager to befriend the Afghanistan leader in Kabul, not only for the pacification of the Muslim minority in Russia, but also to create an Afghan-Soviet allegiance that would serve as a threat to Britain. Upholding his beliefs in Afghan independence from the British, Amanullah sent an emissary to meet in Moscow with Vladimir Lenin, the then leader of the Russian Soviet Federative Socialist Republic. The Afghan representative was warmly welcomed, and in response Lenin sent his own representative to provide support and aid to Afghanistan. The relationship between the two empires fluctuated between two stances: the Soviet's use of Afghanistan as a pawn in their anti-Bolshevik relationships in Central Asia, and also from the advantage as an allegiance and strategic threat to the British. Meanwhile, the Afghans merely wanted Soviets to abandon control over territory across the Amu Darya that was previously lost to the Russians in the late 19th century. In the first act of establishing foreign relations since winning their independence in August 1919, the Soviets and the Afghans forged ahead in their strategic partnership and signed a cordial Treaty of Friendship in May 1921. Despite the Soviets best efforts, including provisions for gifts such as technological advancements and military equipment to include King Amanullah's highly desired Soviet aircraft, King Amanullah was displeased with the growing oppression of the Islamic minority in Russia. In spite of these differences, Anglo-Afghan relations gradually dwindled from the newly forged Afghan-Soviet friendship. While his efforts with the Soviets had increased, Amanullah's amicable relationship with the British was descending quickly into a maelstrom of disrepair. Recognizing this disparity, the British responded by increasing the restrictions on the shipment of goods through India.

While the atmosphere of Afghanistan's affairs with Britain was unsteady and with Russian concordance in the early stages, Amanullah continued his goal of instituting several reforms in Afghanistan, including social, economic, and political reforms. In this new era after the dawn of Afghan independence, King Amanullah sought to eliminate Afghanistan's traditional role of isolation and seclusion from its neighboring countries. Following the Third Anglo-Afghan War, Amanullah recognized the need to establish diplomatic relations with several major countries. After an influential tour of Europe and Turkey in 1927 in which he witnessed firsthand how these governments operated, he instituted several reforms in an effort to modernize Afghanistan under a strong central government.[7] As the founder of the Turkish republic, Ataturk was also the first president. King Amanullah was deeply impressed with Ataturk's reforms of Turkey and sought to implement such factions in Afghanistan. King Amanullah's foreign minister and father-in-law, Mahmud Tarzi, was a driving force and pivotal component for instituting and developing these reforms. Furthermore, Mahmud Tarzi was an avid supporter of the education and advancement of women. In this regard, he intently fought for and won a constitutional legislative law that made elementary education in Afghanistan mandatory. His daughter, Queen Soraya Tarzi, was a driving force and the political face of championing women independence in Afghanistan. Queen Soraya was a prominent ruler for her pioneering efforts in the women's rights movement in Afghanistan. Her feminine-based advancement efforts included such reforms as education for females and the inclusion of women in political activities. She was a devout supporter of the enlightenment period for women, and her efforts have often given her the distinction of being the first and one of the most powerful Afghani female activists.

King Amanullah continued with implementing his revolutionary judicial and political reformation efforts. Most notably in 1923, he instituted the First Constitution of Afghanistan and furthermore implemented a code of civil rights for the Afghan people. Amanullah also instituted a system of national identification through registration

King Amir Amanullah Khan, ruler of Afghanistan from 1919 to 1929, when he was overthrown by tribal forces and forced into exile. He is well known for leading Afghanistan to independence from the British. (AP Photo)

and citizen identification cards. In the judicial improvements, he established a legislative assembly, a court system with multiple factions of code enforcement, and he even further eradicated subsidized payments that were granted to tribal chiefs. However, these revolutionary concepts for the advancement of Afghanistan were not met with excitement, and as such many orders established under Habibullah Khan were alienated by some of Amanullah's efforts, including religious leaders.

As a respected leader, King Amanullah is regarded as a modern thinker, and he successfully initiated many reforms, but most of his ideas never achieved full fruition. He transformed Afghanistan by bringing the country into the 20th century with his social, economic, and political reforms. In this manner, he was successful in achieving social reforms such as adopting the Western style of dress, the elimination of the veiled headdress for women, and the abolishment of slavery and forced labor. His education reforms included secular education for both young men and women, and he further instituted education policies for nomads and farmers. Over the tenure of his reign, his economic reforms included such facets as a complete overhaul of the country's taxation system, the implementation of the country's first budget structure in 1922, the establishment of the afghani as the single form of currency, and even the formation of a national bank in 1928 (known as Bank-i-Melli).

While many applauded these revolutionary concepts for advancement, some of these reforms moved too quickly for such an antiquated society. Movements supporting the abolition of the traditional Muslim veil that was required for women to wear, in addition to the increasing amount of coeducational schools, were considered too extreme and radical. For many, these revolutionary concepts quickly estranged several tribal leaders from Afghanistan's reform movement. In January 1929, faced with overwhelming opposition and resistance for his renovation of Afghanistan, King Amanullah was forced to resign after Habibullah Kalakani captured Kabul.

Afghanistan Civil War and Tajik Rule by Habibullah Kalakani (1929)

Amanullah's reform movement began to unravel when Shinwari Pashtun tribesmen led a rebellion in Jalalabad in 1928. As the armed tribal warriors advanced upon the capital, many troops in the king's bodyguard deserted. Additionally, another tribal revolt was marching toward Kabul, led by a Tajik rebel. With no other option, Amanullah fled the throne and left it in the hands of his brother Inayatullah, and his rule as king lasted for a mere three days before he fled to refuge in India. In the meantime, Amanullah had assembled a small fleet of troops to return to Kabul and seize the capital back from the Tajik vanquisher Habibollah Kalakani. His efforts to reestablish order to his dream of reforming Afghanistan into a modern state were futile, and he fled to Italy and lived in exile until his death in 1960.

The Tajik rule lasted for only 10 months, from January to October in 1929, under a rebellious leader and Tajik bandit who assumed the throne and titled himself Habibullah Kalakani. He was a native of the Kala Khan village north of Kabul, and his siege of Kabul was in shrewd succession to the Shinwari rebellion and the abandonment of the king's army. He was briefly supported by several of the Pashtun tribes to overthrow Amanullah, but since he was not of Pashtun descent, Afghan customs and principles would not allow him to rule on the throne for long. As such, the Musahiban brothers were the next in line for the throne as the descendants of Dost Mohammad and also of the Barakzai lineage. Nadir Shah was the oldest and also Amanullah's former minister of war, and after several months of gaining tribal support, the Musahiban brothers were able to cross the Durand Line into Afghanistan. As such, the large force defeated the Tajik ruler and seized Kabul on October 10, 1929. Habibullah Kalakani escaped but several days later was captured and executed early in November. Soon after, Nadir Shah was declared the king of Afghanistan.

REIGN OF KING NADIR SHAH (1929–1933)

Mohammad Nadir Shah became the king of Afghanistan and began to reconsolidate the country in support of a more gradual approach to modernism, and he quickly abolished the majority of Amanullah's reform programs. In 1930, despite his efforts to rebuild the army, the religious and tribal leaders in Afghanistan grew strong and instigated a rebellion in 1930. The uprising of the Shinwari Pashtuns coupled with the Soviet pursuit of an Uzbek tribal leader created internal friction in the country. In spite of this, by the end of 1931, many of the rebellions were quelled as the country moved from a hub of extremism to a stabilized center.

As part of his abolishment of the previously instated reforms, Nadir Shah appointed a cabinet of 10 members, and in 1931 he developed a new constitution of Afghanistan. As part of the new doctrine, the government was converted into a royal oligarchy. His tenure as king was not only to dispose of previous reforms, as he continued to support some of the efforts as instigated by his cousin and predecessor King Amanullah. King Nadir Shah continued to modernize Afghanistan with roadways and communication networks. Further, he promulgated regeneration efforts when he continued diplomatic relations with foreign countries, expanded economic reforms as the banking centers, and developed a regimented army of nearly 40,000 troops.

However, in spite of the positive reforms, Nadir Shah limited the rights to free speech, and as such thousands of Afghan intellectuals were imprisoned or killed. In November 1933, King Nadir Shah was shot and killed by an Afghan teenager, Abdul Khaliq Hazara, who as a Kabul student, was displeased with the state of Afghanistan under the new legislation and rule of King Nadir. As punishment for the assassination of the king, Khaliq was tortured to death by literally being cut into pieces, starting with his fingers, nose, ears, and tongue. He was hung along with his parents, uncle, friends, and siblings, including his seven-year-old sister. After Nadir's assassination, his son Zadir, who was only 19, succeeded Nadir Shah to the throne.

THE LAST KING OF AFGHANISTAN: ZADIR SHAH (1933–1973)

Mohammad Zadir Shah has the triumvirate honor of being the youngest, the longest-serving, and also the last king of Afghanistan. After attaining the title of king at the young age of 19, Zadir Shah spent the majority of his time as a ruler under the guidance of several more experienced advisors in the royal family. These family members, including his uncles and his cousin Mohammed Daoud Khan, worked with Zadir until 1963. His first 20 years on the throne would be largely influenced by his uncle Sardar Mohammad Hashim Khan, who previously served as the prime minister under Nadir Shah. During his last decade of rule, Zadir's reign would be independent from the sovereign advisement and oversight of his family.

Soon after establishing his sovereignty as king, his uncle Hashim guided King Zahir to make decisions for the nation. Afghanistan became acknowledged in the world by joining the League of Nations in 1934, and subsequently Afghanistan was also officially recognized as a country by the United States. Afghanistan established a new government with the objective to strengthen and increase such aspects as the army, the economy, the transportation system, and the methods of communication in Afghanistan. However, in order to successfully implement and achieve these goals, Hashim knew this would require the aid of foreign countries. After the long history of the Great Game, Hashim was reluctant to turn to the countries of Britain and the Soviet Union for support. Instead, the Afghan government sought new relations with Germany, and by 1935, there were a multitude of German factories and business projects in Afghanistan. Other projects and development efforts were initiated with Japan and Italy. The Treaty of Saadabad on July 9, 1937, established additional relations with neighboring countries. The treaty was a non-aggression pact that increased Afghanistan's regional ties with the Islamic states of Iran, Iraq, and Turkey and lasted for five years.

In the early stages of World War II, Afghanistan quickly announced its neutrality in the war on August 17, 1940. However in spite of this declaration of impartiality, the Allied forces were displeased with the allowance and tolerance of German personnel stationed in Afghanistan. In this regard, the Allied forces of the British and Russians insisted that Afghanistan must expel from its borders any non-diplomatic people who were representatives of the Axis countries. Despite his feelings of insult at this request, King Zahir requested *loya jirga* where he once again reiterated the Afghan stance on neutrality in the war, but he eventually ordered the Afghan government to comply with the Allies' request.

Shortly after the end of World War II in 1946, another of Zahir Shah's uncles replaced the prime minister. After taking the place of his older brother, Sardar Shah Mahmud Khan tried to implement both internal and external policies with the intention to initiate a period of new beginnings and great changes in Afghanistan. One such policy was in regards to political freedom, but he was forced to abort the strategy once it had spun out of his control and in consequence he was forced to overturn any beneficial results from the annulled policy. However, the prime minister successfully presided over the irrigation venture known as the Helmand Valley Project, which created a closer relationship with the United States, especially after the country provided much of the financial backing for the effort.

In 1947, the Durand Line would once again surface as an issue with the government of Afghanistan. At the first implementation of the Pashtunistan demarcation line in 1893, the reigning Amir Abdur Rahman felt anger and resentment over the terms of the agreement with the British, often complaining how he had been forced into signing the agreement. This notion still carried through several decades in the Afghan government, even in light of the years of cooperation and diplomacy with the British. Gradually over time, the Durand Line became a point of contention between the political regimes of Afghanistan and Pakistan, with the Pashtun tribesmen caught in the middle. As a further increase to the difficulty of the situation, new British policy in the North-West Frontier Province complicated relations with India. The North-West Frontier Province was established on November 9, 1901. As part of this new policy, the Muslims of the region were forced to choose between the Hindu-dominated state of India and the Muslim population of Pakistan. In July 1947, the

Pashtun inhabitants in the North-West Frontier Province overwhelmingly elected to be part of Pakistan. Further, the tribal agencies held a *loya jirga*, and once again the tribes chose allegiance to Pakistan. Afghanistan accepted the decision with diplomacy, but the matter continued to remain unresolved until 1949 when a Pakistani air force plane bombarded a local Pashtun village. In light of these new events, Afghanistan took a firm stance in a *loya jirga*, deciding the artificial Durand Line and any similar line was invalid, and furthermore all agreements and treaties regarding the issue since 1893 would not be recognized by Afghanistan. Relations between the governments of Pakistan and Afghanistan suffered, and as consequence, Pakistan ceased the transport of a petroleum shipment into Afghanistan in 1950 and held the cargo for three months in an act of defiance. The incident forced the hand of the Afghan government to sign a treaty with the Soviet Union several months later in July 1950. The agreement involved the amicable trade of Soviet commodities, such as oil and textiles, in exchange for Afghan wool and cotton. The Soviets also offered aid in several construction efforts in Afghanistan, such as petroleum storage facilities. Additionally as a further benefit to the Afghan economy, the agreement offered the free transportation of goods across Soviet territory. Prime Minister Shah Mahmud's efforts during the Pashtunistan issue and the Soviet agreement would have a profound impact on the political aspirations and liberalization of Afghanistan. This agreement not only benefited Afghanistan by providing a viable alternative to the Pakistan blockage of trade, which had severely disrupted the economy of Afghanistan, but the agreement with the Soviets also robustly increased interaction and technological advancements in Afghanistan.

THE LIBERAL PARLIAMENT OF 1949

After World War II, Afghanistan began to move toward an outlook of political open-mindedness, freedom, and liberalization. This newly developed sphere of tolerance had been highly advanced by the emergence and support of the Western style of thinking. The influential political leaders garnered support for the prime minister to hold less controlled elections for the National Assembly, thus leading to the first "liberal parliament." As such, Prime Minister Sardar Shah Mahmud recognized the importance of diverse political groups to represent the spectrum of political interests in Afghanistan, and many of these groups supported a more open political system. These groups contributed to such social acts as conducting debates, producing theatrical plays on subjects such as the monarchy or the role of Islam in Afghanistan, and publishing newspaper articles.

Unfortunately, the multitude of diverse groups emerged in rapid succession and ultimately overwhelmed the prime minister, and he vainly tried to counter this effort by forming his own overarching political party. After his unsuccessful attempts to form his own governmental interest group, the prime minister determined that since his own party was not worthy enough, then none of the other groups would be either. As such in 1951, he terminated all of the previously created political groups and eliminated the virtual abundance of political liberalization. The student union in Kabul was closed, and the newspapers that once were valued for free speech regarding governmental plans and political themes were also shut down. The following year, the elected parliament was a dramatic difference from the liberal assembly that had been elected three years previously. After the new parliament election, the brief period of liberalism in Afghanistan was over. The government cleanup of political tolerance in 1951 alienated many of the young Afghans who were trying to improve the political structure for the benefit of the country, and not as the government believed, which was to create a radically different stance and insurgence in Afghanistan.

PRIME MINISTER DAOUD AND THE URBANIZATION OF AFGHANISTAN (1953)

The failed political and liberalization reforms in the early 1950s created a rift in the royal Afghan house and began to challenge the control held by the king's uncles. Mohammed Daoud Khan became prime minister in September 1953. The placement of Daoud as prime minister was a public recognition of the royal family's attempts at embracing Western thought, for Daoud was the first Western-educated member of the royal family to hold a position of power, as Daoud was both the cousin of the king and also his brother-in-law. Daoud's main concern as prime minister was to eradicate the Afghan governments' stance and bias on the Western way of thought. Daoud would continue to support the Helmand Project as begun under his predecessor, Prime Minister Sardar Shah Mahmud Khan. To further his stance on modernism and in conjunction with the Durand Line ramifications, Daoud sought to expand relations with the Soviet Union and continued to increase his disparity against Pakistan.

In the 30 years since the dawn of reformation under King Amanullah, Afghanistan was still trying to transform out of its antiquated doldrums into a more modern society. Prime Minister Daoud also supported the emancipation of the women of Afghanistan, and these included social advancements for women, once again leading the effort to end the requirement for women to wear veiled coverings in public. However, Islamic fundamentalists who were not in favor of these urban reforms took matters into their own hands. This period of time marks the first instance of men throwing acid onto the faces of unveiled women, thus hoping in the act of disfiguring their female features, these liberal women would choose to have their faces covered out of embarrassment. However, these extreme measures would not dissuade these early female pioneers, and the multitude of women bravely defended their freedom by walking out in public without veiled faces. These vicious acts would gain more publicity in nearly 50 years when the Taliban assumed control of Afghanistan and corroborated the custom of defacing women with acid.

In 1959 as Afghanistan was preparing to celebrate their 40th year of independence, Daoud also invited the wives of his ministers to join in the celebration without the typical veiled attire. Religious leaders vehemently protested this so-called shameful request, and Daoud challenged their objections by requesting these conventional leaders to show him the verse in the Qur'an that mandates women must be veiled. When these religious leaders could not find the reference but continued to dispute the unveiled appearance, these antiquated supporters were thrown in jail.

RELATIONS WITH THE SOVIET UNION

Daoud achieved some success in his reforms of foreign policy, but in consequence, these reforms created economic instability in the country. His goals in foreign policy were to improve relations with the Soviet Union without harming economic aid from the United States, and also to pursue and resolve the Pashtunistan issue, the one standpoint that would consume him throughout his career. Due to the increasing hostile relations encouraged by Pakistan, the economic trade of Afghanistan began to suffer. Afghanistan had little choice as a land-locked country with no access to an independent port, and furthermore the country could no longer interact on cordial terms with Pakistan. For these reasons, Afghanistan was forced to ally with the Soviet Union. However, Prime Minister Daoud recognized that Afghanistan needed to consider other avenues and thus he sought to expand foreign policy for aid and assistance from the other superpowers in the world.

To further intensify the already-strained situation, the border between Afghanistan and Pakistan was closed for five months in 1955, and both Iran and the United States were unable to create another viable trade route for Afghanistan. Prime Minister Daoud's desire for improved relations became imperative with the Soviet Union, and in striding toward the achievement of this objective, the treaty established in 1950 would be amended and ratified again in June 1955 to allow the transit of bartered goods. In an effort to renew the treaty and secure an amicable partnership, Nikita Khruschev visited Kabul and the Soviet-Afghan relationship was once again renewed, and this also included a $100 million development loan for mutual Afghan-Soviet projects.

Despite the escalation of the Cold War between the United States and the Soviet Union, Afghanistan continued to engage in trade and expand relations with both countries. Over the years, the United States had become more and more interested in the countries known as the "Northern Tier," which included the countries of Iran, Iraq, Pakistan, Turkey, and most notably Afghanistan. The United States diligently worked to foster an allegiance agreement with the government, but Prime Minister Daoud continued the traditional stance of nonpartisan politics. Despite the continuous encouragement from the United States, Afghanistan refused to join the Baghdad Pact with the countries of Iraq, Turkey, and Iran as mandated by the United States and Great Britain. The agreement was part of the superpowers' anticommunist regime against the USSR, and it is largely speculated Afghanistan's non-concurrence was due to a lack of guaranteed protection for Afghanistan in the case of a retaliatory Soviet attack with no political infringement from these superpowers. As a result, the United States would not provide Afghanistan with any military assistance.[8] The pact later became known as the Central Treaty Organization (CENTO), which was the term used after Iraq left the agreement in 1959. Once again, Afghanistan turned to its allies the Soviets to provide support, and Daoud received over $25 million in military aid and supplies. Likewise the Soviets also began to build several military airfields in Mazari Sharif, Bagram, and Shindand.

STRAIN WITH PAKISTAN: THE PASHTUNISTAN ISSUE

The Pashtunistan issue was the second topic of greatest concern to Daoud and would continue to consume his efforts to the point that no other issues mattered more than the Pashtunistan resolution.

Previously throughout the early 1950s, Daoud offered payments to the Pashtun tribesman in a dual effort to destabilize the government and policy of Pakistan while also increasing the distribution of propaganda. The situation heightened in 1955 when Pakistan abolished the four governments of West Pakistan and formed one conjoined unit, despite the Afghan government protest of this formation. The Pakistan-Afghan border would close in the spring of 1955, which severed the ability for trade transit and increased the Afghan need for relations with the Soviet Union. The Pashtunistan issue would continue for several more years and relations improved only slightly between the two countries. In 1960, Prime Minister Daoud ordered Afghan forces into Pakistan in an endeavor to finally subdue the Pashtunistan issue once and for all, and throughout the effort propaganda was relentlessly played on the radio. On September 6, 1961, relations between the two countries were completely severed when Pakistan immediately ceased all transit for the country, both for imports and for exports. One such shipment was a crop export of grapes and pomegranates that were bound for India, which the Soviets graciously offered to purchase and transport via aircraft from Afghanistan. The United States made attempts to arbitrate the dispute between Pakistan and Afghanistan, but Pakistan continued to hold supplies, some of which were meant for development projects in Afghanistan. Consequentially, the economy continued to decline due to the lack of income from trade revenue and foreign exchange.

As a further impediment to any form of resolution, Pakistan closed the border to the seasonal travelers who frequently crossed the border to spend winters in Pakistan and summers in Afghanistan. By 1963, it was abundantly clear that neither country would acquiesce on the situation. Both Prime Minister Daoud of Afghanistan and Ayub Khan of Pakistan were resolute in their own stance, and the only option for progress was to remove one of these men from power. While both men were strong in their own positions, for each had attained the duality of both praise and criticism during their tenure in office, the weakened economy in Afghanistan would lead to the downfall for Daoud as prime minister. Consequentially, King Zahir Shah asked for Daoud's resignation based on the depleting economy that was the result of both his incessant perseverance and his lack of resolution to the Pashtunistan issue. Alas with no other option after the dispute in Pakistan resulted in an economic crisis for the country, Daoud was asked to resign as prime minister in 1963.[9] Upon Daoud's resignation, Muhammad Yousuf became prime minister, a non-Pashtun whose limited experience previously included being the minister of mines and industries.

THE LAST DECADE OF MONARCHY IN AFGHANISTAN (1963–1973)

During this final decade of rule for Zahir, he was free from the influence of his uncles and relatives, and the king began to take a more active stance in the affairs of his country. Independent from other control and free to experiment with democracy, in 1964 King Zahir championed the need for a liberal constitution that provided a bicameral legislature. As part of this legislature, the representatives would be appointed in a ratio of one-third each by the king, the provincial assemblies, and the Afghan people.

The replacement of Daoud Khan resulted in swift change in the diplomatic and trade relations with Pakistan. Issues that were once pushed to the side by Daoud were finally able to be resolved. Within weeks of Daoud's resignation, the king designated a new council to outline and plan a new charter for Afghanistan. As such, the greatest achievement of this era would be the resolution of the 1964 Constitution. Earlier in the year, King Zahir ordered a *loya jirga* that required members of the National Assembly, the Senate, the Supreme Court, and the constitutional board to convene with the intention of electing new representatives. At the *loya jirga*, new representatives were elected or appointed by the king, and in September 1964 the constitutional assembly included 452 representatives from the country, six of whom were women. All 452 members signed the new constitution on September 20, and King Zahir officially ratified the document 10 days later.

The signing of the Constitution of 1964 marked a historically significant moment in the formation of the nation. Primarily, the multiple steps required in the involvement, planning, and drafting of the constitution ultimately represented changes that had been made in traditional political thinking. The championing of individual rights and freedoms by provincial delegates rather than tribal chiefs demonstrated the movement of Afghanistan from a tribal society into a contemporary era, a dream that was begun under Ahmad Shah Durrani in 1747 for tribal autonomy. Further, the iconic backbone and belief in the Muslim faith had existed in Afghanistan since 652 c.e. and was affirmed by establishing Islam as the national religion in Afghanistan. Similarly, the constitution also identified that the word *Afghan* would henceforth denote all citizens in the nation, and would no longer only represent those of Pashtun origin. By implementing such measures as the freedoms of press, assembly, and association, the constitution supported new developments in the country and furthered the women's movement by increasing women's involvement in political parties and the fight for equal rights. Additionally, the constitution established an independent judiciary system that was unconstrained by the previous legal system, which was based on religion and obviously favored by religious leaders. Recognizing the importance and need to enact an unbiased and fair system, the constitution implemented the supremacy of secular law. Furthermore, the government of Afghanistan would now be a constitutional monarchy (rather than an absolute monarchy) with a bicameral legislature and elected parliament, which allowed the majority of power to remain with the king.[10] The Wolasi Jirga (House of Representatives) would be known as the lower house of parliament and be composed of 216 members from both ends of the political spectrum. Additionally, King Zahir nominated a new prime minister, Mohammad Hashim Maiwandwal.

The new freedom reforms in the constitution resulted in the development of extremist political parties, such as the communist-based People's Democratic Party of Afghanistan (PDPA) on January 1, 1965. The PDPA was well known to have strong ties to the Soviet Union, and was established with the intention of gaining more seats in the parliament. The leftist party successfully achieved this goal, and four PDPA members were elected. One such elected official, Nur Muhammad Taraki, established the first major radical newspaper in Afghanistan known as *the Khalq*, which endured for only one month before being shut down by the government for the extremist literature it supported.

In 1967, the PDPA split into several different sects, the most prominent two being the Khalq (Masses) faction led by Taraki, and the Parcham (Banner) faction led by Babrak Karmal. The schism would serve to reflect the divisions of ethnicity, class, and ideology within Afghan society. As such, the Khalq supporters were predominately Pashtuns from rural Afghanistan that embodied the Khalq belief in supporting the working class. The Parcham sect was composed of the more urban citizens in Afghanistan who supported the socioeconomic democratic front. While both divisions were regarded as extreme, the king tolerated the Parcham and was more lenient of their publications than that of the Khalq. Karmal was allowed to publish his newspaper *Parcham* from March 1968 to July 1969, while King Zahir officially banned the Khalq newspaper, leading to accusations of Parcham having a hidden association with the king.[11] Part resentment and part suspiciousness over Daoud's tolerance of Parcham, the political party of Khalq propagated Parcham as the Royal Communist Party.

The 1969 elections resulted in the loss of many incumbent seats, including the seats held by all six women in parliament. Further, a great deal of non-Pashtun members were elected, and the new parliament now represented more landowners and businessmen than the previous administration in 1965. As the final upset, Prime Minister Maiwandwal lost his seat as a democratic socialist. As a result of the new election, the next four years left Afghan politics in instability and volatility, as the incongruent political representation in the parliament often resulted in an impasse on any form of progress. Until 1973, the public outcry of their dissatisfaction of the government prompted a clear division with political representation on both ends of the political spectrum. Toward the end of his reign, King Zahir became increasingly criticized for his lack of support he gave to his prime ministers. As this internal dissatisfaction coupled with the political polarization in Afghanistan continued to heighten, a seemingly silent and long-forgotten usurper lay in waiting in the shadows. This chaotic ambiance gave Daoud the opportunity he had been desperately waiting for since he was forced to resign 10 years earlier.

MOHAMMED SARDAR DAOUD KHAN AND THE CREATION OF THE REPUBLIC OF AFGHANISTAN (1973–1978)

In the early 1970s Afghanistan was on the brink of crisis. A severe drought devastated the crops and the harvest, and as a result Afghanistan's economy spiraled downward. The government faced charges of corruption, and while the king was out of the country for medical treatment, Daoud seized control in a nearly bloodless coup. The stability King Zahir had strived for under his "New Democracy" was not achieved. On July 17, 1973, it was under these circumstances that Prime Minister Daoud seized power via a military coup and forced the Shah to exile in Italy. The rebellious coup had been planned for more than a year and was aided by junior officers in the Soviet Union. Further support came from those whom Daoud ironically referred to as his "friends," including factions of Barbrak Karmal's Parcham party. With Daoud's swift action, he abolished the long-standing monarchy in Afghanistan, a precedent that began with Ahmad Shah Durrani in 1747.

Daoud's reemergence in Afghanistan was generally favored, and along with his abolishment of the monarchial rule in Afghanistan, he simultaneously eradicated the 1964 Constitution. He additionally stated Afghanistan would now be a republic government with himself as the first president of the country. He reinstated his previous regime that focused on the Pashtunistan issue, which was still an important topic to conservative Pashtun officers. Previously as prime minister, Daoud had received modern weapons from the Soviet Union, and his experience as a former military officer left him in good standing with the military. In 1976, Daoud established his own political party that would be the nucleus of all political interests, known as the National Revolutionist Party. The following year in a *loya jirga*, the new constitution established by Daoud implemented a presidential system of government.

Over his five-year tenure as president of Afghanistan, Daoud's relationship with the Soviet Union and internal Afghan communists deteriorated gradually, beginning in 1974. This was partly due to Daoud's shift to the right side of the political gamut and his alignment of Afghanistan's stance away from communism. However, Afghanistan continued to side with the Soviets throughout representational voting in the United Nations. Without question, the Soviets had been the chief provider of assistance and support for Afghanistan, and as such the country was highly influential in the economic, political, and social interaction with other countries. Daoud still pushed his state-centered economic strategy in his seven-year plan from 1976 to 1983, which in order to succeed would require a great deal of foreign aid. Since Daoud had shifted away from accepting economic and military support from the Soviets, Afghanistan sought to build relationships with other countries. Daoud recognized any unity with other countries must have the power and strength, both economically and politically, to assist Afghanistan if it was going to completely break ties with the Soviet Union. As such, Daoud turned to several nations for assistance, including the oil-rich countries such as Saudi Arabia, Iraq, and Kuwait to provide financial backing; to India for increased military support; and to Iran for assistance in economic development. However, relations with Pakistan improved by 1977 with the aid of the United States, and in March 1978 President Daoud visited Islamabad. The intention of the meeting was to negotiate an agreement with President Muhammad Zia-ul-Haq of Pakistan for a prisoner exchange and also to agree to the expulsion of Pashtun and Baloch militants from Afghanistan. The meeting proved successful, and relations with Pakistan gradually began to amend. By the spring of 1978, Daoud had achieved little of what he had originally planned five years before.

While there was some economic progress, the standard of living in Afghanistan had not improved, and as a result Daoud was alienated from many political groups. Furthermore, the conservative Pashtunistan supporters still resented Daoud's agreement with Pakistan on the Pashtun militants in Afghanistan.

THE APRIL 1978 COUP

Daoud attempts to renovate and improve the government by implementing economic and social reforms would not be successful, and the new constitution in February of 1977 did nothing to stabilize the political volatility of the country. This mayhem resulted in action from the extremist political party of the formerly banned leftist party of the PDPA. With the political, economic, and social structure in Afghanistan turned upside down, the PDPA successfully implemented and carried out a bloody coup on April 27, 1978.

Daoud feared the rebelliousness pulsing through the communist veins of the country. After the assassination of Mir Akbar Khayber, a member of the PDPA, the funeral served as a gathering point for the Afghan communists, in which an estimated 30,000 persons gathered to hear speeches by the communist leaders Nur Muhammad Taraki and Babrak Karmal. Appalled at this collective demonstration and shocked by the striking unity of the crowd, Daoud ordered the arrest of these PDPA leaders, but he did not direct this soon enough due to his misconception that Parcham was the more immediate threat. For over a week the PDPA leaders escaped punishment until Taraki was arrested and Hafizullah Amin was placed under house arrest, which allowed him to detail the plans for the coup from home while using his family as messengers. The organization and execution of the coup was so well planned that many believe Soviet officials, the KGB, or the CIA had assisted the Khalq.[12] On 27 April 1978, the coup began with troops and tanks moving into Kabul International Airport. Insurgent units formed around the capital, and over the course of the day, the number of rebel units steadily increased throughout the city. Within 24 hours, President Daoud and his family were killed in the Presidential Palace. These plans were successfully executed while the civilian leaders of the PDPA were all imprisoned, and the military coup ended the republican rule begun by Ahmad Shah Durrani over 230 years earlier. Now under control of the communist regime, Nur Muhammad Taraki became president of the Revolutionary Council and prime minister of the USSR-supported Democratic Republic of Afghanistan.

NOTES

1. Nawid, *Religious Response to Social Change in Afghanistan 1919–29*, 108–129.

2. Oliver Roy, *Islam and Resistance in Afghanistan.* 2nd ed. (Cambridge: Cambridge University Press, 1990), 57–68.

3. Peter Tomsen, *The Wars in Afghanistan: Messianic Terrorism, Tribal Conflicts, and the Failures of Great Powers* (New York: Public Affairs, 2011), 69.

4. Nawid, *Religious Response to Social Change in Afghanistan 1919–29*, 108–129.

5. Tanner, *Afghanistan*, 155–188.

6. Stewart, *The Khyber Rifles*.

7. Lewis, *The Middle East*, 111–132.

8. Ewans, *Afghanistan*, 118–136.

9. Ibid., 159–164.

10. Farahi, *Afghanistan during Democracy and Republic*.

11. Roy, *Islam and Resistance in Afghanistan*, 57–68.

12. Ewans, *Afghanistan*, 159–164.

9

The Soviet Invasion and Occupation of Afghanistan (1979–1989)

Prior to the Soviet occupation of Afghanistan, the United States had limited foreign policy involvement with Afghanistan. The origins of American foreign policy in Afghanistan began in the 1950s when the United States was at the precipice of what would become the decades-long Cold War with Russia. As time progressed and the United States was resolute in winning the Cold War, a great strategy towards the end of the Cold War involved foreign policy in Afghanistan. Once again serving as a barrier state, much like the country was under the Great Game, the United States initially viewed Afghanistan as a pawn in a game to prevent Soviet encroachment in territories overseas. When the Afghans signed economic and military agreements with Russia in 1953, relations between the United States and Afghanistan deteriorated mostly due to the U.S. refusal to provide military and economic assistance. Once the coalition occurred between Afghanistan and the Soviet Union, Afghanistan was of little interest to the United States until Russia's increased involvement beginning in 1978.

The U.S. foreign policy shifted from containment of the Soviet Union to influence in the region. No longer seeking to usurp the Soviet Union directly, the United States instead focused on strengthening relations with the Middle East, Afghanistan, and Central America.[1] Leading up to the Soviet occupation, President Carter and U.S. policy makers envisioned how the communist invasion of Afghanistan could become the Soviet Union's Vietnam War.[2] The culmination of the Cold War sentiment, the 1978 coup against Prime Minister Daoud, and the fall of the shah of Iran during the Iranian Revolution in 1979 forced a shift in American foreign policy. These global events caused America to pivot their stance on foreign policy in the region, and focused on Afghanistan as a priority.

The Soviet invasion officially began with the deployment of the 40th Army into Kabul airport on December 25, 1979, and would last until the Soviets began their troop withdrawal on May 15, 1988. Over the duration of nine years, the conflict resulted from the Soviet Union support of the Marxist-based People's Democratic Party of Afghanistan (PDPA) against the rebel forces of the mujahideen (mujahidin). Specifically, the term *mujahideen* refers to a group of Afghan insurgents who fought to overthrow the communist rule of Afghanistan, and were assisted by such countries as the United States, Great Britain, and China.[3] The mujahideen received additional support from other Muslim countries such as Pakistan, Saudi Arabia, Iran, Egypt, and Jordan, not only to champion Afghanistan's freedom from communist rule, but also as a primary effort to stop the Cold War aggression into the Persian Gulf. By the middle of the 1980s, the Afghan resistance movement had received a substantial amount of aid by these countries, and the Afghan fighters had been trained extensively by the United States and Pakistan as part of the Cold War struggle.[4] The United States secretly funded the mujahideen rebel forces during the Soviet war in Afghanistan under the covert program referred to as Operation Cyclone.[5] Led by the U.S. Central Intelligence Agency (CIA), the program provided assistance to the mujahideen not only with funds for weapons, but also with a partnership with neighboring Pakistan. Some authors view this covert funding and support as the U.S. baiting the Soviet Union to a military intervention in Afghanistan, with American money being covertly funneled into Pakistan via the Pakistani Inter-Services Intelligence (ISI).[6] The ISI, the largest and most powerful of the three intelligence services in Pakistan, was formed for intelligence gathering and training spies, in addition to supporting the Pakistan nuclear program and assuring the security of the top Pakistani army generals.[7] Operation Cyclone utilized the militant Islamic groups in neighboring

Pakistan to work with the Afghan resistance groups fighting against the PDPA and Soviet presence.[8] Billions of U.S. dollars and Stinger missiles were covertly provided to the Afghan mujahedeen and through these actions, coupled with the CIA operatives actively monitoring the conflict under Operation Cyclone, resulted in the Soviet Union's Vietnam in Afghanistan. [9] The Soviet occupation ended in defeat and the Soviets withdrew from Afghanistan.

THE BEGINNING OF THE SOVIET INVASION: KHALQ CONTROL (1978–1980)

The assassination of President Daoud on April 28, 1978, symbolized the overthrow of 200 years of democracy in Afghanistan. After the Saur Revolution, the country was thrust under the control of the veiled communist regime of the PDPA. *Saur* is the Dari term for the second month of the Persian calendar, referring to April when the coup occurred. The origins of the PDPA can be traced back to Marxist ideals and communist ideology, which tied hand-in-hand with the communist system of the Soviet Union at the time. The PDPA was founded in 1965 by Muhammad Taraki, Babrak Karmal, and Hafizullah Amin, and based its roots on deeply implemented Marxist ideals which were flowing through the policies trying to be implemented in Afghanistan.

Nur Muhammad Taraki assumed the threefold role of president of the Revolutionary Council, prime minister, and general secretary of the USSR-supported Democratic Republic of Afghanistan (DPA). The PDPA government structure was divided among partisan lines, including the Khalq faction led by Muhammad Taraki and Hafizullah Amin, and also the Parcham leaders of Babrak Karmal and Mohammad Najibullah. Khalq was a more radical faction of the PDPA who advocated the immediate overthrow of the Afghan government with a communist-style regime. Parcham, meaning "banner" or "flag," advocated a gradual advancement toward socialism in Afghanistan. In 1992 the Parcham Party became the Watan Party of Afghanistan. President Abdul Rahim Hatif briefly ruled as president of Afghanistan in April 1992 as the leader of the Democratic Watan Party. The Khalq faction sanctioned a violent overthrow of the Afghan government, with an immediate establishment of a communist-based regime in Afghanistan. The Parcham faction, however, employed a more gradual stance and eventual evolution in Afghanistan toward socialism. In contrast, the goal of the Khalq party was to completely reform Afghanistan under a socialist agenda, if not willingly then by force. The internal struggle between the Khalq and the Parcham parties eventually led to the banishment of Babrak Kamal, which gave way to the Khalq party. The overthrow furthermore led to the arrest and execution of many Parcahmi supporters, which included members of the Afghan elite, religious associates, and community intelligentsia.[10]

When the PDPA began its rule of Afghanistan, many citizens initially were unaware of the existence of the Khalq party. If they were aware, it was certainly possible they were unsure of the true political allegiance behind the PDPA, as the PDPA initially said little about their ties to a communist regime. Shrouded in obscurity at first, the Khalq propaganda used words such as *democratic* and *nationalist* to obscure their true party alliance. Despite the PDPA attempts to mask any ties to communist rule, this allegiance was widely believed to be the case.[11] Still unsure of the preliminary party agenda and evolution to communism one way or another, the United States was initially apprehensive to provide any support to Afghanistan. President Jimmy Carter was an advocate of foreign policy as related to human rights, which created several challenges globally with regards to his foreign policy. However, these challenges were particularly difficult to address in Afghanistan, a country in which the United States to date had very little involvement. Carter was further restricted because while Afghanistan was not openly a communist country yet, the Foreign Assistance Act prohibited assistance to any foreign countries that were under communist control.[12]

In May 1978, the regime government in Afghanistan signed an agreement with Soviet forces to provide nearly 400 military advisors for the Afghan army, a decision that would eventually cripple the Afghan forces when the Soviets invaded 18 months later. If there was any doubt of the communist ties of the Khalq and the PDPA, the mask of the Khalq regime disintegrated at the unveiling of the new flag of Afghanistan in October 1978. Any lingering doubts were cast aside when the Khalq revealed the new communist-themed Afghan banner at a rally in Kabul. The Afghan flag would no longer primarily be green and white, but a flag covered in crimson red. The flag was practically almost a replica of other communist flags, and after the rally the situation became brilliantly clear that the future of Afghanistan had been declared communist under the Khalq control. Furthering communist alliances in December 1978, the Khalq signed an amicable partnership with the Soviet Union to permit the deployment of Soviet military assistance at the request of the Afghan government. These actions committed the country to the Soviet communist regime, and these policy implementation efforts were the genesis of the Soviet invasion.[13] Through the requested alliances and the agreements for Soviet support to modernize the economic infrastructure of Afghanistan, the PDPA regime had become increasingly reliant on Soviet assistance and depended on the Soviets for military support. The new Afghan government under the PDPA looked to the Soviets for economic assistance to build roads, harvest natural resources, and train the Afghan army.

The Khalq grew increasingly stronger with men like Taraki and Amin at the forefront, and the Khalq issued various economic and social decrees as part of their Marxist policies. Furthermore, the objective of the Khalq was to destroy the frontier power structures and educate the Afghan laborers to support the Khalq. These measures, however, failed to create a cohesive movement, as these plans did not take into account Afghan social structure, customs, or formation. As a result these reforms deeply offended the tribal and family structures in Afghanistan. As an example, the Khalq measures included the radical concept of instituting educational requirements for both men and women. Additional reforms included the establishment of marriage rules, which included "bridal choice" which banned forced marriages, implemented a minimum age, and ceased *mehr*, the requirement for a bridal dowry to be paid. These reforms also included land restructuring measures to spread the land distribution among the poor residents of Afghanistan. These methods both reduced the land holding requirements in Afghanistan and eliminated *usury*, the charging of significantly high sums of interest on Afghan loans.[14] Interestingly enough, the land reforms were instituted swiftly, without documentation or accuracy, as many were intimidated by the complicated contractual processes in the banking and legal systems. At the core of the situation, these initial reform measures undermined the Afghan system and social foundation. The difficulty increased with further additions to the education reforms and also the establishment of a national language for the Nuristani, Uzbek, Turkmen, and Baluchi ethnic clans. Traditional religious laws had been replaced by Marxist rules, and once these reforms joined with the liberation and education efforts for women, it was only a matter of time before these Khalq regimes were perceived as an attack against Islam.

The backlash was forthcoming against the monopolistic rule of the PDPA, and as a result, revolts emerged everywhere in Afghanistan. The rebellions against these reforms were often violent, and often increased into all-out tribal attacks. In October, the Nuristani tribe in the Kunar valley rebelled, and this initial rebellion inspired other ethnic revolts. Those who tried to oppose the Khalq communist regime were severely punished, and more often than not, these traitors were executed. The Khalq scoured the countryside for such infidels under a sweeping reign of terror, and these violators included not only Afghan professionals but also military officials, religious leaders, and former political leaders. Prison conditions were the most extreme at Pul-i-Charki, an infamous prison located on the outskirts of Kabul. Even though the prison was not yet completed, the Khalq used the unfinished prison to accommodate prisoners and offenders against the PDPA; most often until these detainees were executed for their actions.[15] Nearly six months after the Daoud coup in the fall of 1978, Amnesty International estimated there were as many as 4,000 prisoners held in Pul-i-Charki prison. The following year, estimates tripled to 12,000 prisoners who were detained without trial.[16] In the 18 months between the Daoud coup in April 1978 and the Soviet invasion in December 1979, as many as 27,000 prisoners were executed at Pul-i-Charki. Many prisoners were captured and imprisoned swiftly, with no contact to their family. These men seemingly vanished from existence overnight, leaving many families unsure of their whereabouts. By the time family members realized what happened, many of these prisoners had already been killed.[17]

By the beginning of 1979, it is clear Afghanistan was descending into an internal rift sparked by the Khalq party overtly under the Soviet Union communist influence. The United States had continued to watch as these series of events unfolded. However, in February 1979, the American involvement in the communist overthrow was escalated when the U.S. ambassador to Kabul, Adolph Dubs, was captured by four members of a leftist group and held hostage. Soviet counsel and advisors guided the Afghan leaders in the resolution of the conflict, but they refused to negotiate with Dubs captors and ultimately decided to storm the room without consulting with the United States. Unfortunately, the situation resulted in the death not only of Dubs's captors but also of Dubs himself. President Carter had to take a firm stance, and the lack of concurrence from the United States prompted an immediate withdrawal and denial of additional support to Afghanistan.[18] Many accounts place the blame for the incident scattered among several individuals, with implications the culprits behind the idea were the Parcham trying to enact revenge on the Khalq. In another allegation, the Soviets alleged the Dubs plot was the result of the CIA to further intensify the situation and discredit the Khalq regime.[19] Nonetheless, with both sides pointing fingers and devising allegations, Hafizullah Amin had gained considerable control and replaced Taraki as prime minister. The situation in Afghanistan was intensifying at an alarming rate and without U.S.-sanctioned support, the Afghani civilians did not have a viable government structure to hear their outrage. With no other alternative to express frustration and anger over the circumstances, the Afghans stormed Herat in a rebellious force and ruthlessly slaughtered Soviet forces. After a month the rebellion was finally sedated, but not before the Afghans killed over 100 Soviets advisors and their families, and paraded the bodies through the streets of Herat by adorning crude spikes with severed Russian heads. Over the next several months the tribal revolts increased and spread like wildfire throughout Afghanistan. Yet despite these reports, the Khalq assembly continued to propagate that these reform measures were being accepted and put into action across Afghanistan with great success. These false claims were a vain attempt to hide the dissention that was boiling within Afghanistan. By the middle of 1979, estimates show over 85 percent of the provinces in Afghanistan had revolted against the Khalq regime.[20] Twenty-four of the 28 provinces in Afghanistan suffered outbreaks from tribal rebellions. Once the truth was finally exposed, Khalq blamed the foreign saboteurs for the unsuccessful land reform measures.

General secretary of the Communist Party of the Soviets, Leonid Breznev, met with Taraki to discuss the situation, and during this meeting the two agreed Amin had gained too much control and influence. The only solution was to remove Amin from power. Knowing the Afghans were on the cusp of fighting the war with the mujahideen, Breznez ordered the Soviet military into Afghanistan to help save the Democratic Republic of Afghanistan (DRA). Upon his return to Kabul, Taraki requested a meeting with Amin, but Amin would only attend on the condition he would be safe from Soviet harm. As such, Amin requested the Soviet ambassador Alexander Puzanov to guarantee his safety. Perhaps the agreement for protection was too hasty, for despite the agreed-upon request, Amin was now highly suspicious of Taraki. Amin deduced instead this was under the guise of a possible assassination attempt, and Amin surmised the guaranteed protection request of the Soviet ambassador was mere lip service. Amin figured if Taraki would agree to such a stipulation so quickly, then something certainly was going to occur. Upon his arrival at the Presidential Palace, a shoot-out occurred and Amin escaped briefly but only to return shortly with his supporters to take Taraki hostage. However, records are not clear whether Taraki was killed during the gunfight, or taken as hostage and later killed. By mid-September 1979, Amin announced his control of the government and on September 16, Amin announced he had to replace Taraki due to medical reasons. In early October, Amin declared Taraki had died of an unknown illness.[21]

The communist regime in Afghanistan became further enmeshed because the Soviets were in complete opposition with Amin. The relations became increasingly distant as Amin believed the Soviets had attempted to kill him. The Soviets were looking for a way to eliminate Amin from power, while Amin demanded the Soviets withdraw ambassador Puzanov from Afghanistan. Amin was aware of several attempts by the Soviets to remove him from power, and as such he worked to make amends for situations in Afghanistan and to gather allies to protect him. Throughout October and November, Amin tried desperately to open communications with Pakistan, and he looked internally into his own country to make reparations by his attempts to implement a new constitution and also his offer of amnesty to refugees to return to the country. While hastily trying to implement these rebuilding efforts, Amin mistakenly drafted a list of some 12,000 prisoners imprisoned and killed since the Saur Revolution. His intentions were most likely an effort to console those grieving the loss of their loved ones and validating what remained unconfirmed for years. Instead, the list created a backlash because the list offered proof to the recent atrocities committed by the Afghan government. By December, the situation in Afghanistan was nearly in full conflict with an internal revolt against Amin, and the Soviets on the apex of invasion.

THE SOVIET INVASION AND OCCUPATION (1979–1988)

The irony of the commencement of the nine-year Soviet occupation is the Afghan government specifically requested the Soviet forces to arrive in Afghanistan as aid in support against rebel forces. Under the backlash of the PDPA, many rebel groups had formed to eradicate the Soviet dependency in Afghanistan, and these groups were gaining momentum. As such, Babrak Kamal requested several times for Soviet assistance throughout 1979 to provide security against the insurgency and the mujahideen rebellions. Some accounts allege Hafizullah Amin also had requested Soviet troops and support, although evidence sustains that Amin stated on several occasions in 1979 that he had no need for Soviet assistance.[22] At the same time, the Russian government in Moscow desperately wanted to remove Hafizullah Amin and replace him with Babrak Karmal, and the Soviets realized this could not be achieved only by an aerial assault. Ground troops would also be necessary in order for the coup to be successful. By early December, the Soviets placed forces around Kabul airport and at the air base at Bagram. The Soviets entered Afghanistan with multiple rifle and airborne divisions and marched into the frontier provinces. By the middle of December, American intelligence sources clearly were aware of the advancing Soviet troops into Afghanistan. By late evening on December 24, Soviet planes began to continuously land into Kabul airport, and by the 27th the Soviets had successfully infiltrated multiple battalions with enough of a military congregation to attack the city. Prior to the invasion, the Soviets had cleverly implemented several tactics against the Afghan troops that unbeknownst to them left them completely incompetent against the invading forces. Previously, Soviet advisors successfully disengaged Afghan troops by using such tactics as removing batteries from tanks citing, "maintenance reasons." The Soviets removed live rounds from weapons and replaced them with blanks, stating the bullets needed to be replaced for upcoming training exercises. The Soviets identified key Afghan military leaders and imprisoned senior officers for miscellaneous petty offenses. In addition, the Soviets had previously dismantled the Afghan communication systems. By covertly instituting these tactics, the Soviets were free to infiltrate Afghanistan with Soviet tanks, troops, and weapons against a force of improperly equipped Afghan soldiers with virtually no armored vehicles, no firepower, and no military leaders. Against a practically paralyzed Afghan army, sometime during the night of the 27th, some of the Soviet troops took over the city and stormed the Presidential Palace, killing Amin and his family. However, within several days Karmal had announced via broadcast over Radio Kabul that Amin had been overthrown and he was now the president of Afghanistan. By January 1, 1980, more than 50,000 Soviet troops and over 1,000 military vehicles had been deployed into Afghanistan, and over the next month the Soviet troops increased to 85,000. Simultaneously, the Afghan army suffered an increasing number of Afghan troops that were deserting due to low morale from their inability to subdue the revolting tribes, with numbers depleting from 90,000 troops to an unreliable force of only 30,000 by 1980.[23]

The world reacted strongly to the invasion, with the United States under President Carter declaring the Soviet undertaking was a threat to world peace. Further, the onslaught into Afghanistan was regarded as the most dangerous menace on the globe since World War II. The Soviets countered by devising allegations and reasons to distract from the root of the cause, even to the point that the Soviets attempted to explain the invasion by arguing Hafizullah Amin had been a spy for America. When pressed further, the Soviets were unable to provide any factual evidence to support these allegations. The United States instated severe measures, which included the restriction of a shipment of 17 tons of grain into the Soviet Union, the immediate cessation of Russian fishing in American waters, the broadcast to boycott the 1980 Moscow Olympics, and furthermore announced the delay of the second sanction of the Strategic Arms Limitation Talks (SALT). The SALT deliberations discussed the issue of armament control, and were composed of two separate panels of bilateral discussions during the Cold War between the United States and the Soviet Union. The discussions consisted of two parts, referred to as SALT I from 1969 to 1972, and SALT II between 1972 and 1979. The U.S. Senate delayed the SALT II Treaty. The treaty became known as the Strategic Arms Reduction Treaty (START), and was signed between Leonid Breznhnev and President Carter in Vienna, Austria on June 18, 1979. However, due to the Soviet invasion of Afghanistan, the U.S. Senate never ratified the treaty, though the terms of the treaty were still honored by both the United States and the Soviet Union. Additionally, the U.S. government emblazoned the Carter Doctrine in an attempt to prevent any Russian aggression and hegemony into the Persian Gulf. President Carter announced the doctrine in his State of the Union address on January 23, 1980, stipulating that the United States had vital interests in the Persian Gulf and any invasion would result in the use of immediate force, if necessary, to protect national interests.[24] In the meantime, the Soviet forces into Afghanistan had grown substantially.

Furthermore, the refugee situation had grown progressively worse. Previously by the end of 1979, Pakistan had accepted nearly 80,000 refugees in the country, and already by the time of the Soviet invasion, resistance groups had formed and were preparing small skirmishes into Afghanistan. The following year, there were as many as 750,000 refugees into Pakistan and over 100,000 in Iran. By 1981, the number of refugees had doubled in Pakistan. By 1984, the numbers were shocking: a total of nearly four million in Pakistan and almost two million in Iran. The numbers would continue to grow until over six million Afghan citizens had fled the country, with estimates of another nearly two million seeking sanctuary inside the country as internal refugees. The United States provided financial support to Pakistan for the Afghan refugees, and also for the multitude of problems that crossed the border with them. Along with the arrival of the Afghan refugees came a sharp increase in drugs and weapons, and the large influx of so many refugees had a profound effect on Pakistan, economically, socially, and politically.

As part of the backlash to the communist regime and Soviet occupation, many rebel groups formed in an attempt to sabotage and destroy
some aspects of the Soviet regime. As such, the mujahideen resistance in Afghanistan was formed, and was comprised of Islamic warrior forces that fought against the Soviet invasion. The United States
secretly provided arms to the mujahideen forces, and the CIA provided funding for these efforts under Operation Cyclone.[25] Throughout the nine-year Soviet occupation, these Afghan rebels and religious
zealots were significantly financed, armed, and trained by the CIA
beginning with the presidency of Jimmy Carter and continuing under
Ronald Reagan, who famously praised the multitude of mujahideen
rebels as "freedom fighters" resisting the Soviet expansion in Afghanistan. Several other countries contributed support to the mujahideen
against the Soviet army, including Saudi Arabia, China, Iran, and also
Pakistan under the Inter-Services Intelligence (ISI).[26] While the CIA
may have provided the funding for the weapons against the Soviets,
the ISI determined how to distribute these weapons among the mujahideen parties, and as such the ISI gave more weapons to the mujahideen forces they favored.[27] Moreover, the ISI distributed weapons to
the mujahideen commanders they could easily control and influence.
After the United Nations National Assembly, the council overwhelmingly voted to call for an end to the recent armed invasion in Afghanistan by immediately withdrawing Soviet troops. However, Leonid
Breznhnev argued the deployment of troops was not an invasion but
rather was in accordance with Article 51 of the United Nations Charter, arguing it was the right of the Afghan government and not of the
United Nations to determine the condition of the Soviet troops.[28]

As a result, the United States began providing covert assistance to
the Afghan resistance fighters via Pakistan as early as January 1980.
Some scholars allege the American government supplied Pakistan
with an emergency shipment of Stinger anti-aircraft missiles for border protection against Soviet aerial assault and bombardment.[29] The
Stinger is a short-range man-held missile known for its portability
as an infra-red surface-to-air homing device. The United States supplied these missiles to provide Pakistan with the ability to stop aerial
skirmishes along the border with the Soviets and to prevent further
bombing raids by the Soviets. During this assistance, a wealthy Saudi
businessman named Osama bin Laden was a central organizer and
financial supporter of the mujahideen, and provided the rebel forces
with money, weapons, training, and additional fighters from around
the globe. Osama bin Laden's office, known as the Maktab al-Khadamat
(MAK), provided these vital services and support for Afghanistan

due to the fundamental Islamic penchant in Saudi Arabia. Osama bin Laden played a limited role in the Soviet resistance, and in 1988 he separated from the MAK to form al-Qaeda with other militant members with the intention of spearheading the anti-Soviet resistance into a global Islamic advancement.

A long-serving Afghani named Ahmad Shah Masood evolved as the primary champion for the mujahideen. Under the fight waged by Masood, the mujahideen forces were heavily armed, trained, and predominately supported by United States and Pakistan.[30] Masood was a legendary military commander in Afghanistan, who not only lived to fight the Soviets but also to fight against the Taliban. The leaders of the mujahideen devoted a great deal of training and operational efforts to sabotage warfare. These efforts included the deliberate damage to power lines, pipelines, and even included the bombing of government office buildings. The mujahideen groups focused on destroying the bridges and major roadways that the Soviets used, and further attacked police stations and Soviet artillery posts. During the middle of the 1980s, the mujahideen forces increased their operational activities against the Soviets, and estimates over a two-year span from 1985 to 1987 reveal over 1,800 episodes of mujahideen-initiated terrorist acts. The mujahideen also relied heavily on mine warfare, and with all of these efforts to force the Soviets out of their country, the mujahideen often enlisted the aid of children and local villagers to assist in the attack of Soviet military installations and air bases. As a result, the Soviets often mercilessly attacked all Afghan residents, blurring the line between the innocent Afghan citizens and the mujahideen rebels by performing blanket attacks on everyone.

While war may be considered a brutal necessity to life, the tactics the Soviets used throughout the invasion were often deemed as cruel to the point of inhumane. One such measure was the use of "butterfly traps," which were tiny bomb-like devices that were decorated and painted brightly to look like small toys. The Soviets designed the bombs with the intention to lure little children into picking up these colorfully decorated devices. These butterfly traps were not meant to kill, but rather to injure and maim so that the individual would require a great deal of care and attention. The rationale behind such contraptions was due to the amount of required medical care, funding, and time needed to assist an injured individual, rather than the shorter amount of time needed to bury a dead body. The Soviets intentionally used these devices to harm children since they struggled to defeat their fierce Afghan opponents, believing the most powerful fighter will abandon the call to defend Islam when their own child is injured.[31] For many foreign countries around the world, it was despicable that these traps were designed like toys to lure and maim innocent children. For the Soviets, however, the children were not innocent victims but a threat, for even young boys were armed with weapons and trained in combat techniques to support the mujahideen rebels. Because of this, the Soviets captured more than 40,000 Afghan youths and relocated them to the USSR for the purpose of Soviet upbringing and integration into the "Soviet way of life."[32] The Soviets perhaps intended to return these youths into Afghanistan one day after they had been conditioned to the Soviet rule, in order to assist the Soviets to control and subdue their native Afghan people. Not only was it increasingly difficult for the Afghans to witness the capture of such young Afghan children, but the lacking medical facilities in Afghanistan contributed to the difficulty of helping those wounded by such heinous butterfly mine contraptions. Those scarce medical facilities that did exist were in deplorable conditions. Even while trying to help the men and children who were wounded in battle, death was common from such minor ailments as heatstroke, hepatitis, and dysentery. Furthermore, the Soviets would invade towns and villages to annihilate mujahideen forces that may be residing in or near the town. Rather than guard the village against these freedom fighters, the Soviets would destroy the villages and kill all of the inhabitants. If the mujahideen fighters escaped death from the Soviets' raids in the villages, the Soviets additionally set up buried mines so if the mujahideen did return, they would be killed or injured by the buried bombs waiting for them.

AFGHANISTAN AS THE SOVIET UNION'S VIETNAM—1985

In May 1985, the seven main mujahideen rebel parties united and formed the Seven Party Mujahideen Alliance, also referred to as the Peshawar Seven. Eventually the party became known as the Islamic Unity of Afghan Mujahideen, which sought to act as a diplomatic representation to the world. In the United Nations, the party sought representation as the Organization of Islamic Conference. The members of the Mujahideen Alliance were composed of two sects as either the political Islamics or the traditionalists.[33] These political parties were not respected by some Afghan citizens, arguing the war for Afghan independence should be fought on the battlefield and not as an armchair warrior in a conference room. The political Islamics were divided into four fundamentalist groups: the Islamic Party led by Yunus Khalis, the Islamic Party led by Gulbuddin Hekmatyar, the Islamic Society led by Burhanuddin Rabbani, and the Islamic Union for the Liberation of Afghanistan led by Rasul Sayyaf. The Mujahideen Alliance was active around Kabul, previously working to coordinate their anti-Soviet operations by administering rocket attacks against the government. Postwar estimates reveal that as many as 800 rockets were launched per day on communist government targets.

Throughout the nine years of occupation, the Soviets tried to hide their casualty and wounded numbers so the Afghanistan forces would not know the severity and impact of these attacks on the communist army. Early in the conflict, the Soviet forces faced extremely problematical challenges in the mountainous terrain of Afghanistan. The Soviet army was unfamiliar with this type of mountainous combat, and as such the Russian armored cars and tanks operated with extreme difficulty and were nearly impossible to maneuver. For the most part, the Russian army was extremely ineffective and highly susceptible to attack in the mountains. Additionally, the Soviets forced those who were injured to be secretly moved to undercover facilities in order to receive care covertly.

After Mikhail Gorbachev assumed the leadership of the Soviet Union early in 1985, the new leader looked for a way to withdraw gracefully from Afghanistan. With the increasing toll in causalities, the severe loss of economic resources, and little Soviet support for the war, making this exit a graceful endeavor was nearly impossible for Gorbachev. The Soviet Union looked to blame Babrak Karmal for his failure in instituting a communist regime in Afghanistan. The Soviets further tried to shift the blame for their failure on Karmal's puppet regime, citing his ineffective rule and leadership of a weakened Afghan government that had been diluted under the PDPA.

In May 1986 Mohammad Najibullah replaced Barak Karmal as secretary general of the PDPA. Najibullah previously served as the head of Khad, the Afghan secret police, and he was also a communist supporter of the Soviets. Once Karmal was relieved of all his government and party posts, the tension among the Banner and People's parties in Afghanistan continued. In May 1986, Babrak was forced to resign as secretary general of the PDPA, finally succumbing to the political pressures of the Soviet Union. His tenure as president would shortly end as well, given that in November 1986, the former chief of the Afghan secret police (known as KHAD) was elected as the fourth and last president of the communist-based DRA. Under the control of his communist advisors from the Soviet Union, President Mohammad Najibullah implemented a policy of "national reconciliation" between the Soviet forces and the rebelling Afghan people.

The Soviet Invasion officially began with the deployment of the 40th Army into Kabul airport on December 25, 1979, and would last until the Soviets began troop withdrawal on May 15, 1988. Pictured is a BMD-1 airborne combat vehicle with Soviet soldiers on maneuvers in Kabul, Afghanistan, in March 1986. (U.S. Department of Defense)

Despite the increasing political unrest with the Soviet forces occupying Afghanistan, a changing of the guard in Afghanistan helped pave the way for better relations. In November 1987 a new constitution changed the name of the country back to the Republic of Afghanistan. Najibullah was elected to the newly strengthened post as president. In his new role, he established a nationalist party and by doing so, this allowed other political parties to participate in the Afghan government. Najibullah's time as president is regarded as one of peace despite the long-standing Soviet forces in Afghanistan.[34]

RETREAT OF SOVIET FORCES (1988–1989)

For over 100 years, the Russian government had tried to break apart Afghanistan and coerce the country into a communist state. Near the end of the Soviet occupation in Afghanistan, the support for the conflict had dwindled along with the depletion of the Soviet forces. Soviet aircrafts had been destroyed on a regular basis, army causalities increased along with the billions of dollars for the cost of the war, and support from the Soviet people had ceased. Instead, they championed to abandon the conflict in Afghanistan. For these reasons, the futile Soviet invasion of Afghanistan is often referred to as the Soviet Union's Vietnam. Yet the Soviet government refused to withdraw forces from Afghanistan until 1988, with the final troops leaving on February 15, 1989. As the last of the Soviet forces left Afghanistan, over 620,000 had served in the country over the nine-year occupation, with the total number of troops peaking at just over 100,000 troops occupying Afghanistan at one time. Throughout the war, over 469,000 troops were wounded or fell ill, and the Soviet Union reported 14,453 troops had been killed in Afghanistan and estimated between 10,700 and 11,600 troops were left disabled or as invalids after the war.[35] Contrastingly, the mujahideen reported losses of up to 1.5 million lives, and tens of thousands were seriously wounded or crippled after the invasion.

NOTES

1. Abdul-Qayum Mohmand, *American Foreign Policy toward Afghanistan: 1919–2001* (Ann Arbor, MI: ProQuest Information and Learning, 2007), 81–84.

2. Mohmand, *American Foreign Policy toward Afghanistan,* 81–84.

3. Peter Bergen, *Holy War, Inc.: Inside the Secret World of Osama Bin Laden* (New York: Free Press, 2001), 44–46.

4. Ibid., 66–78.

5. Ibid.

6. Mohmand, *American Foreign Policy towards Afghanistan,* 71–79.

7. Norm Dixon, "How the CIA Created Osama Bin Laden," *Green Left Weekly,* September 19, 2001.

8. Bergen, *Holy War, Inc.,* 66–78.

9. Mohmand, *American Foreign Policy toward Afghanistan,* 71–79.

10. Tomsen, *The Wars in Afghanistan,* 93–94.

11. Ibid., 93–94.

12. Mohmand, *American Foreign Policy toward Afghanistan,* 75–80.

13. Keegan, "The Ordeal of Afghanistan," *The Atlantic Monthly,* November 1985, Volume 256, No. 5, pages 94–105.

14. Ewans, *Afghanistan,* 118–136.

15. Tomsen, *The Wars in Afghanistan,* 5–6.

16. Robert D. Kaplan, *Soldiers of God: With Islamic Warriors in Afghanistan and Pakistan* (New York: Vintage Departures Edition, 2001), 65, 115–116.

17. Tomsen, *The Wars in Afghanistan,* 71–90.

18. Mohmand, *American Foreign Policy toward Afghanistan,* 75–80.

19. Ewans, *Afghanistan*, 201–210.

20. Goodson, *Afghanistan's Endless War*, 6–10; Tanner, *Afghanistan*.

21. Keegan, "The Ordeal of Afghanistan," 94–105.

22. Ewans, *Afghanistan*, 142, 154.

23. Goodson, *Afghanistan's Endless War*, 10–12.

24. Tomsen, *The Wars in Afghanistan*, 71–78.

25. Bergen, *Holy War, Inc.*, 65–67.

26. Tomsen, *The Wars in Afghanistan*, 71–78; Bergen, *Holy War, Inc.*, 65–67.

27. Kaplan, *Soldiers of God*, 85, 171.

28. Steve Coll, *Ghost Wars: The Secret History of the CIA, Afghanistan, and Bin Laden, from the Soviet Invasion to September 10, 2001* (New York: Penguin Press, 2004), 38–48.

29. Keegan, "The Ordeal of Afghanistan," 94–105.

30. Bergen, *Holy War, Inc.*, 74.

31. Kaplan, *Soldiers of God*, 4–5, 22.

32. Keegan, "The Ordeal of Afghanistan," 94–105.

33. Kaplan, *Soldiers of God*, 167–168, 233–234.

34. Fahiba Nawa, *Opium Nation: Child Brides, Drug Lords, and One Woman's Journey through Afghanistan* (New York: Harper Perennial, 2011), 140–152.

35. Mohmand, *American Foreign Policy toward Afghanistan*, 81–84.

10

Afghan Fundamentalism and the Taliban Regime (1989–2001)

The withdrawal of the Soviet army was regarded as a victory, not only for Afghanistan but also for the United States, which had championed the removal of Russia throughout three presidencies, from Carter to the early presidency of George H. W. Bush. As ignited under the Carter administration, American foreign policy in Afghanistan in the late 1970s played a significant role in ending the Cold War with the Soviets. The Regan administration continued the covert funding of the mujahideen through the Pakistani government and the ISI, which funneled cash and sophisticated weapons to the Afghan freedom fighters.[1] This not only championed American interests but also safeguarded Pakistani interest in Afghanistan. In his February 1985 State of the Union address, President Reagan openly stated his support of the mujahideen and his commitment to the Afghan fighters in order to "defy Soviet-supported aggression and secure rights, which have been ours from birth."[2] Some authors allege the U.S. support of the mujahideen was a method to lure the Soviets into further military entrenchment in Afghanistan, which the United States ultimately hoped this would be a "non-healing wound" to the Soviet Union as Vietnam had been for the United States.[3] The ploy succeeded—the Afghan mujahideen had overthrown the communists, the Cold War ended, and the Soviets left Afghanistan. But what of the Afghan people? The United States, and the world for that matter, was glad to see the mujahideen forces had successfully overthrown the Soviets, thus eliminating the Cold War threat for the control of oil in the Persian Gulf. However, with this victory came challenges and consequences. After the defeat and removal of the Soviet forces, the United States did little to help Afghanistan in the aftermath of the war, and virtually abandoned the mujahedeen forces with no sturdy government in place to restore the country. The U.S. objective was to remove control of the Soviets, not to replace or institute a new government. After establishing control of the oil-rich Persian Gulf, the United States left matters to be handled by Pakistan or Saudi Arabia.[4] The country was in need of serious rehabilitation efforts and large economic investments in order to rebuild this war-torn land. Remnants of the Soviet occupation were abundant, from the crumbled city ruins to the millions of buried landmines still scattered about the countryside, pastures, and farmland. With the Russian forces now vacant from Afghanistan, a country without government stability or control, the mujahedeen rebels effortlessly sought out and achieved their own fiefdoms of power in Afghanistan.

AFGHANISTAN ENTERS CIVIL WAR (1989–1992)

Prior to beginning the removal of the Soviet Red Army in 1989, the foreign ministers of Afghanistan and Pakistan held discussions at the United Nations in Geneva. These discussions, and subsequent agreement, led to the Geneva Accords, which was a four-part settlement on the affairs of Afghanistan. The items of major discord included the timetable for the withdrawal of Soviet troops and the cessation of weapons and supplies to the mujahedeen. In April 1988, the peace accords were finally signed. Soviet general secretary Mikhail Gorbachev, with fevered interest in change on the Afghan front, pledged to withdraw troops from Afghanistan. Honoring his word, he began withdrawing Soviet troops in May, and it would take nearly a year for the last Soviet soldier to leave Afghanistan. Despite the removal of the Soviets, however, the Afghan civil war began with warlords in different provinces all vying for control. The Soviets had helped unite Afghanistan's disparate people, but now Afghanistan faltered under the removal of the Soviet forces coupled with the lapse of any substantial funding to rebuild the economy as pledged by both the United States and Russia.

The retreat of the Soviet army marked the beginning of Afghan civil war from 1989 to 1992. The mujahedeen formed an interim government in Pakistan, but their disunity among the various mujahedeen parties resulted in their inability to successfully dislodge the government. Afghanistan entered into another Afghan civil war, and President Najibullah declared a state of emergency in Afghanistan immediately after the Soviet withdrawal.[5] Despite the Soviet's loss and removal from Afghanistan, the Soviets continued to aid the Afghan government led by Mohammad Najibullah. The fighting continued after the Soviet forces retreated during a harsh winter in Afghanistan, and the Afghan resistance still hungered to attack towns and cities to continue their war to defeat the Kabul government. Interestingly enough, the Soviet Union responded with a massive amount of military and economic supplies, in addition to providing food and fuel for the subsequent two winters. By 1990, the amount of Soviet support provided after the war was approximately $3 billion, which was after the Soviets had already dispensed some $45 billion into Afghanistan during the nine-year Soviet occupation.[6] The resistance was high against Najibullah's reconciliation efforts for the country, even amid predictions of an early collapse of the Najibulah government following the withdrawal of the Soviets. Despite never fully achieving popular support, Najibullah was able to defend the Afghan government from mujahideen attacks during the Afghan civil war from 1989 to 1992. Soviet support to the military continued in the years following the Soviet's withdrawal from Afghanistan and the collapse of the Soviet Union. However by 1992, the eventual decrease in financial support from the Soviets was a key factor in the breakdown of the Najibullah government.[7] The rebel movement began to gain strength, and slowly began to oust President Najibullah from power in order to allow the mujahedeen rebels to overtake Kabul. By early 1992, Najibullah's government was gravely weakened when Russia refused to sell oil products to Afghanistan, thus blocking the much-needed food and fuel during the winter. The government in Kabul was now in a stalemate, and furthermore the defection of General Abdul Rashid Dostam to support Ahmad Shah Massoud gravely weakened Najibullah's government. The following month, the deteriorated government at Kabul finally succumbed to the mujahideen forces led by Dostam and Massoud, and Najibullah and his communist-funded government were overthrown. On April 18, 1992, the two men took control of Kabul and declared the Islamic State of Afghanistan. Representing the National Liberation Front of Afghanistan, Sibghatullah Mojaddedi was named the interim leader of the Islamic State of Afghanistan after the fall of the communist regime in 1992. The Afghan rebel forces regarded Mojaddedi's meeting with then U.S. president George H. W. Bush as a critical victory, and the solution for peace was a complete removal of the Kabul government. However, Mojaddedi served for only two months after transferring his presidential power to Uzbek president Burhanuddin Rabbani for four years, which was based on a previous agreement of the mujahideen forces in Pakistan. Among the disorder and chaos for the control of Kabul, the jockeying for power among dueling mujahideen leaders fostered the rise of the Taliban regime in Afghanistan.

AFGHANISTAN UNDER THE MUJAHIDEEN (1992–1994)

Prior to the inevitable breakdown in Afghanistan in the early 1990s, the foundation was laid during the Soviet occupation for the decades to come in Afghanistan. During the 1980s, Afghanistan was essentially a breeding ground for terrorist training camps. This mind-set to fight against foreign occupation continued into the early 1990s, which is why the mujahedeen forces turned on each other in a fight for power and control after the evacuation of the Soviets. The previously supplied U.S. military weapons were no longer used against the Soviets, but instead among the mujahedeen forces, killing Afghan citizens along the way and thrusting the country deeper into a civil war. The capture of Kabul by the mujahideen forces in 1992 was a devastating blow to the Pashtuns, who had held control for nearly 300 years.[8] Despite their withdrawal, the Russians continued to support President Najibullah of Afghanistan until the mujahideen forces led by Rashid Dostam and Ahmad Shah Massoud captured Kabul. After the overthrow of Kabul and other prominent cities, none of the mujahideen groups could effectively implement a central command in the government. For the next two years until the rise of the Taliban, Afghanistan descended into lawlessness, disorder, and chaos.

The friction among the leaders of the multiple mujahedeen factions resulted in a period of warlordism in Afghanistan. These leaders fought for power among themselves to control the roadways between Pakistan and Afghanistan, capturing much-needed food and relief shipments and selling these supplies on the black market. In order to gain funding for their efforts, mujahedeen rebels set up roadblocks and checkpoints along the roadways which required a toll payment travelers must pay in order to continue on the road. In many instances, there were multiple checkpoints established on one roadway, either by the same mujahedeen group or several. Sometimes these checkpoints were only a few miles apart due to the multiple mujahedeen forces each trying to receive the most optimum amount of money, and if these travelers did not have enough currency to make it through all of the checkpoints, they were beaten and sometimes killed.

In the three years after the Soviets left Afghanistan, by the end of 1992 Afghanistan was utterly disparate and broken as a country. With the ousting of President Najibullah in 1992 by the mujahedeen, this was a pivotal moment that showed the utter collapse of the country into civil war. The capital had fallen to Burhanuddin Rabbani and his Uzbek supporters, and although they successfully defeated Najibullah and the interim government, this accomplishment seems like a nearly improbably feat since the southern Pashtun tribes in Peshawar were more organized and better armed. However, the Pashtun tribes were plagued with feuds and leadership strife which prevented them from ever organizing themselves, let alone leading a successful attack on Kabul. On the contrary, Rabbani's troops were united under his leadership and that of his top commander, Ahmad Shah Massood under the Shura-e Nezar. The troops also had an alliance with General Rashid Dostum in the north and the southern Afghanistan–based Hezb-e Islami Party led by Gulbuddin Hikmetyar.[9] This was seen as a crushing defeat for the Pashtuns as it was the first time in over 300 years the capital had fallen to non-Pashtun ethnic leadership. The unseating of Pashtun leadership was quite an insult for many ethnic tribes, and as a result the country was thrust into an internal civil war. Recognizing the discord and in an attempt to give control back to the Pashtuns, Hikmetyar tried to unite the Pashtuns in the southern and eastern areas of Afghanistan, most notably bombing civilian areas of the capital, one of his favorite tactics. The militarily equipped shell power from Hikmetyar was never enough against the leadership of Rabbani and Massood, though Hikmetyar desperately tried to promulgate this political agenda of the ineffectual leadership of non-Pashtun rulers.

As a result of the bedlam inside its borders, many of Afghanistan's elite and intellectual members of society fled the country as refugees and sought exile in the neighboring countries of Pakistan, and to a less significant degree in Iran. While the exodus of the refugees began during the Soviet occupation, the highest peaks occurred between 1989 and 1992 during the mujahideen rebellion.[10] After the collapse of the Najibullah government, refugees sought to return to the country, and the numbers were particularly staggering in the six-month period after the overthrow of Najibullah. The return of the refugees began in April 1992, with the rush of refugees returning from Pakistan totaling 1.2 million throughout the spring and the summer.

With the influx of people came the overarching sentiment of lawlessness, massive poverty, and the destruction of cities, particularly in Kabul. Women were most susceptible to attack and rape, which occurred even in broad daylight. Many young Afghan girls had been raped multiple times by the mujahedeen forces, oftentimes being taken in the night and made wives of mujahedeen commanders or sold in prostitution. Other women were captured, stripped, raped, and beaten by groups of mujahedeen fighters.[11] Women were afraid to report these rapes and beatings, fearing further repercussions and punishment, or even death. Oftentimes the women received the blame for the rape occurring in the first place, usually for not being in the presence of a male relative. These women were shunned and abandoned by their families for the disgrace they caused, or even in some cases were stoned to death.[12] These killings are referred to as honor killings, intended to restore honor to the family. Resistance to these mujahedeen rebels was often futile, and over 10,000 people had been killed in Kabul alone.

Although there had been no central authority in Afghanistan since 1992, the country was ruled by a handful of geographically located leaders in high positions, existing among a virtually ineffective government. By 1993, Afghanistan was segregated into primary ethnic sections of the country ruled under four different leaders. President Burhanuddin Rabbani and his Tajik government were located in Kabul and controlled the northeast section of Afghanistan. In tandem, Ismael Khan controlled Herat and the western provinces. Close to the Pakistan border in Jallalabad, a Shura (Council) of mujahedeen leaders controlled several Pashtun provinces. Lastly, Gulbuddin Hikmetyar controlled a small section of the country southeast of Kabul. In addition to these four sections, piped throughout the country were the disparate fiefdoms of the mujahedeen: Uzbeks in the north, Hazaras in central Afghanistan near Bamiyan, and the south in tatters among dozens of feuding mujahedeen warlords. The country was nearing its breaking point and was ready for a coup to unseat the president in Kabul. One warlord in particular, General Rashid Dostum in the northern Uzbek area of Afghanistan, controlled six provinces. Previously aligned with President Rabbani in Kabul, Dostum switched sides and made and deal with Gulbuddin Hikmetyar and the Pashtuns as well as Hazara mujahedeen leadership. In January 1994, these forces again tried to overtake Kabul with an onslaught of bombardment and artillery targeted at civilian locations, even to the point where U.N. workers were forced to evacuate the city. Again the leadership of Rabbani and Massood prevailed and prevented Hikmetyar and Dostum from taking the capital in June 1994. The situation in Afghanistan had descended into complete anarchy, with many inhabitants fleeing the country with nothing but the clothes on their backs. Living under the mujahideen was an unimaginable situation—women committed suicide to prevent rape. Armed guards entered homes and kidnapped young children. Women had been forcibly taken or executed in front of their families. One woman recounted her family's decision to flee Afghanistan in June 1994, "There were corpses lying everywhere. No one had time to collect the dead, as the fighting never stopped."[13]

THE ORIGIN OF THE SEEKERS OF KNOWLEDGE (1994–1996)

Afghanistan had swiftly fallen to become a country with no stability in its political environment, no real economy, and incongruent tribal alliances in such a dysfunctional state that prevented any hope of unification throughout the county. This den of chaos in the country gave rise to the Taliban, which means "student" or the "seekers of knowledge." The name itself is born out of the word *talib*, or student of Islam. The Taliban formed as a Sunni Muslim puritanical movement composed of Pashtun students from the southern Helmand and Kandahar regions in Afghanistan. The primary goal of the Taliban was to impose a strict allegiance to Islamic law, and as such they developed a politico-religious force. Almost 98 percent were of the Pashtuns of southern Afghanistan and from northwest Pakistan. The Taliban received training in weaponry and combat from the Pakistani government under the ISI. Since the retreat of the Soviets led to the breakdown of the country into independent mujahedeen fiefdoms, many Afghans had grown tired of the corruption, fighting, and brutality of the mujahedeen warlords. Daily life was consumed by the toleration for such acts by a country that had little choice in the matter.

When the Taliban arrived on the forefront in 1994, this pro-Islamic group seemed like this was the saving answer to the plight of the country under the suffering instilled by the mujahedeen. Born into a country of corruption, disparity, and turmoil, many Westerners find it surprising the origin of the Taliban was with good intentions to unify the country under a purity stance toward Islamic rule. The mujahedeen enjoyed abusing Afghan citizens ruthlessly, breaking into homes and throwing out the occupants in order to turn the home over to favored mujahedeen supporters. Oftentimes mujahedeen commanders enjoyed capturing young Afghan boys and girls and exploiting them for their own sexual gratification. In the early stages of the Taliban, several leaders, including Mullah Mohammed Ghaus, were trying to establish a way to end life under mujahedeen tyranny, and put an end to "this terrible way of life."[14] While the movement to overthrow the mujahedeen had been under way in theory, the early Taliban was unsuccessful in implementing any form of revolt against the oppression instilled by the mujahedeen. After convening at a Shura called by Ismael Khan, the Taliban Mullahs were unable to rally together to find a solution, and traveled to Kandahar to speak with another mullah. Prior to the official establishment of the Taliban, a Muslim cleric named Mohammad Omar was revolted at the disturbing news of several local mujahedeen men who had captured two young girls. Angered by the five years of corruption and debauchery, coupled with an exodus of a large Islamic Afghan population into Pakistan, Omar and other Taliban mullahs had grown tired of the shame these so-called mujahedeen Islamic warriors had brought to Afghanistan. Omar gathered about 50 students from local *madrassas* (regarded as religious schools or seminaries), and led these young students into the local mujahedeen camp, freeing the teenage girls and hanging two of the mujahedeen offenders.[15] Omar was no stranger to war and conflict, having lost his right eye from a rocket explosion at the end of the Soviet occupation in Afghanistan. Hearing of these atrocities caused Omar to react and champion an idea to get back to pro-Islamic roots. Applauded for their efforts against the mujahedeen, and instilling a sense of pride in local Afghans, two months later Omar led these students again into Kandahar to rescue a young boy suffering the same fate by the intolerable mujahedeen. Revitalized by creating this wave of victory against the southern mujahedeen forces in Afghanistan, the Taliban officially banded together to conquer the remaining cities around the country and end the corruption. The newly formed Taliban was a wave of hope that these students under the leadership of Mullah Omar would unite the country in peace and put an end to the insufferable acts endured under the mujahedeen warlords.

The first truly unified Taliban act occurred in the October 1994, when the Pakistani government sent an armored convoy to Turkmenistan via Herat and Kandahar. When armed mujahedeen warlords attacked the convoy, the Taliban ambushed the mujahedeen aggressors, overcame these forces, and allowed the convoy to continue into Kandahar.

The Taliban proceeded into the city as well, fighting the mujahedeen forces and overcoming these warlords by killing many of the leaders and imprisoning the others. The Taliban announced the movement in Kandahar as a way to free the country from the overarching mujahideen corruption, and further sought to generate the Islamic way of life into Afghanistan.

TALIBAN LAW

Many Taliban decrees were strictly enforced, and the punishments were often severe: losing your hand for stealing bread; stoning for women who were not properly clothed; and being arrested for not having a full beard. Some rules included:

A ban on playing or listening to music, dancing
A strict dress code for men and women
Prohibition for women to leave their homes without the escort of a male family member
The requirement for women to wear the burqa, an outer-wear garment to cover the woman from head to toe
A ban on education for girls
A general ban on photographs of people or animals
A ban on flying kites, playing soccer, wearing makeup, nail polish, and watching television
The implementation of stoning, amputation, and public execution as punishment

---

In 1995, Omar announced the Taliban would be more than just a political force against the mujahedeen. He desired the Taliban to act as warriors in a jihad against the Muslims and non-Muslims who harmed the Afghan people. As the leader of the Taliban, he vowed to lead these forces across the country to implement Islamic order. The Taliban repeated this method throughout the cities of Afghanistan, and their reputation for allowing bloodless retreat enabled these religious zealots to overcome mujahedeen forces relatively effortlessly, which was also assisted by instructing a smaller force to march ahead to the village and announce the impending arrival of the Taliban. Thus they encountered little resistance, especially since most villagers were glad to assist the Taliban in eliminating the extortionate comrades of the mujahedeen, since these weary Afghans relatively had not experienced any form of peace since 1979. Thousands of supporters flocked to join the Taliban, strongly optimistic at the sight of the mujahedeen forces that gave up and vanished into the mountains of Afghanistan. Further, Taliban support increased from the students of *madrassas* in Pakistan who crossed the border to join their Afghani brethren. The turning point for the Taliban occurred when Omar and his supporters finally mustered enough strength and power to capture the capital of Kabul in September 1996. By 1996, the Taliban seized control in Kabul under the Islamic Emirate of Afghanistan. Four years later, the Taliban had successfully extended their control throughout 95 percent of the country until being toppled by the Northern Alliance fighters and American aerial bombardment.

After the Taliban overthrow of the mujahideen, the Taliban began to implement their ideological plan to restore peace while championing the integrity of the Islamic way of life in Afghanistan. In order to return to this ideal state, the Taliban issued policies that would bring Afghanistan back to an Islamic-centered way of life. For men, these requirements meant they were not allowed to shave their beards and wear turbans. Men were also forced into certain dress protocols, and were also required to pray five times a day to Mecca in order to receive a higher degree of Islamic observance. The religious police banned "not praying at prayer times," and if caught, the offender was severely punished for insulting Islamic law. Women were required to wear the burqa at all times in public. These Taliban decrees sternly dissuaded women to leave the house, and as such women were not allowed to work since their sole purpose was to raise the future Muslims of Afghanistan. If women did leave the house, it was allowable if the woman was accompanied by a male blood relative. Due to the outlawing of employment for women, many schools closed. Further, schools for female students slowly became dismantled.[16]

THE SPREAD OF THE TALIBAN AND WAR WITH THE NORTHERN ALLIANCE (1996–2001)

The era from 1996 to 2001 under the control of the Taliban may be regarded as one of the darkest periods in the history of Afghanistan. During this time, only three countries offered diplomatic recognition of the Taliban: the United Arab Emirates, Pakistan, and Saudi Arabia.[17] The majority of the other surrounding countries opposed the Taliban and instead supported the Northern Alliance, and these countries included Iran, India, Turkey, Russia, and Central Asian countries.

Taliban fighters destroyed the Buddha statues at Bamyan, Afghanistan, in March 2001. The two, sixth-century monumental statues of the standing Buddhas were carved into the rockface at Bamyan. Mullah Mohammad Omar ordered them to be destroyed after declaring them false idols, and therefore against the beliefs of Islam. (AP Photo/Amir Shah)

The Taliban swept across Afghanistan, removing the mujahedeen city after city in a dominating yet bloodless manner. As support increased substantially, the Afghan people championed and welcome these Islamic students for finally eliminating the plague of Islamic warriors in Afghanistan without, in the prevailing opinion, much violence. It was therefore a severe shock and surprising upset to the community when the Taliban stormed into Kabul and violently demonstrated how the Taliban would punish enemies and offenders of the Islamic faith.

After being removed from power in April 1992, Mohammad Najibullah resided in Kabul and continued to seek refuge in the UN compound in Kabul. When the Taliban were about to invade Kabul, childhood friend Ahmad Shah Massood offered Najibullah the opportunity to flee the city. Najibullah rejected these attempts, believing the Taliban would not harm him. When the Taliban stormed the UN compound on September 28, 1996, Najibullah was castrated, beaten, and hanged.[18] Najibullah's brother, Shahpur Ahmadzai, received the same torture and death. While many citizens were surprised at such a ghastly execution, Najibullah was an abhorred figure in the politics of Afghanistan, and as such a positive outlook still endured about the Taliban. Seen as an insubordinate puppet for the Soviets, his death was a symbolic gesture for the Taliban, and served as the first demonstration of the horrific power the Taliban possessed as they infiltrated the streets of Afghanistan. The Taliban used Najibullah as an example to publicly beat him, tied his feet to a Jeep, and then dragged him through the rocky and jagged streets. The next morning, Afghan residents were shocked to witness his bloated and dead body hanging from a traffic light, his neck so swollen from the beatings and the heat of the Afghan sun that the steel noose continued to cut into him.

While the Taliban overpowered southern Afghanistan with few episodes of violence, the regime changed after moving into the north after seizing control in Kabul in 1996. The Taliban worked to defeat anchor cities such as Mazari Sharif, and in this instance they did not send advance forces to offer bloodless collaboration with the Taliban. Instead, they sent their message by firing rockets and missiles into the city. In 1997, the legendary leader Ahmad Shah Massood, formerly associated as the commander of Rabbani's troops, developed a plan to infiltrate and destroy the Taliban regime north of Kabul in the Shamali plains. Massood infiltrated the villagers that once pledged allegiance to the Taliban, and in doing so he turned these peaceful dwellings into a camouflaged ensnarement. As a result, the Taliban forces arrived in the Shamali plains and walked into a surprising ambush by the villagers and Massoud's forces. However, nearly a year later in August 1998, the Taliban returned to defeat these forces in the city. Known as the massacre of Mazari Sharif, the Taliban sought vengeance on their previous downfall by ruthlessly slaughtering thousands of Afghan citizens and several Iranian diplomats, and the episode is regarded as the worst civilian abomination in the history of the country. Several months prior to the massacre, the Taliban controlled nearly 75 percent of Afghanistan, and more importantly they controlled the major roadways into Pakistan.[19] The massacre is widely believed to have been a form of ethnic cleansing against the Hazara people, as the Taliban was adamantly opposed to these descendants of the Mongols and especially targeted this ethnicity. The Taliban proudly declared the pagans had been slaughtered for their treasons against Islam, and after the massacre of Mazari Sharif, the Northern Alliance held only a small margin of land in Afghanistan with approximately 90 percent in control of the Taliban.

The majority of the population lost all form of independence in addition to many forms of human rights, and as such the Taliban moved from a hub of optimism to a center of controversy over these policies.

Omar enforced his rule through the Ministry of the Promotion of Virtue and the Prevention of Vice (PVPV). The Taliban was notorious in their treatment and policies toward women, and even further, women lost any form of freedom, which included the ability to work and receive an education after the age of eight. The Taliban's interpretation of Muslim law enforced the *hejab*, which required women to be secluded from society. If women were allowed to be in public, all women must be covered by a garment that respected Islamic law in a manner greater than the *chador* provided, which exposed the facial area. Due to the Taliban's interpretation of the Sharia (Islamic law), women were forced to wear the Afghan burqa at all times in public. The burqa is a head-to-toe outer garment which covers every inch of a woman's skin, which was different from the Pakistan or Iranian form of the burqa in which the face and eyes are exposed. The rule of the Taliban was so extreme that while a woman was walking on the road one day, she exposed her hand briefly enough to reveal the nail polish on her fingertips. As punishment for her violation and insult against the code of the Taliban and Islam, several Taliban men held her down and cut off the tips of her fingers. Furthermore, those who resisted the Taliban rule were severely punished, as was the case when a group of women protested the Taliban in Herat. As these women marched through the streets protesting the Islamic law of the Sharia, Taliban members surrounded the leader, doused her with kerosene, and set her on fire to serve as a symbol of the consequences to women if they disobeyed. Women who were caught wearing nail polish, makeup, and even white socks under their burqas were punished by having their fingertips cut off, were sprayed with acid, or beaten with cutting wire.[20] For some women caught wearing nail polish, they were considered lucky if they only received a public beating by the Taliban. The typical white socks under the burqa could not be worn since the Taliban's flag was white and therefore a holy color that represented the purity of the regime. For other crimes such as stealing even minor items, these offenders almost immediately had their hands or feet cut off, depending on the severity of the crime or in some cases, the dollar value of the stolen items. These amputations were held in public locations where the offender was given a minor numbing agent while their limbs were severed from their bodies and then proudly displayed to the crowd. Some attempts were made at nearby hospitals to reattach these limbs, but due to the extremely poor conditions of these hospitals, overwhelmingly the majority of these attempts were unsuccessful.

However, women injured in such punishments sometimes were not even able to receive medical treatment. Even in the dismal medical facilities that existed in Afghanistan. Male doctors were banned on treating women unless they were accompanied by a male chaperone. In many cases, women were turned away for medical care for this reason alone. Furthermore, hospital wards were segregated for women, as they could not be near male patients, and oftentimes the wards were located in a dimly lit basement. Under the Taliban law, no matter the medical situation, the female gender was always the dominant medical infirmity.[21] Female doctors had long been chased out of the hospitals, and the remaining medical facilities for women were painfully lacking and severely limited. Oftentimes hospitals were unable to treat women in childbirth, turning them away or having them deliver on the floor in the hallway. Not surprisingly, many women died from infections due to the inhumane and unsanitary conditions, which included such atrocities as buildings without running water and barely enough electricity to turn on the lights. The Taliban eventually allowed some female doctors to work, but even then, the doctors were required to still wear the burqa during operations and medical procedures. For the most part, these female doctors needed to remove these garments, and would be willing to do if there was a low risk of getting caught. However, the PVPV squads savored the opportunity to catch female doctors who were not wearing appropriate burqa attire. Furthermore, due to overcrowding in some hospitals, the PVPV ordered women to leave the hospitals, even if it was a woman near death compared to a man with only minor injuries. The reasoning behind these feminine expulsions was in these overcrowding conditions, the PVPV could not guarantee the virtue of these women to be protected amid so many men. While many male doctors and dentists disagreed with the Taliban policies toward the medical treatment of women, many were afraid to treat patients in the presence of the PVPV squad for fear of their own execution. Even if not executed, doctors could be reported, and as a result women received little to no medical care. Because of these approaches to female doctors and patients, men in Afghanistan continued to favor and encourage a male dominated environment in other ways. In some extreme cases, a new mother would be seemingly abandoned by her husband in the hospital if she delivered a daughter. This technique was used as a punishment to the mother to ensure for her next pregnancy she will delivers a boy to the family. This is an ironic approach, as students of biology know, the father supplies the Y chromosome, the chromosome needed to produce a male child.

While there are well-publicized atrocities women endured throughout these years in Afghanistan, men also were subjected to similar brutality under the Taliban regime. Men were ordered to grow full beards, and were given only six weeks to do so after the Taliban announced this decree. Further, men were to be properly attired in public, which included the wearing of the *shalwars*, which are baggy-like trousers that must be a specific length just about the ankle. Furthermore, a man's beard could not be longer than his fist, and if his hair was too long, the PVPV stood on street corners with scissors and were prepared to cut the hair. All of these actions were necessary; otherwise these men were considered offenders to Islam and liable to be executed for these treasons. The Hazara tribe especially suffered under the beard requirement, since their biological DNA backbone as descendants of the Mongols did not foster the growth of a full beard. Furthermore, the Taliban also ostracized any form of homosexuality, which was one of the initial reasons Mohammad Omar formed the Taliban due to the mujahedeen notorious rape of young boys.[22]

THE RISE OF THE DRUG TRADE
IN AFGHANISTAN

During the period of Afghan civil war, the country was severely starving and relied on food supplies that were sent to the nation from Pakistan and other world relief organizations. However, the mujahedeen forces frequently captured these shipments and sold these goods on the black market, charging outrageous sums for food that should have been freely administered to the Afghan population. Furthermore, in the mujahideen's quest to acquire more money, the warlords forced the Afghan farmers to cease growing crops and food products, and ordered these farmers to grow and cultivate poppies. The mujahideen recognized that higher-income levels were achieved from the drug production rather than from the crop harvest. The mujahedeen seemed to not mind that the majority of Afghanistan was starving as long as the profits from the drug trade increased. Of the resilient farmers who continued to grow crops and plant orchards, rather than succumb to the mujahideen's orders to destroy these agricultural fields and plant poppies, the mujahideen killed these brave farmers and razed their homes to the ground. Those farmers who did comply with the orders received very little of the opium profits and were still left in poverty. Under the reign of the mujahedeen warlords, the drug production in Afghanistan skyrocketed to launch the country as the world's leading source of heroin and opium production, producing as much as 80 percent of the world's supply.[23]

The Taliban's strict regime on religion, women, and education seems to be in complete contrast to the statements regarding their tolerance of drug production in Afghanistan. When the Taliban first assumed power in Kandahar, they quickly announced the drug trade in Afghanistan must be eliminated. However, the Taliban soon realized the drug cultivation and production was an imperative need in order to pump much-needed income back into the economy, and more importantly to fund their efforts.[24] When the Taliban set out to end the corruption of the mujahedeen, estimates reveal the Taliban controlled 96 percent of the poppy cultivation in Afghanistan, and further reaped substantial profits by taxing the farmers. Additionally, poppy refiners produced morphine and heroin to transport to the West, which the Taliban further taxed and levied fees on the transport of these goods.[25] The result of these taxes created large sums of tens of millions of dollars in revenue for the Taliban, per year. Other accounts allege Taliban officials punished anyone involved in the production and smuggling of hashish, since these users were predominately Muslim. However, according to Abdul Rashid, the chief of the Taliban's antidrug force in Kandahar, the Taliban allowed farmers to grow opium to produce heroin, since these drugs were consumed by the *kafirs* (infidels) in the West and not by the Afghan Muslims.[26] The farmers received impressive profits from the drug trade, and therefore pushed for growing opium in their fields while the country received vital crop shipments of wheat from Pakistan. Thus under Islamic law, the Taliban justified this was a legitimate source of income and continued the poppy cultivation. Believing this was only for the sale of opium to the West, the Taliban continued to collect the large sums of money this revenue generated.

OSAMA BIN LADEN AND THE AFGHAN CAMPS

While the Taliban may have started under good intentions, the inclusion of Osama bin Laden and his radical Islamic group al-Qaeda into the Taliban in Afghanistan in 1996 would drastically impact the future of the Taliban. When the Taliban finally gained momentum in the siege of Kabul of 1996, bin Laden sought to form an alliance with these Islamic fundamentalists and his al-Qaeda organization, and he continued to build terrorist camps free from a similar government oversight he endured in Saudi Arabia. The Taliban was equally as fundamentalist as al-Qaeda, and shared the same views with bin Laden to defeat the infidels of the West. As a result, the Taliban welcomed bin Laden. Further, their terrorist acts resulted in the payment of millions of dollars from bin Laden.[27] After establishing his home in southern Afghanistan, bin Laden raised the call to jihad against Saudi Arabia and the United States, stating it was the duty of the Muslims to kill the American people and their allies.

The fact that bin Laden was willing to stand up to the United States was a beacon of hope for disillusioned young Afghan men who had for years seen one foreign country after another invade Afghanistan. Promises to help rebuild from the United States were never brought to fruition. Osama bin Laden created a private army trained by al-Qaeda known as the 055 Brigade to help support the call to jihad. Members of the Brigade were integrated into the Taliban army using the weapons left behind by the Soviets, and participated in multiple Afghan camps which trained young men with the fighting skills they learned from the Soviets. The Afghan camps served as terrorist training camps to support the jihad and strengthen Taliban fighters. The camps were designed with multiple education levels, and soldiers advanced at the discretion of their instructors and their evaluation of the student's skill and religious fervor. The Taliban and al-Qaeda toiled together to make a strong group of terrorists, and relations were further solidified when one of bin Laden's daughters married Mohammad Omar's son, thus forming a representational allegiance in a matrimonial agreement among these two terrorist organizations. Now with bin Laden's personal army of the 055 Brigade helping to train Taliban, along with unlimited funding from bin Laden, the alliance between al-Qaeda and the Taliban was strong. The training began to raise an army for the jihad against Westerners. These Afghan camps instructed students on covert terrorist operations in order to blend into the Western world of the infidels. Completely contradictory to their social upbringing, terrorist trainees were instructed on Western etiquette, such as being clean-shaven, taking showers, and wearing cologne to hide body odor and be more appealing to Westerners. Further, they were instructed to speak in code in case phone lines were tapped, using words such as "Canada" instead of Afghanistan or "playing with balloons" to infer terrorist-related activities as part of the jihad.[28] Osama bin Laden continued to finance and support the Taliban regime, and through his fusion of al-Qaeda and the Taliban, they are responsible for several terrorist activities around the world. These offenses include the 1998 American embassy bombings in Dar es Salaam in Tanzania and also the bombing in Nairobi, Kenya. After these bombings, Osama bin Laden and several members of al-Qaeda were indicted in a

U.S. criminal court, but the Taliban protected bin Laden from the extradition requests. The Taliban dithered details of bin Laden's whereabouts, and made ambiguous statements he had gone missing, or argued there was no proof in the allegations of these terrorist activities. Furthermore, the bombing of the USS *Cole* while it was docked in the Yemeni port of Aden was not officially accredited to al-Qaeda, though bin Laden publicly praised the attack.[29] For bin Laden, the only way to remove Americans from Muslim lands was to cripple America with a massive and unprecedented numbers of deaths. At the time of the USS *Cole* bombing, plans by bin Laden and his top terrorist strategic manager Kalid Sheikh Mohammed were under way for an attack inside the country itself.

NOTES

1. Mohmand, *American Foreign Policy toward Afghanistan*, 34, 119.

2. The American Presidency Project, "Ronald Reagan State of the Union Address of February 6, 1985"; http://www.presidency.ucsb.edu/ws/index.php?pid=38069 (Accessed November 15, 2015).

3. Mohmand, *American Foreign Policy toward Afghanistan*, 34, 119, 136.

4. Ibid., 13.

5. Ibid., 34.

6. Ahmed Rashid, *Taliban: Militant Islam, Oil, and Fundamentalism in Central Asia* (New Haven, CT: Yale University Press, 2000), 1–2.

7. Marsden, *The Taliban*, 35–37.

8. Rashid, *Taliban*, 1–2.

9. Ibid., 13, 26–27.

10. Bergen, *Holy War, Inc.*, 44–46.

11. Sally Armstrong, *Veiled Threat: The Hidden Power of the Women of Afghanistan* (New York: Four Walls Eight Windows Publishing, 2002), 107–124.

12. Ibid., 107–124.

13. "Women in Afghanistan: A Human Rights Catastrophe," Revolutionary Association of the Women of Afghanistan (RAWA), March 11, 1995, http://www.rawa.org/ai-women.htm (Accessed October 15, 2015).

14. Ibid.

15. Bergen, *Holy War, Inc.*, 165–168.

16. Marsden, *The Taliban*, 103–105.

17. Ibid., 52, 145.

18. Rashid, *Taliban*, 49–50.

19. Neamatollah Nojumi, *The Rise of the Taliban in Afghanistan: Mass Mobilization, Civil War, and the Future of the Region* (New York: Palgrave, 2002), 134–151.

20. Armstrong, *Veiled Threat,* 107–124.

21. Benard, *Veiled Courage: Inside the Afghan Women's Resistance* (New York: Broadway Books, 2002), 6–7.

22. Rashid, *Taliban,* 85–90.

23. Marsden, *The Taliban,* 114–116.

24. Ibid., 9, 116.

25. M. J. Gohari, *The Taliban: Ascent to Power* (Oxford: Oxford University Press, 2001), 90–91.

26. Marsden, *The Taliban,* 116, 144.

27. Gohari, *The Taliban,* 99–103.

28. Fawaz A. Gerges, *The Rise and Fall of Al-Qaeda* (New York: Oxford University Press, 2011), 43–72.

29. Ibid., 43–72.

11

Afghanistan after September 11, 2001

INTRODUCTION

The United States had limited experience with terrorist attacks, and none quite as powerful as the events of September 11th, 2001. The attacks on September 11th resulted in more deaths than any other terrorist attacks in the history of the United States. Although this type of event could hardly be imagined or predicted, it is widely believed there was some credible evidence that an attack was being planned against the United States in the years leading up to 2001. Multiple U.S. government intelligence agencies reported to President Bill Clinton about preliminary speculations regarding al-Qaeda and a terrorist attack plot using aircraft. However, none of these leads or suspicions have ever been confirmed.

In April 2001, the leader of the Northern Alliance in Afghanistan, Ahmad Shah Massoud, spoke to the European Parliament and pleaded for those with the ability to provide help for Afghanistan. At the time, Afghanistan was in desperate need for humanitarian aid, and the vast majority of the people of Afghanistan were suffering.

Nearly 100,000 families had lost the male head of the household to war with the mujahedeen and the Soviets, and for another 63,000 families the patriarch of the family was disabled.[1] The country had endured destruction many times over, and the once-glorious routes that brought wealth to the empires of Afghanistan, such as the illustrious Silk Road, had crumbled away to become nothing more than mere miles of ruins. Afghanistan was a country that had been bombed, invaded, and suffered for years under the corruption of the mujahedeen. The most recent years under the brutal grip of the Taliban had taken a toll on the country, and Massoud pleaded for foreign aid to help rebuild the country, particularly before Afghanistan was devastated again. It was during this speech when Massoud stated he had heard rumblings of plans for a terrorist attack against the United States.[2] Further, Osama bin Laden, leading al-Qaeda from Afghanistan, was at the forefront of witnessing the suffering Afghan families endured every day. Bin Laden blamed the Americans for causing his people to suffer and was possibly formulating a plan for revenge on a scale greater than his previous attacks.[3]

In the months leading up to the attacks of September 11th, intelligence chatter increased regarding some sort of attack on U.S. soil, though the specifics were few and the unknowns were too great to lead to any real ability to act on this intelligence. *Chatter* is a term used to describe signals intelligence (SIGINT) collection of data heard over airwaves. In May 2001, the CIA had gathered enough information to relay to the White House there was some sort of terrorist attack planned on U.S. soil. After two months, the CIA again relayed that the plans for a large-scale attack were in process, presumably led by the mastermind bin Laden, who had already led the USS *Cole* bombing in Yemen and the U.S. embassy bombings. By July, the CIA director George Tenet met with National Security Advisor Condoleezza Rice and the CIA director of Counterterrorism to discuss new information on these speculated terrorist attacks. Additional information had been received that increased the possibility that al-Qaeda was in the process of planning an attack against the United States very soon, possibly within the next few months. While plausible, with few details Rice remained unconvinced of an attack, and Secretary of Defense Donald Rumsfeld questioned the information as well, speculating the information could be a means to determine the U.S. response or a way to glean U.S. intelligence methods. While it is apparent there were pockets of information about the 9/11 attacks, Rice testified in the 9/11 Commission Report there was no way to predict al-Qaeda would attack the United States using commercial airplanes as missiles.

THE DEATH OF THE LION OF PANJSHIR

Ahmad Shah Massoud and his Northern Alliance forces offered critical support as their presence and strategic tactics restricted the Taliban from controlling the entire country of Afghanistan. A mujahedeen leader from the Panjshir region of northern Afghanistan, Massoud was a pivotal military leader who fought against the Soviet occupation and also against the fundamentalist beliefs of the Taliban. As the commander of the Northern Alliance (also known as the United Islamic Front), Massoud was by far the most respected fighter of the Northern Alliance and was known by the respectful title as the "Lion of Panjshir." Massoud was born in the Panjshir valley in Afghanistan, and was regarded as a brilliant military strategist and champion of Afghan freedom. He was pivotal in the war against the Taliban and al-Qaeda, and this title was one of respect and admiration. He was not only a brilliant strategist against the Soviets and the Taliban, but he was also well respected because Massoud genuinely cared for the safety of his fighters. In one such regard, he ordered his commanders to select unmarried men with no children, or men who were not the only sons in the family, for the most dangerous missions against the Taliban. On September 9, 2001, this highly revered Northern Alliance military leader was killed when two young Moroccan suicide bombers and supporters of al-Qaeda posed as interviewers to talk with Massoud about the Northern Alliance. The attack had been planned by al-Qaeda for weeks, who had recruited the two young Moroccans. The suicide attack had been cleverly devised for the two men to pretend to be journalists interviewing Massoud. Included in their guise of news gear was a hollowed-out video camera packed with a bomb. His death was a critical victory for al-Qaeda, which paved the way for the September 11 attacks.[4] A beloved and well-respected leader, Ahmad Shah Massoud was revered and in Afghanistan the date of his death, September 9, is celebrated as a national holiday, Massoud Day. The killing of Massoud was seen as a gift by Osama bin Laden to Mullah Omar, and also as symbol that despite the impending and the certain U.S. retaliation for the upcoming September 11 attacks, al-Qaeda would continue to persevere in Afghanistan.

SEPTEMBER 11, 2001

The morning of September 11, 2001, is day that nearly everyone in America can recall with clarity on the events that fateful day. The former deputy director of the CIA, Michael Morrell, recalled he was riding in the backseat of a van as part of President Bush's presidential entourage in Sarasota, Florida.[5] After the initial crash into the North Tower, the news came to Mike Morrell in the form of a question, "Do you know anything about a plane flying into the World Trade Center?" As the senior White House intelligence officer, Morrell was further asked what the CIA may possibly know about an impending attack—was this event terrorist related, or just an unfortunate accident? Morrell internally speculated due to the weather conditions it was most likely a pilot caught in bad weather, and perhaps had become disoriented. Morrell called his analysts at CIA headquarters in Langley, Virginia, with the hope that his internal suspicion was correct.[6] However, CIA analysts confirmed a commercial airplane hit into the middle of the North Tower of the World Trade Center. Morrell relayed this information to the White House press secretary Ari Fleisher. At that point, it was still plausible this random event was just a coincidence. Though suspicious, it was still too preliminary to call this event a terrorist attack.

The presidential motorcade continued on to Emma E. Booker Elementary School, where the president planned to greet the students, and also read a book to the class. As some later recalled, the items on the agenda that day seem trivial in comparison to the events that began to unfold. While Bush was sitting in front of an audience of first-graders, the news of the second plane was relayed to the president's security team. Andrew Card, the White House chief of staff, walked to the front of the room and quietly delivered the news to the president, "Sir, a second plane has hit the second tower. America is under attack."[7] The scene was captured by local news agencies: Card whispering the news to the president while he processed the news and tried to remain calm in front of the school children. This scene was hotly debated by both sides of the political gamut, as President Bush continued to sit with the children in the room for several minutes. Many critics have expressed appall at how Bush continued to stay seated in the room after Card informed him that the second plane had hit, and there was no question that America was now under attack. Many argue his stance to remain seated in reality serves as proof Bush was an indecisive and ineffective leader. In the aftermath of the events, a 9/11 Commission Staff Report entitled *Improvising a Homeland Defense* stated: "The President felt he should project strength and calm until he could better understand what was happening."

As a way to further antagonize the events of that day, Osama bin Laden publicly rejoiced in how the president continued to remain seated, allowing more time for the al-Qaeda operatives to continue the siege against America. Prior to the 2004 U.S. presidential election, bin Laden applauded the lack of response from President Bush that day, and mockingly stated how President Bush continued to read the book, which provided the hijackers with more than enough time to continue to implement the attacks on America. Bin Laden is quoted as saying:

> But because it seemed to him that occupying himself by talking to the little girl about the goat and its butting was more important than occupying himself with the planes and their butting of the skyscrapers, we were given three times the period required to execute the operations—all praise is due to Allah.[8]

However, in the years following this intensely debated moment in American history, the faculty and students of Emma Elementary School are quick to defend Bush's actions, or seemingly lack thereof. In one such instance, Principal Gwendolyn Tose-Rigell stated, "I don't think anyone could have handled it better. What would it have served if [Bush] had jumped out of his chair and ran out of the room?"[9]

As the debate continued of how America should respond to these unprecedented and tragic acts of terror, America continued to look to the president to bring Osama bin Laden to justice. The attacks had killed more than 3,000 civilians, a far greater amount of causalities than the Japanese aerial attack on Pearl Harbor in 1941. In order to achieve the objective of bringing bin Laden to justice, a complete overhaul of Afghanistan's government to a democratic regime would be undertaken. This would pave a partnership with Afghanistan and a new government, help the country rebuild, and by eradicating the corruption of the Taliban regime this would also help expose bin Laden and bring him to justice.

THE COLLAPSE OF THE TALIBAN

After the September 11 attacks on the World Trade Center in New York and also at the Pentagon in Washington, D.C., the United States quickly implemented its response under the military campaign Operation Enduring Freedom with the multifaceted goal to remove the Taliban from power and bring bin Laden to justice. As President Bush stated in his address to the nation, the United States would "make no distinction between the terrorists who committed these acts and those who harbor them." As part of this objective, in uniting with the Afghan Northern Alliance, the United States sought to eliminate the Taliban regime and the al-Qaeda terrorist network in Afghanistan, and further demanded the Taliban turn over bin Laden to the United States. At the initial reports of the attack, the blame quickly centered on bin Laden, who was living in Afghanistan. On September 13, President Bush stated his number one priority: "The most important thing is for us to find Osama bin Laden." Though other terrorist organizations were also suspected to be the force behind the attacks, the then secretary of state Colin Powell believed bin Laden and his al-Qaeda network were the most probably suspects. With a signature attack method that was easily recognized as al-Qaeda, coupled with the attacks against the World Trade Center, which had been a long-standing target of bin Laden's, these factors left many in the Intelligence Community without any doubt that the mastermind behind the attacks had to be Osama bin Laden. While at the time neither bin Laden nor al-Qaeda had officially claimed the attack, many were left with little question on the origins of the plot. Osama bin Laden even published a statement on September 16, stating he was not responsible for these acts against the United States.[10]

The Taliban refused repeated demands from the United States to extradite bin Laden and his associates. The Taliban also refused to respond to the demands of President Bush and other world governments, including Britain, to dismantle the Afghan camps and any terrorist training facilities in Afghanistan. Other world governments with reason to fear Islamic acts of terror either supported the U.S. regime or did nothing to oppose it, such as Russia, China, India, and even Pakistan. Mullah Mohammad Omar refused to cooperate with the United States, even after the urging of Pakistan's Inter Services Intelligence (ISI) chief Faiz Gilani. For Muslims in Afghanistan and around the world, bin Laden was seen again as a hero who had stood up to the true terrorist, America. Mullah Omar would not be persuaded and refused to give in to these demands. With little hesitation, America decided Afghanistan could no longer be a den of hiding for terrorists like bin Laden and al-Qaeda. Further, other countries around the world also feared of any further attacks to their own nations if nothing was done. If the Taliban was unwilling to cooperate, then they must be overthrown.

Acting quickly in the days after September 11, 2001, the United Nations released an initial assessment of the Afghan population to determine the conditions and circumstances of food provisions if there was an aerial invasion. Believing many of the civilians in

Afghanistan were ill-equipped and had little food, possibly due to Taliban restrictions, the UN advised some 3.8 million Afghanistan citizens would have enough provisions only for two to three weeks, and were completely dependent on external aid. With the assistance of other countries, the United States began to drop food rations and first-aid necessities into the country via a paramilitary campaign. However, the Taliban quickly manipulated these efforts by broadcasting the United States had poisoned the food in an effort to deter the population. Likewise, the United States was also afraid the Taliban was deliberately poisoning the food with the intention to kill any Afghan citizens or children indirectly supporting the United States and its efforts to overthrow the Taliban. As a result, the campaign was quickly abandoned.

Within weeks of the attacks, the United States and Great Britain launched an intensive campaign known as Operation Enduring Freedom against the Taliban. The United States provided significant logistical support to the Northern Alliance forces in an attempt to force the regime to yield to its demands. The Taliban refused repeated demands from the United States to extradite bin Laden and his associates, even after President Bush gave the Taliban numerous opportunities to do so. Utterly devastated by the U.S. bombardment, Taliban forces folded within days of a well-coordinated ground offensive launched in mid-November by Northern Alliance troops and U.S. special forces. On December 7, Mullah Omar and the Taliban surrendered the city of Kandahar, which was the militia's base of power and the last city under its control in Afghanistan. The previous day, representatives of several anti-Taliban groups met in Bonn, Germany, and with the help of the international community, named an interim administration which was installed two weeks later. After five years of rule, the Taliban had been quickly unseated from power, but key leaders like Omar and bin Laden sought refuge in local supporters across the border in Pakistan.

FOCUS ON OSAMA BIN LADEN

The U.S. Intelligence Community quickly launched into a full-scale effort to determine the exact location of Osama bin Laden, which would eventually result in the CIA-led Abbottabad raid in 2011. The hunt began with a fragment of information unearthed in 2002, resulting in years of consequent investigation in Afghanistan. After the attacks, the Taliban was implicated as terrorists, and as part of their terrorist regime, they were condemned for the continual harboring of Osama bin Laden and his al-Qaeda network. The United States launched the military campaign in October 2001 and by November the Taliban had been removed from power in the country.

Although Osama bin Laden had not been captured and was presumably seeking refuge in the mountains of Afghanistan, the Taliban regime had been successfully driven from their last seat of power in Kandahar and forced to retreat to the wilderness of Afghanistan as a guerilla warfare operation. While these Taliban forces continued to recruit new forces and work to devise plans to restore their power in Afghanistan, the United States was able to focus efforts now on bring bin Laden to justice for the 9/11 attacks. In the years after 9/11, the hunt for bin Laden stretched onward for so long that many analysts speculated he was dead already. Others in the IC felt he was constantly on the move and always just outside the grasp of any real intelligence leads. As al-Qaeda continued to resurge throughout the mid-2000s, the CIA hunt for bin Laden had dwindled. No longer focusing on capturing Al-Qaeda operatives, or even achieving success taking out al-Qaeda leaders, the manhunt diminished. The then CIA director Porter Goss stated the CIA "had an excellent idea" of where bin Laden was located; however for many it was widely believed the CIA in fact had no clue where he was located.[11] Top CIA analysts and operatives believed he was located in the Pakistani tribal region along the border of Afghanistan, seeking refuge with other top Taliban and al-Qaeda leaders who were safely harbored by Taliban sympathetic Pakistani tribal groups. With little evidence, it was extremely difficult to find bin Laden. How would America bring him to justice?

NOTES

1. Rashid, *Taliban*, 31–41.

2. Mike Boettcher and Henry Schuster, "How Much Did Afghan Leader Know?" CNN.com, November 6, 2003. http://www.cnn.com/2003/US/11/06/massoud.cable/.

3. Ibid.

4. Rashid, *Taliban*, 218–219.

5. Mark Bowden, *The Finish: The Killing of Osama Bin Laden* (New York: Atlantic Monthly Press, 2012), 3–4; Martin, *Beyond Neptune Spear*.

6. Bowden, *The Finish*, 3–4.

7. Martin, *Beyond Neptune Spear*.

8. Osama bin Laden, "Full Transcript of Bin Laden's Speech." *Aljazeera.net* (Al Jazeera), November 1, 2004, http://www.aljazeera.com/archive/2004/11/200849163336457223.html (Accessed April 30, 2014).

9. Tim Padgett, "The Interrupted Reading: The Kids with George W. Bush on 9/11," *TIME Magazine*, May 3, 2011.

10. Bre Baier, Ina McCaleb, and Anna Persky, "Bin Laden Claims Responsibility for 9/11," Fox News, October 30, 2004, http://www.foxnews.com/story/2004/10/30/bin-laden-claims-responsibility-for-11/.

11. Peter L. Bergen, *Manhunt: The Ten Year Search for Bin Laden from 9/11 to Abbottabad* (New York: Crown Publishing Group, 2012), 42–46.

12

The Decade to Find Osama Bin Laden

Born to a Saudi Arabian family with billions of dollars from their lucrative oil business, Osama bin Laden had a privileged and wealthy upbringing. While his brothers received educations overseas, young bin Laden remained close to home and studied at school in Jeddah. He joined the Islamist Muslim Brotherhood and, after relocating from Saudi Arabia in 1979, bin Laden was drawn to Afghanistan to help the mujahedeen fight against the Soviet occupation. Just prior to the withdrawal of the Red Army, bin Laden met with Ayman al-Zawahiri, the man accredited with being the dogma behind al-Qaeda. With roots grounded in this radical ideology and the Muslim Brotherhood, bin Laden founded al-Qaeda or "the base" in 1988, which was heavily fueled by the Soviet occupation and the need to return to a true Islamic-centered state. Al-Qaeda has long been designated as a terrorist organization for its strict Muslim beliefs and call for a global jihad. Under bin Laden, al-Qaeda has successfully carried out several terrorist attacks, most notably the 1998 U.S. embassy bombings, and the attacks on the United States on September 11, 2001.

The search to bring Osama bin Laden to justice for his terrorist acts ended when he was shot and killed on May 2, 2011. After a
nearly 10-year hunt to bring him to justice, bin Laden was killed at
his compound in Pakistan where he and his team had lived in hiding
for several years. The al-Qaeda leader was killed by Navy SEALs
in a CIA-led operation launched from Afghanistan. The secret mission, code named Operation Neptune Spear, also categorized bin
Laden under the code name Geronimo.[1] The heavily protected compound in Abottabad, Pakistan, located approximately 160 miles from
Afghanistan, was believed to have been the residence of bin Laden
and his family since 2005. Several days after his death, bin Laden's
death was confirmed via several militant websites. In response to the

A headline from the *Los Angeles Times* announces the death of Osama bin Laden,
former Islamic militant and leader of al-Qaeda. Bin Laden and al-Qaeda had allegedly carried out a number of terrorist and guerrilla attacks worldwide including
the 9/11 attacks on the World Trade Center and the Pentagon. Bin Laden was
sought as one of the FBI's Ten Most Wanted for his involvement in the September 11 attacks, the 1998 U.S. embassy bombings in Dar es Salaam, Tanzania, and
Nairobi, Kenya, and other international attacks. (AP Phone/Damian Dovarganes)

death of their leader, several militant groups vowed to avenge the killing by retaliating against the United States.

THE KEY TO SUCCESS: THE IDENTITY OF HIS COURIER

After it was revealed the United States had tapped into bin Laden's Inmarsat satellite phone, he ceased all use of his phones after August 1998.[2] At that time, the United States had just attacked terrorist bases in Afghanistan and Sudan with ties to bin Laden, and the United States was able to locate these bases by tracking an associate's satellite phone.[3] With this method of tradecraft now eliminated, the CIA needed a new way to find bin Laden and where he could possibly be located. The focus shifted to al-Qaeda couriers as the next priority for CIA interrogators questioning known terrorists and extremists who may have information on known couriers used by bin Laden. Through the use of an extensive network of couriers, bin Laden was able to communicate with his al-Qaeda leaders without revealing his location.

By 2002, CIA interrogators had heard unconfirmed statements about Abu Ahmed al-Kuwaiti, a courier in the inner sanctum of al-Qaeda.[4] Further, in late 2003, the operational chief of al-Qaeda, Khalid Sheikh Mohammed (often referred to as, by his initials, KSM) allegedly revealed more information about the courier.[5] In further providing credence to the importance of this courier, in 2007, officials learned al-Kuwaiti's true identity. U.S. officials would not disclose his true name or the source of revelation. In August 2010, while al-Kuwaiti was under surveillance, the unique situation and oddities led officials to speculate this exclusive fortress could in fact be the hiding location of bin Laden.[6]

THE COMPOUND

Located near the city of Abottabad about 160 miles from the Afghanistan border, the compound itself was only a few years old, three-stories high, and isolated down a dirt road with limited means of getting in or out. Images from satellite photos show the compound had not been built in 2001. The compound appeared in photos by 2005, which is presumably when bin Laden started to live there. Key geographical features and the location made the compound suspicious to intelligence analysts. Primarily, the compound was near the Pakistan military academy, a top military training academy for the training and advancement of the Pakistan military. The size of the land itself was suspect compared to neighboring areas, with much more land than those of neighboring homes. For added security, there was a gradient concrete wall with barbed wire that entirely surrounded the compound. Other suspect features include two heavy security gates. Of further interest, the top floor of the compound had a private covered balcony with its own privacy wall with virtually no visibility onto the balcony. For such a well-protected fortress, it also seemed odd that the compound had telecommunications access in and out of the facility. Surveillance continued to uncover more puzzling incidents. One such instance included the disposal of the garbage, as the compound inhabitants did not deposit garbage in the street like the neighbors. Rather, the inhabitants instead chose to burn all garbage inside the facility, preventing any analytical research to help further identify the occupants inside the facility.[7]

The design, including a concrete barrier with barb wire, heavy security gates, and other peculiar details, led many to believe someone of significance was staying in this facility. Through surveillance and intelligence gathering, analysts tried to glean whatever information they could about the occupants of the household. For officials, there were too many strange incidents surrounding this particular facility. Analysts were puzzled by oddities such as an extremely tall male individual who was seen walking under a concealed platform, but never seemed to step foot outside of this covered pathway. The repeated traveling of the courier to this semi-fortress in Abottabad was perplexing. While the use of couriers is a common practice for higher members of al-Qaeda, the comprehensive environment surrounding this particular compound was extremely curious to officials. Being unable to ascertain details on the comings and goings of the residents further upped the speculation this compound was the residence of someone of great importance who needed extreme security measures and precautions. By the end of the summer in 2010, the CIA deduced this unique environment was very likely home to bin Laden, his youngest wife, and other family members.[8]

A MULTI-INT APPROACH

Using a multiple-intelligence (multi-INT) approach, other U.S. agencies in the Intelligence Community helped to play major roles in the operation. The CIA began "red teaming" on the intelligence collected from the multiple agencies involved in the operation. By red teaming, this provided the ability to independently assess the circumstantial evidence. Through the facts available based on the intelligence gathered, it was overwhelmingly speculated the compound was used to protect a person of very high interest, and it could be bin Laden himself who resided at the Abbottabad compound. This process of red teaming the information gained was necessary because there was no solid concrete proof that it was in fact bin Laden, as no photograph existed proving it was bin Laden at the compound, and there was never an intelligence confirmation for voice or audio recording of bin Laden at the facility.

Due to the extensive structure of the compound, it was adamantly clear this fortress was protecting someone with no intention of surrendering or going quietly without a fight. Due to the extreme sensitivity of the operation, and the need for involvement with so many personnel and agencies, President Obama expressed concern over the potential exposure of the raid, and he wanted to move forward as quickly as possible with carrying out the mission. The speed with which the mission needed to proceed also contributed to the reasons not to include the Pakistani government and military, though it is widely speculated senior military leaders in Pakistan knew of the U.S. mission and hunt for bin Laden, and also of his whereabouts in Abbottabad.[9] Though many believed the compound was the hiding location of bin Laden, Defense Secretary Robert Gates as well as others doubted this was bin Laden's compound. For these reasons, since there was no certain proof, many speculated perhaps the raid simply was not worth the risk. By the time the discussion was over and the pros and cons of the mission debated, President Obama was in favor of a bombing attack on the compound rather than the SEAL's mission. Due to the presumed reinforced structure of the compound, without the inclusion of a bunker, the amount of bombing power needed to destroy the facility would be enough to destroy other homes in the blast radius, as well as a number of civilians.[10] Furthermore, with the amount of bombing material needed for the compound, any evidence to prove it was bin Laden could be destroyed.

THE RAID ON THE ABOTTABAD COMPOUND

Admiral Mullen briefed and outlined the plan for the raid to the National Security Council. In order to support the "fight your way out" situation requested by President Obama to protect the SEALs, several additional helicopters with reinforcements would be on hand in case they were needed to assist in the rescue and removal of team members. With these details confirmed, the raid on the compound was about to be launched. President Obama had a final "go or no-go" session with his advisors, and it was ultimately President Obama who gave the final order to proceed with the raid. At that point, the raid was planned to start the following day. However, due to inclement weather conditions, that evening the president was informed they needed to delay the raid.

On the afternoon of May 1, CIA director Leon Panetta authorized the raid under the president's authority. The SEALs flew into Pakistan from an air base in Afghanistan, purposefully timed to be under the cover of darkness. Per the raid plan, there were two teams to be deployed: one to advance on the compound itself and one to land outside the compound perimeter. After landing, in which one helicopter crashed, the teams advanced into the facility. At the guest house on the compound, the SEALs had the first encounter with the inhabitants. Bin Laden's courier Abu Ahmed al-Kuwaiti and the one identified in the CIA interrogations of Khalid Sheikh Mohammed opened fire with an AK-47 rifle on the first team of SEALs from behind the guest house door. Al-Kuwaiti was killed in the firefight with the SEALs. As the SEAL team progressed into the main house, the team first discovered Osama bin Laden and he had been shot while retreating. He was laying on the floor next to the bed with several of his wives around him trying to protect him. Two SEAL team members approached and fatally shot bin Laden. Using the code name Geronimo to refer to bin Laden, the SEAL leader radioed, "For God and country, Geronimo, Geronimo, Geronimo." After the raid concluded, bin Laden's body was taken in a Chinook helicopters on standby to Bagram Air Base in Afghanistan for identification.

On the evening of May 1, 2011, President Obama began his speech to the nation by remembering the victims of the September 11 attacks against America. President Obama praised the efforts of all those involved in the 10-year operation to bring bin Laden to justice. Although it had taken 10 years, the efforts by all those involved were vital to achieve numerous feats such as disrupting terrorist acts, strengthening the defense of the nation, and unseating the Taliban from control in Afghanistan. These efforts helped to kill top al-Qaeda operatives, including bin Laden. President Obama reminded the nation of his pledge when he came into office, citing the top priority was to find bin Laden. President Obama went on to clarify American was not in a war against Islam, "To those families who have lost loved ones to al-Qaeda's terror," he said, "justice has been done." This remark was directly linked to the beginning of the U.S. quest for justice, as quoted by then president George W. Bush to Congress, stating "justice will be done."[11]

The death of bin Laden after multiple terrorist acts that spanned across the globe was generally welcomed by many foreign governments. Some countries condemned the actions surrounding his death, and further debated the legal and ethical aspects of the killing. In particular, Amnesty International questioned the death and the aspects surrounding the disposal of his body. Other questionable actions included not releasing certain evidence to the public, which had been collected of bin Laden and his family members killed in the raid.

IDENTIFICATION OF OSAMA BIN LADEN'S BODY

The United States used several identification methods and techniques in order to authenticate the true identity of the body. Techniques include body measurements, facial recognition software, in-person identification from those living with him at the facility, DNA testing and analysis, and data collection inference based on the information gathered at the Abottabad compound after the raid. First, bin Laden was unusually tall and his height was 6 feet 4 inches. In order to measure the body, a Navy SEAL of exactly 6 feet in height lay down next to the corpse as a way to measure the differences between the two lengths. The height was approximated by comparison, and resulted in as close of a measurement as possible which determined the corpse was 6 feet 4 inches. This exercise caused President Obama to quip, "We donated a $60 million helicopter to this operation. Could we not afford to buy a tape measure?"

For additional confirmation, photographs of bin Laden's body and face were transmitted by the SEALs to CIA headquarters in Langley, Virginia, for further analysis. The photograph comparison of the body to known photos of bin Laden generated an over 90 percent correlation which was arguably the most decisive evidence the corpse and bin Laden were the same person. Additionally, several women living in the compound were used in the identification of bin Laden's body. The most specific method of identification would be the DNA testing analysis performed on the body. DNA information had been collected on bin Laden's extensive family, including samples from his sister who died of brain cancer. Finally, the department "assessed that much of this information, including personal correspondence between Osama bin Laden and others, as well as some of the video footage . . . would only have been in his possession."

OSAMA BIN LADEN AND CONSPIRACY
THEORIES AROUND HIS DEATH

Though explicit details on the compound raid in Abbottabad have been described in several books written by those involved in the operation, to date there has not been any collected evidence which would confirm "proof of death" that has been shared with the public. This evidence has been requested; however, under the Freedom of Information Act (FOIA) this information is exempt from being released to the public. Under the FOIA, members of the press or the public can request information on events such as the raid on Abottabad. Further, there are numerous organizations that have requested under the FOIA to provide some of the information, including a release of photographs, any videos around the event, or the DNA evidence collected and the test results. The vast majority of this information, including any techniques, sources, or methods, that assisted in the hunt and raid for Intelligence Community agencies to determine and plan the raid on the compound, is classified information and is exempt from FOIA requests.

The reports of bin Laden's death have been contested, particularly by those in the Muslim community. Conspiracy theories remain despite the multiple sources of information that confirmed his death, including the unreleased DNA testing which confirmed his identity, the personal accounts of those who witnessed bin Laden's death (including his wife and daughter), and finally a statement issued on May 6, 2011, by al-Qaeda which confirmed bin Laden's death. Several conspiracy theories exist which question aspects surrounding the events, including factors such as his true burial at sea according to Muslim tradition, the credibility of DNA samples, as well as the lack of any photographic evidence of his dead body. These details have given credence to several beliefs that bin Laden was not the one killed in the Abbottabad compound.

Boxes of evidence were seized from the compound, and included electronic media such as cell phones, computers, hard drives, and computer storage devices including disks, thumb drives, and DVDs. The material seized from the compound included a variety of documents and an assortment of personal items. Also discovered were thousands of electronic memos which held conversations and discussions with top al-Qaeda leaders around the world.[12] As outlined in the recovered documents, bin Laden sought to regain control from Yemen to Somalia, and wanted to gain control over the disparate jihadists who had developed in the world. The information recovered from the raid helped to provide greater insight into bin Laden and his plans for al-Qaeda and Afghanistan.

THE IMPACT OF BIN LADEN'S DEATH ON THE WAR IN AFGHANISTAN

Overall the sentiment regarding the death of bin Laden was met with mixed emotions from the Afghani population. For many, he was a man who represented the very essence of evil in society. He was an albatross for Afghanistan, and his death meant the end of the oppressive founder of al-Qaeda which the country had endured for over 15 years after his involvement with the Taliban.[13] For the majority of Afghanis, the emotions around his death were also mixed with a great deal of shock. Bin Laden hiding in Pakistan was perhaps not so much of a surprise, but the fact he was living in a large mansion in which he had been successfully hiding for so many years. Furthermore, the compound was located in a known Pakistani tribal region and unfriendly section of land near Afghanistan. For many, this led to questions regarding the Pakistani governments' involvement and knowledge of his comfortable accommodations, and the likelihood the Pakistani government had provided protection.[14]

The overwhelming sentiment though was many Afghanis knew his death would bring about more violence and upheaval, especially from al-Qaeda and Taliban members who would surely seek to avenge his death. Not only was bin Laden revered for his role as the founder of al-Qaeda and for his influence in the Taliban, but he was also glorified for his role in the expulsion of the Soviets from Afghanistan while he was a freedom fighter with the mujahedeen. Further, his ability to elude key intelligence agencies in the United States made him almost a legendary sensation, and he was revered as an elusive enigma of the Afghan people.[15] For these reasons, some feared reprisal and upheavals would break out across Afghanistan as the reverberance of his death spread across the globe.

How did the death of bin Laden impact the future of Afghanistan? First and foremost, the death of bin Laden did not end the Afghan war. Moreover, his death did not result in the removal of foreign security forces or American involvement in the country, at least not immediately. These factors have influenced the rise of the Taliban again in Afghanistan. While the Taliban and al-Qaeda are similar and share some same goals, the two organizations are different in their leadership chain and in how they operate. The Taliban has always remained an Afghanistan-grown and independent group focused on the state of affairs in Afghanistan, including foreign ownership and control of the country. A reverberation regarding bin Laden's death may be the inability to negotiate and work with Taliban leaders, which still exist and operate in the country. The outcome of Afghanistan will be shaped not only by bin Laden's death but also by the success of the newly democratic regime in Afghanistan. The removal of U.S. forces and transition to Afghan security forces will occur if the Taliban negotiations continue. These factors in Afghanistan will be crucial to determine the stability of neighboring nations, and the country's relations with leading nations.

NOTES

1. Martin, *Beyond Neptune Spear*.

2. Mary Lu Carnevale, "Tracking Use of Bin Laden's Satellite Phone," *The Wall Street Journal*, May 28, 2008, http://blogs.wsj.com/washwire/2008/05/28/tracking-use-of-bin-ladens-satellite-phone/ (Accessed May 8, 2015).

3. Martin Sief, "Terrorist Is Driven by Hated for U.S., Israel," *The Washington Times*, August 21, 1998, https://www.highbeam.com/doc/1G1-56776487.html (Accessed May 8, 2015).

4. John Woodward, "Death of Osama Bin Laden: Phone Call Pointed U.S. to Compound—and to 'the Pacer,'" *The Washington Post*, May 6, 2011, https://www.washingtonpost.com/world/national-security/death-of-osama-bin-laden-phone-call-pointed-us-to-compound—and-to-the-pacer/2011/05/06/AFnSVaCG_story.html (Accessed October 25, 2015).

5. Adam Goldman and Matt Apuzzo, "Osama Bin Laden Dead: How One Phone Call Led U.S. to Bin Laden's Doorstep," *Huffington Post*, May 2, 2011, http://www.huffingtonpost.com/2011/05/02/osama-bin-laden-dead-one-phone-call_n_856674.html (Accessed October 25, 2015); also Bergen, *Manhunt*, 99–103. Also Woodward, "Death of Osama bin Laden."

6. Woodward, "Death of Osama bin Laden."

7. Bergen, *Manhunt*, 130–132, 190.

8. Greg Miller, "CIA Spied on Bin Laden from Safe House," *The Washington Post*, May 5, 2011, https://www.washingtonpost.com/world/cia-spied-on-bin-laden-from-safe-house/2011/05/05/AFXbG31F_story.html?utm_term=.a0fde03b9c25 (Accessed October 25, 2015).

9. Seymour Hersh, "The Killing of Osama Bin Laden," *The London Review of Books*, May 21, 2015, http://www.lrb.co.uk/v37/n10/seymour-m-hersh/the-killing-of-osama-bin-laden (Accessed October 25, 2015).

10. Bergen, *Manhunt*, 130–132, 190.

11. Ibid., 230, 236–240.

12. Ibid., 246, 250–257.

13. Jonathan Partlow, "Osama Bin Laden Is Killed; Afghanistan Reacts," *The Washington Post*, May 2, 2011, https://www.washingtonpost.com/national/osama-bin-laden-is-killed-afghanistan-reacts/2011/05/01/AFioA9VF_story.html (Accessed October 25, 2015).

14. Ibid.

15. Vanda Felbab-Brown, "The Implications of Osama Bin Laden's Death for the War in Afghanistan and Global Counterterrorism Efforts," *Brookings.Edu*, May 2, 2011, http://www.brookings.edu/blogs/up-front/posts/2011/05/02-bin-laden-afghanistan-felbabbrown (Accessed October 25, 2015).

13

Looking Back: The Road to Democracy in Afghanistan

Years of war, devastation, and conflict have saturated the history of Afghanistan. During the 19th century, the confrontation between the expanding British and Russian empires for territory in Central Asia drastically impacted the history, culture, and environment of Afghanistan. While the country was predominately used as a pawn in the Great Game in the 19th century, Afghanistan often served as a buffer state in the midst of the surrounding Anglo-Afghan aggression and the lack of concern for the Afghan people. The 20th century continued the tension and warfare into the country with Third Anglo-Afghan Civil War in 1919, the result of which at least solidified Afghanistan's independence from the British and heralded respect from neighboring countries. The Soviets, however, continued their struggle for the control of the country, which finally cumulated into the Soviet invasion in 1979. For 10 years the country endured a communist-controlled government, savage war techniques, and constant bombardment and destruction. The mujahideen forces successfully worked to cast out the Soviets, but the retreat of the Soviet forces was just the beginning of the impending mayhem and strife to come. The Afghan Civil War from 1989 to 1992 was a time of corruption, rape, and disillusionment as the mujahideen forces turned on each other to gain control of the country. The constant corruption and bribery the mujahideen required was a bitterly hated sentiment among the Afghan citizens caught in the middle. When the Taliban regime surfaced to expel these corrupt warlords, the country welcomed these religious madrasa students with open arms. However, once the Taliban united with the fundamentalists of al-Qaeda under the guidance of Osama bin Laden, Afghanistan was thrust into an Islamic maelstrom of darkness and despair. The continued struggle for Afghan independence from war, civil unrest, and foreign government occupation continued into the turn of the millennia. It was clear there was a need for change in Afghanistan. Yet for changes to be effective, these reforms needed to include an integrated ideological approach for the Afghan people and the establishment of a well-defined government democratic structure.

The implementation of the current democratic republic in Afghanistan did not occur overnight, or even in a matter of years since the fall of the Taliban in 2001. Rather, the quest for a legitimate government structure in Afghanistan as a democratic republic was a political objective which plagued the country for nearly three decades. The invasion of the Soviets and their communist regime can be seen as the genesis of the need for democracy in Afghanistan. After the withdrawal of the Soviets in 1989, Afghanistan suffered under a period of civil war with various mujahedeen warlords vying for control. For seven years Afghanistan struggled with many factors, including the economy, government policy, foreign affairs, to the point the country was both physically and politically in ruins. On the brink of collapse, the country was virtually defenseless when the Taliban assumed control in 1996. The transition to a democratic government clearly occurred after the removal of the Taliban, though there are several significant events that helped pave the way for this to occur. As the first democratically elected president of Afghanistan, Hamid Karzai announced that his plan for the road ahead in Afghanistan was one of a prosperous and secure Afghanistan. Karzai again won the vote in the elections held in 2004 and again in 2009 which aided in the recovery of the country. The implementation of a communist regime, the period of corruption under the mujahedeen, and the suffering under the extreme pro-Islamic state of the Taliban are key events in the history of the country that signify Afghanistan's struggle for democracy and lead up to present-day Afghanistan. Since the establishment of the Democratic Republic of Afghanistan, the country has been on the road to rebuilding the economy, and has also helped to provide much-needed stability to the Afghan citizens who suffered for so long under the unstable regimes of the mujahedeen and the oppression of the Taliban.

SOVIET AND COMMUNIST INFLUENCE ON DEMOCRACY

As the Soviets began to invade Afghanistan in December 1979, the Soviets special army stormed the presidential palace and assassinated President Hafizullah Amin on December 27. His predecessor, Babrak Karmal, became the new president of Afghanistan in a puppet regime for the Soviets, which helped support the Soviet invasion. This era from 1979 to 1986 under Karmal saw the support of the Soviets and their foreign control of Afghanistan in order to stabilize the country. However, Karmal was eventually ousted due to his inability to bring peace and stability to war-torn Afghanistan. In May 1986, Mohammad Najibullah replaced Barak Karmal as the secretary-general of the People's Democratic Party of Afghanistan (PDPA), a communist-supported party in Afghanistan under the strong influence of the Soviet Union. Karmal was removed from his government role and all associated political posts, yet the tension among the Banner and PDPA parties in Afghanistan continued to escalate. A new constitution was established in November 1987, in which one of the new guidelines changed the country to the new title, the Republic of Afghanistan. Also under the constitution, Najibullah was appointed as the president.

In tandem with these events in Afghanistan, the political landscape in Russia was evolving as well. Michael Gorbachov became the newly elected prime minister, and one of his major goals was the removal of Soviet forces in Afghanistan. Likewise, despite renewals of the official cease-fire, Afghan resistance to the Soviet presence continued while the war waged on. The effects of the war were not only felt in Afghanistan but also expanded beyond the borders. Many Afghanis fled the country, and Afghan refugees in Pakistan and Iran numbered more than five million. In 1989, with 15,000 Soviet soldiers dead, more than 1.5 million Afghans had lost their lives during the war. An even staggering amount had been maimed or crippled from the nonstop carpet bombing and landmines, a favorite technique of the Soviets. Within the span of nine years, the Afghan military was reduced from 105,000 troops to approximately 25,000 by 1987.[1] Understandably, with troop support reduced to one-fourth the original amount, the Afghan military struggled with morale and the military continued to downsize as desertion was rampant.[2]

Despite the removal of the Red Army, the Afghan Civil War from 1989 to 1992 continued with warlords in different provinces all vying for control. The Soviets had helped unite Afghanistan's disparate people, but now Afghanistan faltered under the removal of the Soviet forces. Also coupled with the lapse of any substantial funding to rebuild the economy as pledged by both the United States and Russia, Afghanistan was struggling to keep the economy alive. Now with the Russian forces vacant from Afghanistan, the mujahedeen rebels effortlessly sought out and gained their own fiefdoms of power in the government. However, their disunity among the various mujahedeen parties resulted in their inability to successfully centralize the Afghan government. The resistance was high against Najibullah's reconciliation efforts for the country. Further, many predicted the Najibullah regime would crumble soon, as a result of the withdrawal of the Soviets and their backing of the insubordinate puppet Mohammad Najibullah.

After the fall of the communist Najibullah regime, the Peshawar Accords were enacted to create the Islamic State of Afghanistan. In this new government structure, an interim president was appointed as endorsed by a coalition of the mujahedeen groups seeking to implement an initial government. As rival mujahedeen factions vied for influence in the capital, the tensions once again flared between the diverse ethnic tribes existing under no true political structure in the country. The Afghan economy, without the much-needed Soviet funding, lay in ruins. In tandem with the lack of stability in the Afghan government, external Middle Eastern countries saw an opportunity for influence and control among the chaos. Neighboring governments such as Saudi Arabia and Iran assisted and championed different Afghan militias in an effort to push their own political agendas, power, and influence in Afghanistan.[3] Kabul descended into lawlessness and disorder, while both sides jockeyed for power in the capital.[4] Beyond Kabul, the country existed in chaos.

THE TALIBAN AND NORTHERN ALLIANCE ATTEMPTS AT DEMOCRATIC REPUBLIC

Afghanistan did not have a unifying government to keep peace and order. Instead, divergent militia fiefdoms reigned across the countryside, mountains, and desert. Afghanistan had become a country ruled by differing mujahedeen warlords, and the people as well as their cities generally fell into a state of despair. The interim government in Kabul had little control over the far-reaching external sections of the country. Southern Afghanistan was ruled by the Pashtun governor Gul Aha Sherzai. After the collapse of the PDPA government in 1992, Sherzai served as governor of Kandahar. He was known outside of Afghanistan as one of the major warlords until around September 1994 when the Taliban began their conquest in Kandahar.[5] The capital did not have any influence, and as a result Kandahar was overrun by long-standing Pashtun rivalries.[6]

For several years this feud for power continued. Afghanistan needed a leader, and this time opportunity arrived under the auspice of the Taliban in 1994. As Gulbuddin Hekmatyar remained unsuccessful in conquering Kabul, the Taliban gained strong support from neighboring countries covertly trying to gain influence in Afghanistan, most notably countries such as Saudi Arabia and Pakistan.[7] Many analysts have described the Taliban was established for Pakistan's regional interests, an allegation to which the Taliban harshly declines in spite of the vast amounts of funding provided by Pakistan.[8] In 1994, the Taliban took control in Kabul with no formal education, experience in politics, or skill in running a country. The religious school, or madrassa, provided students from Pakistan and the southern province of Kandahar to form the early group of the Taliban. These students gained international attention when they defeated the Kandahar council and removed the corrupt governors. Soon thereafter, the students were joined by others, who were not necessarily ready to fight but rather they were war-weary Afghanis ready to support the noble cause of the Taliban. With the intention of reducing the perversion and the corruption that had sieged the government in Afghanistan, the Taliban was enabled by additional fighters formerly associated with the communists and a number of mujahedeen defectors. In order to support their mission, the Taliban received financial support from several key places. It is alleged the Taliban received initial funding provided from Pakistan and Saudi Arabia, which helped to entice some mujahedeen fighters to switch sides to support the Taliban.[9] Not only did the Taliban allegedly receive financial backing from Saudi Arabia, but it is also alleged the Taliban also gained significant assistance early on from members of Pakistan's government as well as the ISI.[10] Pakistan had long since been plagued by the disparate warlords and rebel forces taxing the Afghanistan roadways. The Pakistani government saw this union as a way to secure its road access to Central Asia through Afghanistan, which would also help garner funding from companies interested in cross-border trading. As a result, numerous Pakistani officials supported funding the Taliban in order to wrestle control from these corrupt warlords. Further, Pakistan was struggling with the implementation of gas and oil pipelines from the fields of Central Asian into Pakistan.[11] Many officials believed the involvement of the Taliban would help achieve this goal. In receipt of funding and support, the Taliban pledged Pakistan would have a pliant, friendly regime in Kabul. This was in opposition to previous experiences with the Afghan governments that often deflected regarding any foreign control or influence from neighboring countries such as India or Pakistan in any domestic issues in Afghanistan.[12] Despite predominant Pashtun membership in the Taliban, the absence of any advocacy to the Pashtunistan issue, a sensitive and long-standing rift between the Pashtun regions of Pakistan and Afghanistan, made the Taliban a seemingly safe choice for Pakistan to fund and support the Taliban regime.

In 1995 several disparate warlords, including Gulbuddin Hekmatyar and Rashid Dostum's forces, were defeated militarily in the capital city of Kabul by Ahmad Shah Massoud and the Northern Alliance. Massoud tried unsuccessfully to unite the various ethnic regions of Afghanistan, one of the pivotal steps in forming a democratic republic by offering to hold democratic elections. Even though he was a large opponent to the Taliban, Massoud invited leaders from the Taliban to join in the discussions.[13] With the additional funding and backing from other Middle Eastern countries, the power of the Taliban spread across Afghanistan and neighboring regions. The majority of these areas were under the control of the Taliban, and the militia succeeded in disarming the local inhabitants. The Northern Alliance and a loose coalition of mujahedeen militias remained in control of the northern areas of Afghanistan. These freedom fighters, led by Ahmad Shah Massoud, were a key reason why the Taliban was never able to gain full control of the country. The Taliban and the Northern Alliance would continue to fight each other for control of the country, or at least from the stance of the Northern Alliance, the objective to fight was more to keep the Taliban from sustaining power. Options for a cease-fire and invitations to peace talks were continually turned down by the Taliban, despite Massoud's continual offers to negotiate peace. Meanwhile assistance from foreign aid relief organizations continued to be provided to Afghanistan during the conflict. However, there was virtually little to no headway made regarding major reconstruction efforts for the country that had already endured years of civil war and conflict with the Soviets. Though the Taliban was more organized and united than the mujahedeen had been, the Taliban had no experience in managing or rebuilding the country and made virtually no efforts to do so. The only focus was on rebuilding the Islamic code of character for Afghan men and women that had seemingly abandoned the pillars of Islam according to the Taliban.

THE FIGHT FOR DEMOCRACY

Conditions across Afghanistan continued to deteriorate into late 2001.[14] After the events of September 11, it was clear al-Qaeda and bin Laden were operating from Afghanistan. Responsible for the 9/11 attacks, though never admitting it until three years later, many countries saw Afghanistan as a haven for terrorists and radical Islamic extremists. With the Taliban now ousted from power, the next step was to help Afghanistan rebuild and recover from years of physical damage caused by war. The interim administration sought to create the democratic foundation of a more peaceful and united country under a new type of government. On November 28, 2001, several major political parties in Afghanistan, including the Northern Alliance and the Peshawar parties, met with the United Nations in Bonn, Germany, to decide Afghanistan's political future. Many of the details

Election workers count presidential ballots following Afghanistan's first democratic presidential election in October 2004. A series of ballot recounts followed the contested election. Ultimately, Harmid Karzai garnered 55 percent of the vote, far surpassing the closest challenger, Abdullah, making Karzai the undisputed winner of the election. (U.S. Department of Defense)

had already been discussed several weeks earlier with the neighboring Afghan countries, as well as the United States and also Russia. The country needed a leader who would help unite the Afghans and the multiple ethnicities. Burhanuddin Rabbani was put in place again as the interim president of the country, much like after the removal of Soviet troops in the early 1990s. However, in a step toward ethnic reconciliation, Hamid Karzai was highly supported to be the new president. The following month, plans were outlined in order to institute a new democratic government in Afghanistan, and in the interim, the future president Hamid Karzai was established as the chairman of the Afghan Interim Authority. Furthermore, in a *loya jirga* in 2002, Karzai was also chosen as the interim president of Afghanistan until the new elections would be held after the establishment and ratification of a new constitution for the country.

AFGHAN DEMOCRATIC ELECTIONS 2004

For many Afghan citizens, the dawn of a promising era began when the country held the first historically significant national democratic elections in October 2004. The determination of the national assembly allowed Afghanistan to become an Islamic republic, but after centuries of mayhem, it was likely that many Afghans were still distrustful of any type of political control.[15] Several ethnic groups hold their own opinion on how Afghanistan should be governed, including the Pashtuns, the Tajiks, and the Hazaras. As evident throughout numerous events in the history of the country, the inclusion of the varying ethnic tribes in Afghanistan is paramount in order to successfully implement new regime changes. When the leaders of these ethnic groups are not consulted in political situations, or worse are consulted and ignored, these ethnic tribes do not hesitate to respond in rebellion. As such, the implementation of a democratically elected government needed to have support from the disparate ethnic groups in order to unite and reconstruct Afghanistan. The hope was this united front would simultaneously reduce the turmoil, strife, and violence within the country. Yet as a testament to the resentment still lingering from some dissimilar Afghan ethnic groups, Vice President Haji Abdul Qadir was assassinated in July 2002 outside of his government office as a stance against the rise of a democratic republic in Afghanistan.[16]

The interim administration held power until June 2002 when a *loya jirga* was convened in order to select a transitional government to rule the country until national elections could be held. In addition, a new constitution would be drafted to establish the country as a democratic republic. The work for democracy continued, and by the beginning of the 2004 campaign, Afghanistan had 18 candidates for President. Candidates were able to include two nominations for Vice President on their presidential ballot. For some candidates, they saw this as an opportunity to balance the nomination with representatives across the three largest ethic tribes. After delays from July and September, the first democratically held elections occurred in October 2004, and the people elected the country's current president, Hamid Karzai.[17]

AFGHAN DEMOCRATIC ELECTIONS 2009

The country held the second official democratic elections in the history of Afghanistan on August 20, 2009. While accounts vary, the BBC released in the first round of elections, President Hamid Karzi as the incumbent received 49 percent of the vote. Abdullah Abdullah was the second rival for the presidency, receiving just over 30 percent of the vote.[18] Abdullah has been involved in Afghan politics for a number of years, and was previously friends with the Northern Alliance commander Ahmad Shah Massoud prior to his death in 2001. After the Taliban was removed from power, Abdullah became the minister of foreign affairs until 2005. However, the August 2009 elections were marred with instances of fraud and ballot stuffing at voting locations and created a period of political turmoil.[19] After another counting of the ballots in September, the voting totals revised to show Karzai had actually garnered 55 percent of the vote, far surpassing the closest challenger Abdullah and marking Karzai as the unquestionable winner.[20] However, numerous complaints of fraud at voting stations led the Electoral Complaints Commission (ECC), an entity endorsed by the United Nations, to investigate any wrongdoings at questioned polling stations, estimated to be over 200.[21] The audit revealed some polling stations had a voter turnout of over 100 percent, and these questionable results launched a formal investigation of fraud and abuse. The results of the ECC audit indicated there were more than 200 instances of fraud at these polling places across the country. The election results were invalidated from these 200 voting stations, which reduced President Karzai's percentage from 55 percent to 49.7 percent of the vote. Since the votes were now below the majority needed in the country, a new round of voting needed to be conducted. At first President Karzai resisted the need for the second round of elections. Finally abdicating to the political pressures, and particular under the embarrassment of the fraudulent voting stations, Karzai agreed to the second round of elections to be held on November 7. However, only a few days before the new election, Abdullah announced he was withdrawing from the race, citing it was in the best interest of the country. After canceling the runoff election, Karzai was inaugurated as the president of Afghanistan.

During the 2009 presidential campaign, the number of insurgent attacks in Afghanistan continued to increase. The newly elected U.S. president Barack Obama had pledged in his campaign the war in Afghanistan would need more assistance from the United States, as top U.S. officials determined the numbers of troops in Afghanistan were far too low to help implement reconstruction efforts for the country. Additional forces were needed to protect the population from the insurgents that planned to attack and hinder these rebuilding efforts. In early 2009 the president announced another 17,000 American troops would be sent to Afghanistan that year alone. By the end of that same year, Obama doubled the number of troops needed in Afghanistan as a temporary basis to assist in reconstruction efforts.

NATO SUPPORT TO DEMOCRATIC ADVANCEMENT

In order to help facilitate the transition of troop support to NATO forces, a changeover timeline was established to help facilitate training and to provide a smooth transition from NATO forces to the democratic government in Afghanistan. By 2010, NATO troops had increased to 150,000, the highest levels yet experienced. While the increase in troops was necessary to help rebuild the country and to help provide protection from any insurgent Taliban attacks, the mere presence of NATO forces was met with mixed results. While the troops were successful in preventing some Taliban attacks and removing remaining insurgents from heavily dominated Taliban areas, in truth the NATO forces were unable to squash many Taliban or other militant attacks. These surprise attacks usually targeted civilians as well as military and government targets, which made it difficult to predict or prevent. These attacks succeeded for several reasons, mostly due to the constant uncomfortable sentiment the Afghan population likely felt regarding NATO forces in their country.[22] Further, possible sympathetic support by neighboring Pakistan provided a safe zone for Taliban fighters, and allowed a base from which to plan and launch attacks in Afghanistan. By 2010, it was readily apparent a military-enforced cease-fire to the conflict would be unsuccessful. Political tensions were also mounting at the press of the public and lack of support for continuing to send troops into Afghanistan under the evident stalemate existing between the Taliban and the troops. As a response to these declining sentiments, as well as a lack of improvement in Afghanistan, NATO agreed to withdraw all troops by the end of 2014. Prior to the removal of all troops, the United States had hoped to establish a political agreement with the Taliban which required support from President Karzai. Further relations between the Afghan government and the United States continued to deteriorate, and with the relationship strained, the likelihood of preventing any form of peace accords with the Taliban ceased to exist. President Karzai worked with the United States to keep progress moving forward on this front.

THE FUTURE OF DEMOCRACY IN AFGHANISTAN

After the 2014 presidential elections, Afghanistan faces an arduous challenge for the future. The political relationship between central government in Afghanistan and with other foreign powers was precarious in the last years of the Karzai administration. Further, the faith of the Afghan citizens in this democratic governance is faltering, mostly due to the corruption which still plagues the government at all levels.[23] In addition to the fraudulent presidential elections in 2009, the 2010 parliamentary elections were again marred with vote fraud that further smeared the sanctity of the voter election process.[24] Attacks and threats from the Taliban continue to keep citizens away from polling stations, resulting in low voter turnout for the elections. The year 2014 proved to be interesting for Afghanistan, both politically and security wise. The decrease of American and NATO forces with the intended transition of security responsibilities to Afghan forces by the end of 2015 will surely pose a strain to the new Afghan administration. Many have already questioned the ability of the newly elected democratic government to retain control of the country while the NATO forces withdraw.

Despite the numerous impediments and problems the country faces, Afghani citizens remain both optimistic and yet cautiously reserved about the future of this war-torn land. In a country that was utterly at the brink of collapse under the oppression of the Taliban in 2001, it is a remarkable feat that within the next decade, the country would hold two presidential and parliamentary elections and provide stability to key areas. Afghanistan has without question advanced over the past several years on a number of fronts, including democracy, the government, and removal of the Taliban. Yet these ambitious achievements also need to be balanced with decades of corruption, political skepticism, and foreign control as evident by American and NATO security forces. Yet it is the removal of these very security forces that could potentially shut down the democratic government, perhaps one of the reasons why the Taliban focused on this as a political demand in the hopes of coercing the removal of troops to proceed on any form of political negotiations. Criminal activity and violence in Afghanistan remains high in a country ensnared in an ongoing threat of insurgency by the Taliban, al-Qaeda, and other regimes hoping to overthrow the government amid the withdrawal of NATO troops. The failure to implement a successful security regime will likely undermine the central government, leave Afghanistan's social and economic network vulnerable to attack, and trigger the same issues that led to the foreign involvement in the first place. This in turn could threaten global security, including the United States, and undermine any form of political advancement again between Afghanistan and foreign nations.

In light of overcoming these political feats, Afghanistan still faces numerous obstacles to rebuild the fragile economy. Since the establishment of the democratic government in Afghanistan, genuine efforts have been made to eliminate the continued opium drug trafficking that has widely occurred within the country. Afghanistan still struggles with eradicating this source of revenue for the farmers who depend on this income to survive in a land of austere poverty. It seems logical that the work begun under the Karzai administration will continue in order to eliminate the refuge of terrorist activity, safely recover the millions of buried landmines from constant wars, and assist with the repatriation of millions of refugees after years of exile. To implement these measures, President Karzai was resolute in his goal to unify the country and put an end to the war, violence, and resentment that Afghanistan has fostered for so long. With hope, the new democratically elected government will carry the torch and continue to help transform this war-torn country into a land of peace and prosperity in the 21st century. In spite of the many obstacles the country faces in rebuilding Afghanistan, though the Taliban is no longer in control, the extremist group is still a threat. Hope remains on the horizon for the country to withstand as a democratic republic.

NOTES

1. Rashid, *Taliban*, 1–2.

2. Tomsen, *The Wars of Afghanistan*, 93–94.

3. Amin Saikal, *Modern Afghanistan: A History of Struggle and Survival*. 1st ed. (London; New York: I.B. Tauris & Co. 2006), 352.

4. Kamal Matinuddin, *The Taliban Phenomenon: Afghanistan 1994–1997* (Oxford: Oxford University Press 1999), 87, 218.

5. Marsden, *The Taliban*, 40–48.

6. Ibid., 40–48.

7. Tomsen, *The Wars of Afghanistan*, 196–198, 223, 243–245, 372, 437.

8. Rashid, *Taliban*, 95–104, 232.

9. Ibid., 124, 224, 232, 236.

10. Saikal, *Modern Afghanistan*; Rashid, *Taliban*, 224.

11. Robert M. Shelala, Nori Kasting, Sam Khazai, and Sean Mann. "U.S. and Iranian Strategic Competition: The Impact of Afghanistan, Pakistan, India, and Central Asia," Center for Strategic and International Studies (CSIS), June 26, 2012, http://csis.org/files/publication/130626_AfPak_Asia.pdf (Accessed October 25, 2015).

12. Ibid.

13. Steve Coll, *Ghost Wars: The Secret History of the CIA, Afghanistan, and Bin Laden, from the Soviet Invasion to September 10, 2001* (London: Penguin Press. 2004), 107–124.

14. Ernesto Londoño, "Study: Iraq, Afghan War Costs to top $4 Trillion," *The Washington Post*, March 28, 2013, https://www.washingtonpost.com/world/national-security/study-iraq-afghan-war-costs-to-top-4-trillion/2013/03/28/b82a5dce-97ed-11e2-814b-063623d80a60_story.html?utm_term=.5cf92e52d3f9 (Accessed October 25, 2015).

15. Elizabeth Rubin, "Karzai in His Labrinth," *The New Yok Times*, August 9, 2009, http://www.nytimes.com/2009/08/09/magazine/09Karzai-t.html?_r=0 (Accessed October 25, 2015).

16. Ibid.

17. Ibid.

18. Dexter Filkins and Carlotta Gall, "Fake Afghan Poll Sites Favored Karzai, Officials Assert," *The New York Times*, September 6, 2009.

19. David Ibsy, *Afghanistan: Graveyard of Empires: A New History of the Borderland* (New York: Pegasus 2010), 7, 146–152.

20. Filkins and Gall, "Fake Afghan Poll Sites Favored Karzai, Officials Assert."

21. Anthony H. Cordesman, "Afghan Metrics: How to Lose a War—and Possibly How to Win One," Center for Strategic and International Studies (CSIS), January 12, 2010, https://www.csis.org/analysis/afghan-metrics (Accessed August 10, 2016).

22. Ibid.

23. Ibsy, *Afghanistan*.

24. Rubin, "Karzai in His Labrinth."

14

The Future of Afghanistan

The United States seemingly obliterated the Taliban forces in December 2001 which allowed for a new democratic assembly in Afghanistan. The country once again emerged into the international community, this time with a more hopeful approach toward building a credible government free of Taliban influence. Leaders worked to establish diplomatic relations with the countries that could not support Afghanistan while under the Taliban-controlled Islamic state of Afghanistan. One year after the overthrow of the Taliban regime which forced many militants into exile, Afghanistan signed the Kabul Declaration on Good Neighborly Relations with the nearby countries of Iran, Pakistan, China, Turkmenistan, Uzbekistan, and Tajikistan. The declaration was a symbolic agreement, which recognized Afghanistan's independence and outlined territorial boundaries. Furthermore, countries around the globe, including the United States and Japan, pledged financial support to assist in the rebuilding of a country peppered with destroyed fields, orchards, and villages.

THE PATH TO REBUILDING WAR-TORN AFGHANISTAN

The initial rebuilding of battle-weary Afghanistan commenced in 2002, while the Taliban began regrouping inside Pakistan. It has been over 15 years since Operation Enduring Freedom ended and great progress has been made for a country yearning to stand on its own. Yet as the neophyte Afghan government continues to devise plans to rebuild and restore Afghanistan, the country grapples with a weakened Taliban insurgency devising new plans to overthrow the government and control Afghanistan once more. Reginal stability continues to be threatened as attacks are a frequent occurrence from remaining al-Qaeda and Taliban militants. Further, the country struggles against impediments such as poverty, poor economic infrastructure, landmines, as well as the illegal opium production and trade. While improvements regarding medicinal initiatives have been made, health issues continue to plaque the nation. Medical facilities have substantially improved, but these efforts alone are not enough. Swift, drastic measures need to be implemented, especially for the women and children of Afghanistan. Under the oppression of the Taliban regime, Afghan women were forced to stay home and remain indoors. Outside activity could occur only in the presence of a male relative. As a result, many women are unhealthy and require substantial medical treatment. Preliminary estimates speculate it can take decades to completely rebuild Afghanistan.

Afghanistan has been in a state of conflict for centuries, and many argue this is the result of foreign involvement in the country. Afghanistan is hungry to demonstrate competence and integrity in an approach that demonstrates successful Afghan governance independent of foreign involvement. From 2002 to 2014, estimates show nearly $18 billion had been sent to Afghanistan in the form of economic aid.[1] With this aid and economic relief, the Afghan people worked toward reclaiming their communities, a challenge in areas with a lack of government control or influence. In order to continue the transition, several significant factors should be assessed to perform a peaceful progression toward true democracy. This includes the challenges of terrorism threats from the Taliban and other insurgencies, decrease of the opium drug trade, economic and social reform strategies free from foreign intervention, reduction in corrupt warlords, and a transparent approach to improve strained U.S. relations.

PEACE TALKS WITH THE TALIBAN

The Taliban insurgency still lingers on the horizon, assessing perhaps for the opportune time to crush the U.S.-supported Afghan government.[2] The number of insurgent attacks has steadily begun to increase, along with the illegal production of opium. President Karzai held negotiation talks with the Taliban beginning in April 2007, amid the long-standing dispute on how to rectify the situation with the Taliban. The options were polarized on the ends of an extreme spectrum: to eradicate the regime through capture and execution, or work at peace negotiations and end the need to resolve conflicts with violence. As such President Karzai initially sought approval from the United States and the North Atlantic Treaty Organization (NATO) prior to meeting with the Taliban leaders. However, many believe these peace talks should have occurred much earlier to foster more amicable relations which would have hindered attacks from the Taliban. These polar options consequentially formed a rift between the Tajiks of the north and the Taliban-inclined Pashtuns of southern Afghanistan.[3]

Following Karzai's initial Taliban talks in 2007, substantial peace efforts did not fully begin with the Taliban until early January 2010.[4] During a London conference, Afghan president Hamid Karzai informed world leaders he intended to reach a peace agreement with top echelons of the Taliban. Karzai set the framework for dialogue with Taliban leaders when he called on the group's leadership to take part in a *loya jirga*—or large assembly of elders—to initiate peace talks.[5] At the end of January 2010, at a conference in London with more than 70 organizations, President Hamid Karzai stated his intentions to reach out to members of the Taliban leadership. Dr. Abdullah stated:

> I should say that Taliban are not fighting in order to be accommodated. They are fighting in order to bring the state down. So it's a futile exercise, and it's just misleading. . . . There are groups that will fight to the death. Whether we like to talk to them or we don't like to talk to them, they will continue to fight. So, for them, I don't think that we have a way forward with talks or negotiations or contacts or anything as such. Then we have to be prepared to tackle and deal with them militarily. In terms of the Taliban on the ground, there are lots of possibilities and opportunities that with the help of the people in different parts of

the country, we can attract them to the peace process; provided, we create a favorable environment on this side of the line. At the moment, the people are leaving support for the government because of corruption. So that expectation is also not realistic at this stage.[6]

Along with the Taliban, other radical terrorist groups continue to thrive in Afghanistan or in the neighboring countries along its borders. The Taliban continues to support other terrorist groups around the world, which adds strength to this draconian order for the advancement of Islam. The Taliban continues to fight to restore Afghanistan to the belief of a true "Islamic Emirate." The ongoing threat of terrorist insurgency is just a recent example that has occurred in the history of Afghanistan within the last 20 years. For centuries before the Taliban, countless leaders and countries have gloriously failed to break the hard-engrained Islamic principles and true roots of Afghan culture. It is this very foundation of unyielding Islamic faith that continues to fuel the Taliban and other extremists.

PRESSURE AGAINST OPIUM PRODUCTION

Early in 2007, the Afghan government embarked upon a quest to destroy the opium croplands in the country with a poppy eradication team. Already an unpopular government regime, the Karzai administration faced severe criticism in removing this generous source of income from the farmers without providing a realistic source of substitute income. Over the last decade, the drug trade in Afghanistan has continued to be quite lucrative, with figures in 2016 reaching an all-time peak at more than 6,000 tons harvested.[7] This even occurred after the previously highest record in 2015. Because of these steadily increasing numbers, the Afghan government recognizes the need to eliminate this illegal drug trade. Billions of dollars have been poured into Afghanistan to assist farmers with pivoting the use of their fields to crops such as wheat, fruit, and saffron. Yet despite these investments, after surveying winter planting trends in Afghanistan there is a 10 percent increase in 2016, and a potential opium production increase of 43 percent, which could be the biggest crop yield to date.[8] These estimates revealed an increase in half of the agricultural provinces that planned to harvest more poppies in the following years.[9] The Karzai administration worked diligently to destroy these poppy fields, and it is with hope the work will continue under President Ghani.

LIBERTY FROM FOREIGN INTERVENTION

Afghanistan is trying to evolve as a country, independent from foreign occupation or control. Afghanistan has experienced a significant change in the population as a result of foreign influence. Throughout the 1980s due to the Soviet occupation, almost one-third of the Afghani people were forced into exile as more than six million Afghani refugees fled to Pakistan and Iran, one of the largest recorded exodus episodes in history.[10] After the Soviets withdrawal of all forces in 1989, millions of refugees repatriated to Afghanistan, only to face more instability and turmoil under hardships such as the corrupt mujahedeen warlords, economic disparity, food shortages, inflation, and severe drought. Since Afghanistan is primarily agricultural and rural based, many of those Afghanis raised in refugee camps lack the essential farming expertise needed to survive.[11] From 2009 to 2010, the United States resettled an incredibly small number of refugees—328 refugees total—from Afghanistan.[12]

While the presence of NATO forces has been helpful, President Hamid Karzai was unsuccessful in his efforts to reach an agreement with America for remaining troops. President Obama pledged a slow withdrawal of NATO forces from Afghanistan by the end of 2016; however significant progress has been made with the Taliban prior to the full removal of NATO forces. In September 2016, the Afghan government signed the first peace treaty with the Taliban since 2011.[13] President Ghani successfully formalized a treaty with Hezb-i-Islami, the second-largest insurgency group of the Taliban led by Gulbuddin Hekmatyar. Through this initial peace accord, President Ghani hopes other Taliban and militant groups will follow suit. Afghanistan continues to work to counter these long-standing rifts with the disparate Taliban insurgency, regarding the treaty as a template for other peace deals with the Taliban.[14] The strategic significance for Afghanistan as a nation is this agreement was void of foreign, and particularly Western, intervention. As a result, this arrangement is not necessarily one which is seen to end violence, or regarded as a true peace agreement, with the Taliban. Rather, Afghanistan as a country wanted to demonstrate to the world the nation is able to achieve amity in the country free of foreign influence or interference.

THE THREAT OF CORRUPTION

Further significant obstacles for Afghanistan include the warlords who claim certain territories as their own. These warlords enslave the inhabitants of that region and for the most part operate beyond the control of the government. When the Taliban was removed from power, this gave the warlords the opportunity to quickly claim these abandoned territories. These warlords however are split between enemies of the Taliban and also silent supporters, and despite which side of the Taliban partisan line, warlords are a severe threat to the new Afghan government and the stability of Afghanistan's future. In order to remove these warlords, who substantially contribute to the increasing illegal drug trade, the Ghani administration has the opportunity to address these issues which threaten peace and prosperity in Afghanistan.

STRAIN ON WESTERN RELATIONS

The democratically elected Afghan government has faced a long, arduous road to democracy. Looking back, President Hamid Karzai was reelected as the president of Afghanistan in August 2009 for another four-year term. During that time, President Karzai pledged to help rebuild Afghanistan, yet some believe he failed in his efforts. For the presidential elections held in June 2014, time had run out for Karzai to make further progress on his intentions, as President Karzai served his constitutionally allotted two-terms and was ineligible to run for a third term. As President Karzai prepared to transition out of office, he was particularly focused on his legacy and the enduring image Afghanis would hold of him. At the forefront of this was the haunting of errors past in Afghanistan, in which previous leaders were seen as puppets in a foreign-controlled regime. Karzai worked to pivot from this image and present himself more as one for the people of Afghanistan. Oftentimes his decisions reflected this sentiment, rather than merely opposed Western views. In response to his refusal to sign the security agreement, Karzai referenced this episode to another haunting one in Afghanistan's past—the Treaty of Gandamak in 1879.[15] The Treaty of Gandamak was drafted very heavily in favor of the British, which gave control of large swaths of Afghan land to the British in India in order to prevent encroachment from other nations. Additionally, the treaty gave the British complete control over Afghan foreign policy, which is what was at the forefront of President Karzai's justification to not sign the security agreement. As Karzai continued to distance himself from the Western allies, it was perceived as more endearing to the hardened Afghanis who wanted to see more of an independent stance from their Afghan president. Of all the multiply ethnicities found in Afghanistan, this stance against American control was particularly relevant for the Pashtuns, who have ethnic domination in the Taliban. In order for his peace talks to be successful with the Taliban, and in order for Karzai to secure a lasting image with his people, a hard stance against American control and power would be necessary.

One challenge for Afghanistan may be the handling of U.S. relations, which some leaders believe Karzai's relationship with the United States deteriorated over the years mainly due to Karzai's handling of the hunt for Osama bin Laden. The secret Taliban talks also resulted in a strain on U.S. and Afghan relations after it was revealed Karzai had been secretly meeting with the Taliban without his Western supporters. Many in Washington felt this enigmatic meeting was a ploy by the Taliban to distract Karzai from signing the long-term security agreement for the future of Afghanistan.[16] After his refusal to sign the agreement, which would allow U.S. troops to remain in Afghanistan for counterterrorism training of Afghan security forces, Karzai's meeting with the Taliban further corroded U.S. relations. This was also on the cusp of what some believe were antagonizing actions by Karzai. In the previous months, Karzai had released several Taliban prisoners, which the United States opposed. Karzai also engaged in propaganda campaigns against the United States on distorted facts that Karzai referred to as war crimes.[17] These events coupled with his secret Taliban meetings continued to disintegrate U.S. and Afghan relations and create a wall of distrust between the two governments. From Karzai's perspective, he was trying to reach a deal with the Taliban for peace absent of any U.S. influence. The Taliban had long stated there would be no peace talks as long as there was an American presence in Afghanistan. Regardless of intention, the secret peace talks did not yield any substantial movement toward peace in Afghanistan. The years since 2001 have included a series of ebb and flows with the Taliban. Yet by the end of Karzai's eight-year tenure, progress for the international community as well as Afghanistan would have to wait until the new Afghan president was elected. After a turbulent election season, Dr. Ashraf Ghani Ahmadzai was elected president of Afghanistan on September 21, 2014. The election was particularly contentious as there were overwhelming accusations of corruption and inability to get accurate ballot results. Contender Abdullah, who ran against Karzai in the 2009 election, received overwhelming Pashtun support for the presidency. This divided many Afghanis and resulted in multiple election polling dates.

The government of Afghanistan seeks to address key issues in order to rebuild relations across the globe, as well as address internal strife with the Taliban. Progress has been made, and recent years have been unlike any other year in Afghanistan. The country has much to be proud of, and remarkable progress has been made toward a stance of peace in the country. Yet the status quo changed significantly at the end of July with the announcement of the death of Mullah Omar. The death of the founder and 20-year leader of the Taliban ignited a firestorm, and forced the Taliban to revert to conservative tactics. Due to his prestigious role in the Taliban, Mullah Omar was the only voice that could unite the Taliban to support a peace agreement. If the Afghan government made any kind of deal with another, it would be illegitimate without Omar's blessing. Since his death, the peace talks have somewhat stalled under the Taliban's new leadership, Mullah Akhtar Mohammed Mansour. Almost immediately after assuming power, Mansour issued a new call to jihad against both the Afghan government and the United States. In less than a week, attacks and bombings in Kabul claimed the lives of 400 Afghans. Has the chance for peace in Afghanistan passed?

IS PEACE POSSIBLE?

In order to achieve peace, Afghanistan certainly has a long road ahead paved with several critical obstacles. Today, Afghanistan faces threats not only from terrorists such as ISIS and the Taliban, but the Afghan government's difficulty in extending applicable laws and standards across Afghanistan challenges the future economic growth of the country. In tandem, Afghanistan's living standards are among the lowest in the world. The majority of the Afghan population continues to experience health and community issues. Despite the help from many foreign countries, the government of Afghanistan will need to address a number of challenges and issues in order to rebuild the economy. This includes new methods to address low revenue collection, a reduction in corruption, threat of insurgency, and how to improve the poor public infrastructure.

One of the key debates is questioning how Afghanistan will respond to the withdrawal of the NATO troops. The fear remains that another civil war may break out in the country again amid the unrest and lawlessness. Yet it is clear the British policy was one of a temporary presence in Afghanistan. The British recognize the complex structure of Afghanistan, meaning the multiple ethnicities will need to harmonize on their own terms, and the British or any other foreign power will have little say into the outcome. Rather, the NATO occupation in Afghanistan was a means to protect Britain's own security, instead of meaning to dominate Afghanistan's.

POSSIBLE STEPS ON THE ROAD TO RECOVERY IN AFGHANISTAN

Investing and rebuilding in Afghanistan is not only critical for the country, but also for the protection of the United States and its allies. Over $2 billion was requested in 2014 to rebuild the country, and this funding would both protect and advance work that has progressed in the last 10 years and continue investments in several areas. First, the democratic government must continue to work to advance peace talks with the Taliban, and continue to overcome the threat of insurgency. Second, economic growth must be championed with a focus on agricultural efforts away from opium cultivation. Third, the justice system in Afghanistan must evolve and embrace new methods to strengthen the judicial role in the Afghan government. Finally, addressing the needs of basic human rights is critical for development. Once these components are addressed, the Afghan government can move into more control for transforming the country. All of these investments in the country rely on a successful transition of security forces, and empowerment free of foreign control.

Several major areas will need to be addressed on the road to recovery. It is without question that the people of Afghanistan have endured many years of terror and battle. Within the last 30 years alone, Afghanistan has seen conflict with the Soviets lasting through the 1980s, control by the Taliban and al-Qaeda since 1995, and the NATO offensive, which still lingers. Despite these tumultuous conditions facing the people of Afghanistan, many refugees from neighboring Pakistan are returning to the country, mostly young children seeking a new way of life. Primarily, the rights of all Afghan people must be at the foreground of any settlement with the Taliban. The importance of open elections under the democratic republic is a vision that must endure. In addition to this mind-set, basic human rights for women in Afghanistan must also be considered. In order to ensure these basic human rights remain on the horizon, women should be involved in the road-map to peace.[18]

The country has overcome many challenges and yet regarding society, Afghanistan needs to address some basic services needed for the population. A critical success component throughout the restructure is how to protect the vulnerabilities of those less fortunate in

Afghanistan. Namely, the women and children of Afghanistan have possibly the hardiest challenges to overcome. There remains a lack of access to general aspects of human life, including health care, education, and other basic services such as food and clean water. Many sections of Afghanistan have been completely ravaged from decades of war. Focusing on stabilizing the government structure is one part. For many women, significant strides should be made to no longer marginalize their role in a profoundly conservative and male-dominated society. Many women are the victims of domestic abuse and oftentimes are married at a young age because they are seen as property or are for financial remuneration. However, some women are able to break through the barriers to their education and views in Afghan society. One such woman, Captain Niloofar Rahmani is the first woman pilot in the Afghan Air Force (AAF) since the fall of the Taliban. Her role is unprecedented in the history of Afghanistan. Her journey to this prestigious title began when she was 18, and she overheard a media recruitment announcement for young women to join the AAF. Rahmani continued to push barriers after her graduation from flight school and proceeded to pass advanced flight training. These examples of strong women serve as role models for the younger generation in Afghanistan.

If the vision of peace is possible in Afghanistan, then some concessions may need to be made in any negotiations with the Taliban. Steps must be taken, and if lasting peace is the vision of success, the international community must realize this will not be achieved overnight. President Ghani will oversee a tumultuous period as the country responds to the threat of insurgents as a result of the withdrawal of NATO forces from Afghanistan. The removal of U.S. forces has been delayed at the request of President Ghani, requesting that U.S. president Barak Obama allow troops to remain in the country and continue support to the Afghan forces. The Taliban insurgency has been on the rise, and the capture of the northern city of Kunduz in northern Afghanistan, which occurred seamlessly in a matter of hours, has increased concern on the preparedness of the Afghan forces.

Despite these numerous challenges to be overcome in Afghanistan, many remain hopeful that one day Afghanistan will be seen as a land of optimism, freedom, and new beginnings. History has clearly demonstrated that the control of a foreign power in Afghanistan is fleeting. Undoubtedly the future of Afghanistan needs to be left in the hands of its people. This is the goal of supporting countries such as Great Britain and the United States. The ability for Afghanistan to be a prosperous and flourishing country is attainable. However, it must be on the terms of the Afghan citizens. The country is currently in such a delicate state that it could easily descend into another period of civil war and continued unrest in Afghanistan. Only the Afghan people can rebuild this war-ravaged land and cultivate the future of the country.

NOTES

1. Anthony Cordesman, *Afghanistan at Transition: The Lessons of the Longest War* (Washington, DC: Center for Strategic and International Studies [CSIS], 2014), 141–142.

2. Cordesman, "Afghan Metrics."

3. Philip Smucker, "Taliban Talks Open Rift in Kabul Leadership," *The Washington Times*, April 9, 2007, http://www.washingtontimes.com/news/2007/apr/8/20070408–111652–7309r/.

4. Cordesman, *Afghanistan at Transition*, 36.

5. Rashid, *Pakistan on the Brink*, 10, 23–45.

6. Paul Richter, "U.S. Cool to Karzai Plan on Taliban," *Los Angeles Times*, January 29, 2010, http://articles.latimes.com/2010/jan/29/world/la-fg-afghan-meeting-29–2010jan29.

7. The Associated Press, "Report Shows Increase in Afghanistan Opium Poppy Cultivation," *The New York Times*, October 23, 2016. http://www.nytimes.com/aponline/2016/10/23/world/asia/ap-as-afghanistan.html?_r=0.

8. Ibid.

9. Carlotta Gall, "Record Opium Crop Possible in Afghanistan, U.N. Study Predicts," *The New York Times*, March 6, 2007, http://www.nytimes.com/2007/03/06/world/asia/06poppy.html?ei=5090&en=98429154f8b66121&ex=1330837200&partner=rssuserland&emc=rss&pagewanted=print.

10. Goodson, *Afghanistan's Endless War*, 3–4.

11. Ibid., 91–132.

12. Nolan, R. "Global Views: Iraq's Refugees," *Foreign Policy Association Features*, Resource Library, June 12, 2007.

13. "Afghanistan: Ghani, Hekmatya Sign Peace Deal," *Al Jazeera*, http://www.aljazeera.com/news/2016/09/afghanistan-ghani-hekmatyar-sign-peace-deal-160929092524754.html.

14. Ibid.

15. A. Ahmed and M. Rosenberg, "Karzai's Secret Taliban Talks Put Strain on US Relations," *The Irish Times (Dublin)*, February 10, 2014, http://www.irishtimes.com/news/world/asia-pacific/karzai-s-secret-taliban-talks-put-strain-on-us-relations-1.1679167.

16. Ibid.

17. Ibid.

18. Richard Norton-Taylor and Sam Jones, "Afghanistan's Future after NATO Troops Leave Uncertain, Admits Hammond," *The Guardian*, April 10, 2013, http://www.theguardian.com/world/2013/apr/10/afghanistan-future-uncertain-hammond (Accessed October 15, 2015).

Notable People in the History of Afghanistan

Abdali, Ahmad Shah (1720–1772). First emir and ruler of Afghanistan from 1747 to 1772, and he is considered to be the founder of modern Afghanistan. During his reign he continuously worked to expand Afghanistan's borders and created an extensive empire that extended from eastern Persia to northern India. Elected as Ahmad Khan and assumed the name Ahmad Shah Durrani.

Abdullah, Abdullah (1960–). Abdullah Abdullah is an Afghan politician and a doctor of medicine. He was an adviser and a close friend of Ahmad Shah Massoud, the Northern Alliance leader and commander known as the "Lion of Panjshir," who was assassinated in September 2001. Abdullah, who ran against former president Karzai in the 2009 election, received overwhelming Pashtun support for the presidency. Abdullah also ran for president of Afghanistan in the 2014 elections but was defeated by current president Ghani.

Alexander the Great (356 B.C.E.–323 B.C.E.). Considered one of the greatest military leaders in all of history, the king of Macedon conquered most of the known world before his death. In 331 B.C.E., Alexander and his Greek armies deposed the Persian Empire and seized the land known today as Afghanistan.

Asoka the Great (304 B.C.E.–232 B.C.E.). King of the Indian Mauryan Empire and ruler of the Mauryan dynasty from 273 to 232 B.C.E. In 262 B.C.E. at the Battle of Kalinga, after witnessing great destruction and death, he abandoned the life of the sword and embraced Buddhism. His teachings and beliefs in moral behavior were widespread in the southern region of Afghanistan. As the first great political apostle of Buddhism, his teachings are carved on the Rock Pillar Edicts in such locations as Kandahar.

Bashardost, Ramazan (1965–). Ramazan Bashardost is Afghanistan's former planning minister, is a current member of the National Assembly of Afghanistan, and was an independent candidate in the Afghan presidential election in 2009.

Bin Laden, Osama (1957–2011). Former Islamic militant and leader of al-Qaeda, and believed to be the mastermind behind 9/11. Bin Laden and al-Qaeda had allegedly carried out a number of terrorist and guerrilla attacks worldwide including the 9/11 attacks on the World Trade Center and the Pentagon. Bin Laden was sought as one of the FBI's Ten Most Wanted for his involvement in the September 11 attacks, the 1998 U.S. embassy bombings in Dar es Salaam, Tanzania, and Nairobi, Kenya, and also for other world attacks.

Cyrus the Great (590 B.C.E.–530 B.C.E.). Also known as Cyrus II of Persia, he is the founder of the Persian Empire. After conquering the Medes and assuming control of their lands, including in Afghanistan, Cyrus became king of Persia in 559 B.C.E.

Daoud, Zohra Yousuf (1954–). Former Afghani model who won the title of Miss Afghanistan, and used her title to promote literacy throughout the country. She currently works as a social activist for women's rights in Afghanistan.

Darius III (380 B.C.E.–330 B.C.E.). Last king of the Archamenid Empire of Persia and rival of Alexander the Great. Sparring for many years with Alexander, Darius led the Persian army in the Battle of Gaugamela in 330 B.C.E. At the battle, Alexander the Great defeated the Persian Empire. Darius was chased off the battlefield by Alexander and ultimately defeated, but Darius was overthrown and killed by his trusted advisor Bessus.

Daud Daud, Mohammed (1969–2011). Mohammed Daud Daud, also known as General Daud Daud, an ethnic Tajik, was the police chief in northern Afghanistan and the commander of the 303 Pamir Corps. He was an opponent of the Afghan Taliban. In the 1980s, he joined the forces of Ahmad Shah Massoud against the Soviet invasion of Afghanistan. Ahmad Shah Massoud had ordered him to guard northern areas and to keep his forces out of the capital Kabul. When the Taliban took power in Kabul, Daud served as a leading military commander of the anti-Taliban United Front under the command of Ahmad Shah Massoud, which later spearheaded the defeat of the Taliban. After the fall of the Taliban regime, he was appointed deputy interior minister for counter narcotics in Afghanistan. His campaign against poppy cultivation was successful in several provinces, including Ogar, Ghazni, Wardak, Paktia, Paktika, and Panjshir. In 2010 he was appointed police chief of Afghanistan's northern provinces, overseeing interior ministry forces and directly commanding his own police elite force called 303 Pamir Corps. An opponent of the Taliban, Daud was assassinated on May 28, 2011, in a Taliban bomb attack in Taloqan, Afghanistan.

Dostum, Abdul Rashid (1954–). Abdul Rashid Dostum is a former army general during the Soviet war in Afghanistan and is considered by many to be the leader of Afghanistan's Uzbek community. He is currently part of the leadership council of the National Front of Afghanistan along with Ahmad Zia Massoud and Mohammad Mohaqiq, and chairman of his own political party Junbish-e Milli-yi Islami-yi Afghanistan (National Islamic Movement of Afghanistan) or commonly known as *Jumbish*. He is also chairman joint chiefs of staff of the Afghan National Army, a role often viewed as ceremonial. He participated in battles against the mujahideen fighters in the 1980s as well as against the Taliban in the 1990s.

Durand, Sir Henry Mortimer (1850–1924). Diplomat and civil servant to colonial British India, and served as a political secretary in Kabul during the Second Anglo-Afghan War from 1878 to 1880. He is most notably remembered for his negations in 1893 with Amir Abdur Rahman of Afghanistan over what would come to be known as the Pashtunian Issue. His self-created Durand Line was an ethnographic delineation which separated the frontier province between British India and Afghanistan, which eventually resulted in the international border between Afghanistan and Pakistan.

Ghani Ahmadzai, Ashraf (1949–). Ashraf Ghani Ahmadzai is an Afghan politician and was a candidate in the 2014 presidential election. In the 2009 presidential election, he ranked fourth in the polls, behind Hamid Karzai, Abdullah Abdullah, and Ramazan Bashardost. He previously served as finance minister and as a chancellor of Kabul University. As finance minister of Afghanistan between July 2002 and December 2004, he led Afghanistan's attempted economic recovery after the collapse of the Taliban government.

Hamidi, Ghulam Haider (1947–2011). Ghulam Haidar Hamidi and also known as Henry Hamidi was the mayor of Kandahar in Afghanistan. Hamidi graduated with a degree in finance from Kabul University. He spent a brief period in Pakistan and lived in the United States for almost 19 years. In 2007, he returned to Afghanistan when the country was under the Karzai administration. On July 27, 2011, Hamidi was killed in Kandahar by a man who had hidden explosives inside his turban. The target killing or assassination was blamed on the Taliban insurgents, who are guided and supported by foreign elements such as Pakistan's ISI spy agency.

Haqqani, Sirajuddin (1970–). Sirajuddin "Siraj" Haqqani is a Pashtun warlord and military leader from Afghanistan who fights against American and coalition forces from his base within North Waziristan in Pakistan, where it is claimed he provides shelter to al-Qaeda operatives.

Hekmatyar, Gulbuddin (1947–). An Afghan warlord under the mujahideen forces, and served as the prime minister twice during the 1990s. He was also the founder of the Hezb-i-Islami party in 1975, and he is regarded for his measures against Soviet occupation as well as the United States. In 2003 the United States declared Hekmatyar as a global terrorist and longtime ally to Osama bin Laden until his death. Gulbuddin Hekmatyar is a designated "global terrorist" by the United States.

Hotak, Mirwais Khan (1673–1715). A legendary figure and Afghan hero, he was the leader of the Ghilzai tribe and also mayor of Kandahar. In 1709, he assassinated Gurgin Khan, the Georgian governor and tyrant from the Persian court. After the assassination, Mirwais Khan successfully defeated the Persians and ejected them from Afghanistan. Mirwais remained in power until his death in 1715, and is regarded as Afghanistan's first nationalist. As a symbol of his historical significance in Afghanistan, he is entombed in a blue mosque outside of Kandahar.

Jebe (ca. 1165–1225). One of the four prominent generals under Genghis Khan referred to as his "Four Dogs of War." After he wounded Genghis Khan with an arrow in the Battle of the Thirteen Sides in 1201 C.E. and killed his prized war horse, Genghis Khan interrogated the soldiers on who had tried to kill him. Jebe voluntarily confessed his deeds, and Genghis Khan rewarded his honesty and bravery and appointed him to a top position in his army. His birth name was Zurgadai, but Genghis Khan also renamed him Jebe, which means arrowhead in Mongolian. Jebe became one of the best and most loyal commanders to serve under Genghis Khan, and was believed to be second in command to Subutai, his greatest general.

Jelme (ca. 1160– ?). One of the four great generals under Genghis Khan referred to as his "Four Dogs of War." He is the older brother of another of the four generals, Subutai. A descendant of the Uriankhan clan of the Mongols, he served in a high position under Genghis Khan and was a leader of 1,000 men known as a *Mingghan*.

Kanishka I (304 B.C.E.–232 B.C.E.). Indian emperor and ruler of the Kushan dynasty from 273 to 232 B.C.E. He encouraged Asoka's beliefs in Buddhism and promoted a moral way of life. As a tribute to Asoka's teachings and beliefs of Buddhism, King Kanishka had carved into the mountains two large Buddha's statues. Known as the "Buddha's at Bamyan," these stunning figures regrettably were destroyed as part of the Taliban's regime in 2001.

Karmal, Babrak (1929–1996). Karmal was the third president of Afghanistan from 1979 to 1986, reigning during the Soviet invasion of Afghanistan, and was often regarded as a puppet leader for the Soviets. Prior to his political career, he was arrested for his involvement in Marxist activities at Kabul University, and after his time in prison he became a devote communist and friend to the Soviets. Karmal was the leader of the communist regime Parcham after the split in the People's Democratic Party of Afghanistan in 1967.

Karzai, Ahmed Wali (1961–2011). Ahmed Wali Karzai was a prominent politician in Afghanistan and the younger paternal half-brother of Afghan president Hamid Karzai and son of Abdul Ahad Karzai. As an elder of the Popalzai Pashtun tribe, he was elected as chairman of the Kandahar Provincial Council in 2005. Karzai formerly lived in the U.S. city of Chicago, Illinois, where he worked in a restaurant owned by his family. He returned to Afghanistan following the removal of the Taliban government in late 2001. He was shot and killed by one of his bodyguards on July 12, 2011, in an assignation fostered by the Taliban.

Karzai, Hamid (1957–). Hamid Karzai is first and second democratically elected president of Afghanistan. After winning the election in 2004 and again in 2009, Karzai removed many of the former Northern Alliance warlords from his cabinet. During his tenure as president, he worked to form a peace alliance with these warlords rather than fighting to help ensure Afghanistan was not caught in another civil war.

Khalis, Younas Mohammad (1919–2006). As a devote fundamentalist, he assisted in the launching of the Taliban regime in Afghanistan as a mujahideen commander during the Soviet invasion of Afghanistan in 1979. He was a leader of the Hezb-i-Islami (the Party of Islam), the same as Gulbuddin Hekmatyar's party.

Khan, Abdur Rahman (1844–1901). Amir of Afghanistan from 1881 to 1901, he was a strong ruler who reestablished the Afghan government structure after the Second Anglo-Afghan War.

Khan, Amir Amanullah (1892–1960). Ruler of Afghanistan from 1919 to 1929 until he was overthrown by tribal forces and forced into exile. He was well known for leading Afghanistan to achieve complete independence from the British.

Khan, Daoud Mohammed (1909–1978). The first president of Afghanistan from 1973 to 1978 until being killed in a military coup by the Khalq regime. He previously served as the prime minister under King Zahir Shah until being forced to resign in 1963 due to his incessant involvement in the Pashtunian Issue, which contributed to the failing economy in Afghanistan. As president, he was known for his advancement of women's rights and his efforts for increasing employment in Afghanistan.

Khan, Dost Mohammad (1793–1863). He was regarded as an eminent player in the development of Central Asia, particularly as the founder of the Barakzai dynasty in Afghanistan, and ousted Mahmud Khan in 1826. Ruling during the First Anglo-Afghan War in Afghanistan, he was ousted from power by the British and forced into exile.

After his surrender and subsequent release by the British, he formed a strong alliance with the Sikhs of India. He furthered Afghanistan's tribal efforts but died suddenly several months after his victory in Heart.

Khan, Genghis (Temujin) (ca. 1162–1227). Considered one of the most successful military leaders in all of history, he founded the largest contiguous empire known as the Mongol Empire. His birth name was Temujin; he did not have the title of Genghis Khan, or Universal Ruler, until 1206. The Mongol Empire existed from 1206 to 1368, and Genghis Khan invaded and ravaged the region of Afghanistan in 1219.

Khan, Jan Mohammad (ca. 1960–2011). Jan Mohammad Khan was a politician in Afghanistan, who served as governor of Oruzgan Province from January 2002 to March 2006, member of the National Assembly, and a special adviser to President Hamid Karzai. He was an elder of the Popolzai Pashtun tribe in Oruzgan and a close ally of Hamid Karzai.

Lang, Timur (1336–1405). A 14th-century Mongol warrior and conqueror of much of Western and Central Asia. Founder of the Timurid Empire in Central Asia, he conquered and dominated much of Afghanistan in the late 14th century. Due to an injury to his right leg, he was forced to limp, earning him the name Timur Lang, or Timur the Lame.

Mansour, Mullah Akhtar Mohammed (ca. 1968–2015). Leader (emir) of the Taliban after the death of Mullah Mohammed Omar. Mansour was elected on July 29, 2015, although his election was debated and denounced by some Taliban members. He was a mujahedeen fighter during the Soviet occupation of Afghanistan,

Massoud, Ahmad Shah (1953–2001). A well-respected and prominent Afghan mujahedeen leader known as the commander of the Northern Alliance. Massoud was highly regarded for his role in driving the Soviets out of Afghanistan, which earned him the name "The Lion of Panjshir." His ethnic background was of Tajik descent, and he was a Kabul University engineering student who became a prominent Afghan military leader. He became the leader of the United Islamic Front for the Salvation of Afghanistan, and was assassinated by al-Qaeda suicide attackers on September 9, 2001. He was later declared a national hero for his efforts in Afghanistan.

Massoud, Ahmad Zia (1956–). Ahmad Zia Massoud was the vice president of Afghanistan in the first elected administration of President Hamid Karzai, from December 2004 to November 2009. He is a younger brother of Ahmad Shah Massoud, the legendary resistance leader against the Soviet invasion of Afghanistan and against the Taliban. In late 2011, Ahmad Zia Massoud joined hands with major leaders in the National Front of Afghanistan, which strongly opposes a return of the Taliban to power. The National Front is generally regarded as a reformation of the United Front (formerly known as the Northern Alliance) which, with U.S. air support, removed the Taliban from power in late 2001.

Mohaqiq, Mohammad (1955–). Mohammad Mohaqiq is the founder and chairman of the People's Islamic Unity Party of Afghanistan. He had an active role in the war against the Soviet invasion of Afghanistan in 1979, fighting the Soviet army from the northern Balkh Province. After the withdrawal of the Soviet Union from Afghanistan in 1989, Ustad Mohaqiq was appointed as the leader of the Hezb-e Wahdat for northern Afghanistan. During the rule of the Taliban from 1996 onward, Mohaqiq remained one of the few mujahideen leaders who never left the country. He led United Front (Northern Alliance) Hazara resistance forces around Dar-e Suf in Samangan Province and in Yakawlang and Panjab of Bamiyan Province. After the fall of the Taliban, he was appointed as the vice president and the minister of planning in the interim government of Afghanistan. Due to differences between him and the new Afghan president Hamid Karzai as well as Ashraf Ghani (the former finance minister), Mohaqiq was ousted from the cabinet by Hamid Karzai.

Parmenio (400–330 b.c.e.). Macedonian general to Phillip II of Macedon and his successor and son, Alexander the Great. Also known as Parmenion, he was the trusted advisor of Alexander the Great and his second in command of his army. He was stabbed to death under Alexander's orders, believing Parmenion was planning to assassinate him, but alas this was a false charge of treason.

Qublai (ca. 1160– ?). One of the four great generals under Genghis Khan referred to as his "Four Dogs of War."

Rabbani, Burhanuddin (1940–2011). Former president of Afghanistan from 1992 to 1996 until he was ousted by the Taliban invasion in Kabul. He was the leader of Jamiat-e Islami Afghanistan, also known as the Islamic society of Afghanistan. Rabbani also served as the leader of the United Islamic Front for the Salvation of Afghanistan (UIFSA), which allied with various political groups against the Taliban regime.

Rahmani, Nilloofar (1992–). The first female fixed-wing aviator in the Afghan Air Force. Despite continued threats against her and her family from the Taliban, Rahmani continued her training and graduated in July 2012. She received the State Department's International Women of Courage Award in 2015.

Samar, Sima (1957–). The first deputy chair and minister of women's affairs in Afghanistan, she is currently the chairperson of the Afghanistan Independent Human Rights Commission (AIHRC). She is a pioneer for women's rights in Afghanistan, refusing to accept that women must be kept secluded from the public, and she speaks out against wearing the burqa garment. Under the Taliban regime, women were required to wear the burqa and be covered from head to toe, and many women in Afghanistan today suffer from osteomalacia, a softening of the bones due to an insufficient diet and a lack of sunlight.

Seleucus Nicator I (358–281 B.C.E.). A Macedonian general under Alexander the Great, he participated in the revolt and assassination of Perdiccas that resulted in the division of Alexander's empire into four large territories. Seleucus gained control of Alexander's lands in the east and thus began the Seleucid Empire in Afghanistan. After signing a treaty with the Mauryan dynasty, Seleucus ceded all lands south of the Hindu Kush Mountains.

Shah, Mohammad Nadir (1880–1933). King of Afghanistan from 1929 to 1933. He reversed all of King Amunella's reforms and reinstated traditional values. During his reign thousands were killed, imprisoned, or forced to flee to the Soviet Union.

Shah, Timur (1748–1793). The second son of Ahmad Shah Durrani, he assumed the throne upon his father's death in 1772. Previously overthrown after his father left him in control of India in 1757, under his rule as king, the Durrani Empire began to crumble. In 1776, Timur Shah Durrani was forced to move the capital from Kandahar and established Kabul as the capital of Afghanistan.

Shah, Zahir (1914–2007). Zahir Shah has the distinct honor of being the youngest, longest-serving, and last king of Afghanistan. He ruled from 1933 to 1973 until he was ousted in a bloodless coup by the former prime minister Daoud and forced into exile in Italy. Most notably during his reign, he ratified the 1964 constitution and implemented multiple political and economic reforms for the country.

Sherazai, Gul Agha (1954–). Gul Agha Sherazai, also known as Mohammad Shafiq, is a politician in Afghanistan. He is the former governor of Nangarhar Province in eastern Afghanistan as well as the former governor of Kandahar Province. He also was a candidate for Afghanistan's 2014 presidential election.

Subutai (ca. 1175–1248). One of the four great generals under Genghis Khan referred to as his "Four Dogs of War" and his primary military strategist known for his imaginative and sophisticated strategies. He was the younger brother of another of the four generals, Jelmei. A descendent of the Uriankhan clan of the Mongols, he served in a high position and directed more than 20 military campaigns, defeating 32 nations, and is credited with conquering more terrains than any other commander in history.

Taraki, Nur Muhammad (1913–1979). Afghan political figure and founder of the People's Democratic Party of Afghanistan (PDPA). Taraki was also a leader in the political coup in April 1978 that ousted President Daoud, after which Taraki assumed power as the president of Afghanistan from 1978 to 1979. He implemented radical Marxist policies and challenged traditional Afghan values under the Khalq regime until he was overthrown in 1979.

Tarzi, Soraya (1899–1968). As the wife of King Amanullah Khan, Queen Soraya Tarzi was the political face of championing women independence in Afghanistan, and she was also the daughter of Mahmud Tarzi. She was a pioneer in the women's rights movement in Afghanistan, and she was a devout supporter of the enlightenment period for women. Her efforts often gave her the distinction as the first Afghani female activists. Her feminine advancement efforts included education for females and the inclusion of women in political activities. She was the only female ruler of Afghanistan, as the king credited her as the minister of education in Afghanistan. She was the first female ruler to appear in public without her veiled facial covering, and many of her actions and efforts were deemed too progressive for antiquated Afghanistan.

Wardak, Abdul Rahim (1945–). General Abdul Rahim Wardak, an ethnic Pashtun, was the defense minister of Afghanistan. He was appointed on December 23, 2004, by Afghan president Hamid Karzai. Before this appointment, Wardak was the deputy defense minister to the former minister, Mohammed Fahim. During the 1980s' Soviet war in Afghanistan, Wardak had been a national mujahideen resistance leader who fought the Soviet forces. He is an ethnic Pashtun from Wardak Province. He signed an accord with NATO commanders for better cooperation and coordination in counterterrorism operations. In August 2012, Wardak resigned after receiving vote of no confidence from the Afghan Parliament. He was also a candidate of the 2014 presidential election in Afghanistan.

Zoroaster. Iranian prophet and founder of the Middle East religion called Zoroastrianism. His date of birth is highly debated, with estimates ranging from 1200 B.C.E. to 600 B.C.E. His religious beliefs were influential in Afghanistan after the conversion of King Vishtaspa, believed to have occurred in the fifth century B.C.E.

Glossary of Frequently Used Terms

Afridi: A powerful and dominant Pashtun tribe located in eastern Afghanistan, in the region of the Khyber Pass. The Afridi are divided into eight clans and are well known for their part in the 1895 Khyber Rifles.

Aimaq: (Aimak) *A* semi nomadic ethnic group living in the northwestern highlands of Afghanistan, principally located immediately north of Heart.

Allah: The word for God in Arabic, and the term for the only deity in Islam.

al-Qaeda: Term that means "the foundation"; used to describe an international terrorist regime formerly led by Osama bin Laden.

Amir: (Emir) term used as a high title of nobility or office, such as commander or ruler.

Areia: Ancient term for western Afghanistan centered near Herat.

azaan: The Islamic call for the five daily prayers.

Bactria: Ancient term for northern Afghanistan.

badal: The Pashtun law of revenge.

bad-dadan: The custom by which a woman was given away in marriage to compensate for a crime.

Badshahgardi: Translated as "ruler turning," term used to describe a period of transition from one ruler family to another.

baksheesh: A Middle Eastern term of several meanings, which can describe a charitable contribution to beggars, a tip as a sign of gratitude or respect, and also as a bribe paid to corrupt government officials.

Barakzai: A major sect of the Pashtun Clan, notably a subtribe of the Durrani Pashtuns and descendants have ruled as kings since 1835.

burqa: Head-to-toe covering designed to conceal the identity of the female.

buzkashi: A traditional Afghani game played on horseback in which the headless carcass of a calf or goat is the object sought after by the opposing teams.

chadari: The traditional veiled clothing for women to wear in public; it is a veiled garment worn by Pashtun women in Afghanistan. The chadari has a mesh opening for the eyes, and is worn over regular clothing. This is different from the Afghan burqa, which covers a woman's facial features so she is completely covered from head to toe.

Dari: A dialect of the Persian language spoken predominantly in Afghanistan, locally known as Farsi.

dupatta: A long shawl or scarf worn by women around the head or neck, and worn when dressed in shalwar kameez.

e'dam: Afghanistan term for capital punishment.

emam: Term to describe a religious leader.

fakir: A holy man, one who is a sufi and especially one who performs unbelievable or magical acts, often used to refer to a spiritual recluse or a beggar.

Farsi: Local name for one of the two main languages spoken in Afghanistan, and of Persian dialect.

Gandamak, Treaty of: Treaty signed on May 26, 1879, by the Afghans and the British to officially end the Second Anglo-Afghan War. The treaty gave the British control of Afghan territory and would prevent further invasion in the country, but many Afghan people saw it as a humiliation.

ghaza: A type of holy war and used as a term for battle.

Ghazi: A 19th-century term for Afghan religious warriors.

Ghilzai: One of the two largest groups of the Pashtun tribe of eastern and northern Afghanistan, and the most populous Pashtun tribe in Afghanistan.

Hajj: The pilgrimage to Mecca, one of five Muslim religious duties and a rite of passage in Islam.

Hajji: A Muslim who has completed the pilgrimage to Mecca.

Hanafi: *The oldest of the* four major schools of Islamic law within Sunni Islam, and is dominant in over 80 percent of the Sunni population in Afghanistan.

Hazara: An ethnic group residing in the mountains of central Afghanistan, mostly of Mongolian origin.

hejab: The Taliban enforcement of the seclusion of women from society.

hoquq-i-zanan: Term that refers to women's rights.

hudud: Term to describe the Islamic law rules of social behavior and the penalties for crimes, including severe punishment for acts such as theft, which includes amputations.

jaza: Term for punishment.

jihad: Religious holy war and struggle in defense of Islam against attackers or infidels.

jirga: An assembly of tribal elders or leaders.

khan: A title used to mean lord of chief, and is considered an elite title of respect.

Khyber Pass: An important and historic pass connecting Pakistan to the Afghan border. Historically it has been a vital trade route and strategic military location.

Khyber Rifles: A paramilitary corps during the British rule, comprised of members of the Afridi tribe and the Pakistani army that protected the Khyber Pass.

Koran (Qu'ran): The sacred book of Islam.

Kurka: The holy cloak of the Prophet Mohammed. The cloak was presented to Ahmad Shah Durrani by the Emir of Bangladesh as a gift for the agreement.

loya jirgah: A tradition that is at least 1,000 years old, the term describes a grand assembly or great council as a large meeting. Participants include great political, military, and religious leaders. There are no time limits, and the meeting is held until a consensus can be reached.

madrasa: The Arabic word for school, usually in reference to an Islamic schoolhouse or college.

mahr: A tradition in Islamic marriage, it is a marriage offering from the groom to the bride, and is a gift only for her and not for her father.

masjid: A mosque or a place of worship in the Islamic faith.

Meli Shura: The highest legislative body in Afghanistan.

Mingghan: A unit of 1,000 men as developed under Genghis Khan and his revolutionary approach to dividing men into military units as small as ten.

Mujabedin (mujahadeen): Arabic term for holy warriors of Islam in the Middle East. In Afghanistan, the best-known mujahadeen were the Afghan opposition groups that fought against the Soviet invasion from 1979 to 1989.

Mullah: A religious priest or teacher on Islamic rules and traditions known as Islamic clergy.

Naan: A popular bread item for food, it is a round flatbread similar to pita bread, and is a staple item to hot meals in Afghanistan.

namaaz (salat): Refers to ritual prayers said five times daily by Islamic followers.

namus: An ethical essence for men and households in Afghanistan, it describes the defense of the honor of women in the household.

Northern Alliance: Led by Ahmed Shah Massoud, a coalition of non-Pashtun parties that fought against the rule of the Taliban and, with the U.S assistance, succeeded in the overthrow of the Taliban in 2001.

Noyan: Mongolian term for general.

Paiza: An amulet worn around the neck of the yam network riders under Genghis Khan. The paiza was a revered item in Mongolian culture.

Pashtun (Pushtun): A major ethnic tribe living in eastern and southern Afghanistan characterized by their Pashto language and their following of Pashtunwali.

Pashtunwali: A pre-Islamic religious code of honor.

Pushto: One of the two main languages spoken in Afghanistan and is predominantly spoken by the people in southeastern Afghanistan.

qarez: An underground aqueduct system unique to Afghanistan and Iran.

rajm: An Arabic term that means "to stone" as a punishment for adultery.

Ramadan (Ramazan): The Fourth Pillar of Islam, it is a month-long period of religious fasting from sunrise to sunset where purity of action and thought are observed throughout the day.

Rawalpindi, Treaty of: A peace treaty signed by the United Kingdom and Afghanistan on August 8, 1919, at the end of the Third Anglo-Afghan War. The terms of the treaty gave Afghanistan independence, established that the British Empire would not extend beyond the Khyber Pass, and ceased British subsidies into Afghanistan.

Salat: The Second Pillar of Islam that calls for ritual prayers or worship.

sarkar (sirkar): Term used to describe the government or an historical administrative unit.

satrap: In ancient history, a term originated by Cyrus the Great, it is the given name of the governors of the empire's provinces. Alexander the Great revised the satrap system when his Macedonian army conquered the Persians, and reduced the satrap powers of such authority as commanding the troops and issuing coinage. In modern times, the term is also used to describe world leaders who are influenced by larger world superpowers.

Sawm: The Third Pillar of Islam, it is the act of fasting during the month of Ramadan.

sayyid: Honorific title given to Afghanistan's holy men and traditional healers.

Shahadat: The First Pillar of Islam, it is the belief that Allah is the only God and that his messenger is the Prophet Mohammed.

Shahria: The body of Islamic law.

Sunni: A major Islamic sect that represents more than 80 percent of Afghanistan's population.

Tajik: A major ethnic group in northeastern Afghanistan and in the cities of Kabul, Mazari Sharif, and Herat.

talib (taleb): The Arabic word for a student of a madrasa school.

Taliban (Taleban): An extreme Islamic fundamentalist group that effectively overthrew Afghanistan in 1996 and remained in control until 2001. The term is a plural form of the word *talib* and represents students of religious madrasas in Pakistan and Afghanistan.

Uzbek: One of the major ethnic groups in Afghanistan, located in the plains and are primarily farmers and herders.

velayat: An administrative division or province.

wazir (vizier): Literally meaning "burden bearer" in Persian, refers to a high-ranking political or religious advisor to a Muslim monarch.

Yam network: A collection of communication points developed by Genghis Khan. Messengers traveled up to 300 kilometers a day to relay messages during battle.

Zakat: The Fourth Pillar of Islam known as charity, it refers to the paying of alms or giving to the poor based on a percentage of income.

Timeline of Rulers of Afghanistan

Ancient Civilization	
Proto-Elamite civilization	2300–1800 B.C.E.
Indus valley civilization	2200–1800 B.C.E.
Oxus civilization	2100–1800 B.C.E.
Aryans	1700–700 B.C.E.
Medes	728–550 B.C.E.
Achaemenids	550–330 B.C.E.
Seleucids	330–150 B.C.E.
Mauryans	305–180 B.C.E.
Greco-Bactrians	256–125 B.C.E.
Indo-Greeks	180–130 B.C.E.
Indo-Scythians (Sakas)	155–80 B.C.E.
Indo-Parthians	20 B.C.–50 C.E.
Kushans	135 B.C.–248 C.E.
Sasanians	230–484

(Continued)

(Continued)

Ancient Civilization	
Kidarites	320–465
Hephthalites	410–557

Medieval Era	
Sasanians	512–651
Kabul Shahi	565–879
Rashidun Caliphate	642–641
Umayyads	661–750
Abbasids	750–821
Tahirids	821–873
Saffarids	863–900
Samanids	875–999
Ghaznavids	963–1187
Ghorids	1149–1215
Khwarezmids	1215–1231
Ilkhanate	1258–1353
Khiljis	1290–1320
Kurts	1245–1381
Timurids	1370–1506
Arghuns	1479–1522
Mughals	1501–1738
Safavids	1510–1709

Modern Afghanistan	
Hotaki Empire	1709–1738
Afsharid dynasty	1738–1747
Durrani Empire	1747–1826
Emirate of Afghanistan	1826–1919
Kingdom of Afghanistan	1919–1973
Republic of Afghanistan	1973–1978
Democratic Republic of Afghanistan	1978–1992
Islamic State of Afghanistan	1992–2001
Islamic Emirate of Afghanistan	1996–2001
Interim/Transitional Administration	2001–2004
Islamic Republic of Afghanistan	2004–Present

Chronological List of Recent Leaders of Afghanistan

Name	Birth–Death	Took Office	Left Office	Political Party
Mohammed Daoud Khan	1909–1978	July 17, 1973	April 28, 1978	Independent (until 1976)
Abdul Qadir	1944–2014	April 28, 1978	April 30, 1978	People's Democratic Party
Nur Muhammad Taraki	1917–1979	April 30, 1978	September 14, 1979	People's Democratic Party
Hafizullah Amin	1929–1979	September 14, 1979	December 27, 1979	People's Democratic Party
Babrak Karmal	1929–1996	December 27, 1979	November 24, 1986	People's Democratic Party
Haji Mohammad Chamkani	1947–2012	November 24, 1986	September 30, 1987	Independent

(*Continued*)

Name	Birth–Death	Took Office	Left Office	Political Party
Mohammad Najibullah	1947–1996	September 30, 1987	April 16, 1992	People's Democratic Party
Abdul Rahim Hatif	1926–2013	April 16, 1992	April 28, 1992	Democratic Watan Party
Sibghatullah Mojaddedi	1926–	April 28, 1992	June 28, 1992	National Liberation Front of Afghanistan
Burhanuddin Rabbani	1940–2011	June 28, 1992	September 27, 1996	Jamiat-e Islami (Northern Alliance)
Mullah Mohammed Omar		September 27, 1996	November 13, 2001	Taliban
Burhanuddin Rabbani	1940–2011	November 13, 2001	December 22, 2001	Jamiat-e Islami (Northern Alliance)
Hamid Karzai	1957–	December 22, 2001	September 29, 2014	Independent
Mohammad Ashraf Ghani	1949–	September 29, 2014	Incumbent	Independent

Bibliography

The author has included books that have been referenced or cited while writing *The History of Afghanistan*. Included are those books that are readily available in most libraries or on the Internet. These texts may also be helpful for those interested in exploring more details on the topics presented in this book in order to perform more in-depth research.

Ahmed, Asam, and Matthew Rosenberg. "Karzai's Secret Taliban Talks Put Strain on US Relations." *The Irish Times*, February 5, 2014. Accessed November 6, 2016. http://www.irishtimes.com/news/world/asia-pacific/karzai-s-secret-taliban-talks-put-strain-on-us-relations-1.1679167.

Aizenman, N. C. "Afghan Jew Becomes Country's One and Only." *The Washington Post*, January 27, 2005. Accessed November 6, 2016. http://www.washingtonpost.com/wp-dyn/articles/A39702–2005Jan26.html.

The American Presidency Project. "Ronald Reagan State of the Union Address of February 6, 1985." Accessed November 15, 2015. http://www.presidency.ucsb.edu/ws/index.php?pid=38069.

Armstrong, Sally. *Veiled Threat: The Hidden Power of the Women of Afghanistan*. New York: Four Walls Eight Windows Publishing, 2002.

The Associated Press. "Navy SEALs Knew bin Laden Mission Was One-Shot Deal." FoxNews.com, May 17, 2011. Accessed April 30, 2014. http://www.foxnews.com/politics/2011/05/17/sources-navy-seals-knew-bin-laden-mission-shot-deal/.

The Associated Press. "Report Shows Increase in Afghanistan Opium Poppy Cultivation." *The New York Times*, October 23, 2016. Accessed November 6, 2016. http://www.nytimes.com/aponline/2016/10/23/world/asia/ap-as-afghanistan.html?_r=0.

Barfield, Thomas. *Afghanistan: A Cultural and Political History*. Princeton, NJ: Princeton University Press, 2010.

Bergen, Peter L. *Holy War, Inc.: Inside the Secret World of Osama Bin Laden*. New York: Free Press, 2001.

Bergen, Peter L. *Man Hunt: The Ten-Year Search for Bin Laden from 9/11 to Abbottabad*. New York: Crown Publishers, 2012.

Bernard, Cheryl. *Veiled Courage: Inside the Afghan Women's Resistance*. New York: Broadway Books, 2002.

Bin Laden, Osama. "Full Transcript of Bin Laden's Speech." Aljazeera.net (Al Jazeera), November 1, 2004. Accessed April 30, 2014. http://www.aljazeera.com/archive/2004/11/200849163336457223.html.

Bowen, Donna Lee, and Evelyn A. Early. *Everyday Life in the Muslim Middle East*. 2nd ed. Bloomington: Indiana University Press, 2002.

Bowden, Mark. *The Finish: The Killing of Osama Bin Laden*. New York: Atlantic Monthly Press, 2012.

Briant, Pierre. *Alexander the Great: Man of Action, Man of Spirit*. New York: Harry N. Abrams, Inc., 1996.

Brulliard, Karin. "Pakistan to Return U.S. Helicopter Tail, Kerry says." *The Washington Post*, May 16, 2011. Accessed April 30, 2014. http://www.washingtonpost.com/world/sen-john-kerry-arrives-in-pakistan-for-meetings-that-could-sway-future-us-aid-prospects/2011/05/16/AFJJIZ4G_story.html.

Bumiller, Elisabeth, Carotta Gall, and Salman Masood. "Bin Laden's Secret Life in a Diminished World." *The New York Times*, May 7, 2011. Accessed October 11, 2015. http://www.nytimes.com/2011/05/08/world/asia/08binladen.html?pagewanted=1&_r=0.

Cantor, Norman F. with Dee Ranieri. *Alexander the Great: Journey to the End of the Earth*. New York: HarperCollins, 2005.

Carnevale, Mary Lu. "Tracking Use of bin Laden's Satellite Phone." *The Wall Street Journal*, May 28, 2008. Accessed May 8, 2015. http://blogs.wsj.com/washwire/2008/05/28/tracking-use-of-bin-ladens-satellite-phone/

Chandrasekaran, Rajiv. *Little America: The War within the War for Afghanistan*. New York: Alfred Knopf, a Division of Random House, 2012.

Constable, Pamela. "A Poor Yield for Afghans' War on Drugs." *The Washington Post Foreign Service*, September 19, 2006.

Cordesman, Anthony H. *Afghanistan at Transition: The Lessons of the Longest War*. Washington, DC: Center for Strategic and International Studies (CSIS), 2014.

Cordesman, Anthony H. *Afghanistan at Transition: The Lessons of the Longest War*. Washington, DC: Center for Strategic and International Studies (CSIS), 2014.

Cordesman, Anthony H. "Afghan Metrics: How to Lose a War— and Possibly How to Win One." *Center for Strategic and International Studies (CSIS)*, January 12, 2010. Accessed August 10, 2016. https://www.csis.org/analysis/afghan-metrics.

Corera, Gordon. "Analysis: Bin Laden Papers Detail." *BBC News*, May 3, 2012. Accessed April 30, 2014. http://www.bbc.com/news/world-us-canada-17943175.

Coll, Steve. *Ghost Wars: The Secret History of the CIA, Afghanistan, and bin Laden, from the Soviet Invasion to September 10, 2001*. New York: Penguin Press. 2004.

Cooley, John K. *Unholy Wars: Afghanistan, America, and International Terrorism*. 2nd ed. Sterling: Pluto Press, 2000.

David, Ibsy, *Afghanistan: Graveyard of Empires: A New History of the Borderland*. New York: Pegasus Books, 2010.

De Vogue, Ariane. "Was Killing of Osama bin Laden Legal under International Law?" *ABC News*, May 6, 2011. Accessed April 30, 2014. http://abcnews.go.com/Politics/osama-bin-laden-killing-legal-international-law/story?id=13538365.

Dixon, Norm. "How the CIA Created Osama bin Laden." *Green Left Weekly*, September 19, 2001, Issue #465.

Dupree, Louis. *Shamir Ghar: Historic Cave Site in Kandahar Province, Afghanistan*. New York: Anthological Papers of the American Museum of Natural History 46, No. 2, 1958.

Dupree, Louis, J. Lawrence Angel, Robert H. Brill, Earle R. Caley, Richard S. Davis, Charles C. Kolb, Alexander Marshack, Dexter Perkins, and Alan Solem. "Prehistoric Research in Afghanistan (1959–1966)." *Transactions of the American Philosophical Society* 62, no. 4 (1972): 1–84. doi:10.2307/1005969.

Dupree, Nancy. "An Historical Guide to Afghanistan." Afghan Tourist Organization. 1970. Referenced at http://www.zharov.com/dupree/chapter23.html.

Emadi, Hafizullah. *Culture and Customs of Afghanistan*. Westport, CT: Greenwood Press, 2005.

Ewans, Martin. *Afghanistan: A Short History of Its People and Politics*. New York: HarperCollins, 2002.

Farahi, Abdul G. Translated by Juma Khan Sufi. *Afghanistan during Democracy and Republic: 1963–1978*. Kabul: UNO Education Press, 2004.

Felbab-Brown, Vanda. "The Implications of Osama bin Laden's Death for the War in Afghanistan and Global Counterterrorism Efforts." *Brookings.Edu*, May 2, 2011. Accessed October 25, 2015. http://www.brookings.edu/blogs/up-front/posts/2011/05/02-bin-laden-afghanistan-felbabbrown.

Filkins, Dexter Carlotta Gall. "Fake Afghan Poll Sites Favored Karzai, Officials Assert." *The New York Times*, September 6, 2009. Accessed August 10, 2016. http://www.nytimes.com/2009/09/07/world/asia/07fraud.html?hpw=&pagewanted=all&_r=0.

Gall, Carlotta. "Record Opium Crop Possible in Afghanistan, U.N. Study Predicts." *The New York Times*, March 6, 2007.

Gannon, Kathy. "Taliban Suspends Talks with U.S. about Exchange of Captive Soldier for Gitmo Detainees." *The Huffington Post*, February 23, 2014. Accessed April 30, 2014. http://www.huffingtonpost.com/2014/02/23/taliban-suspends-talks-with-us-bowe-bergdahl_n_4840770.html?utm_hp_ref=tw.

Gerges, Fawaz A. *The Rise and Fall of Al-Qaeda*. New York: Oxford University Press, 2011.

Gohari, M. J. *The Taliban: Ascent to Power*. Oxford: Oxford University Press, 2001.

Goldman, Adam, and Matt Apuzzo. "Osama bin Laden Dead: How One Phone Call Led U.S. to Bin Laden's Doorstep." *Huffington Post*, May 2, 2011. Accessed October 25, 2015. http://www.huffingtonpost.com/2011/05/02/osama-bin-laden-dead-one-phone-call_n_856674.html.

Goldman, Adam, and Matt Apuzzo. "Phone Call by Kuwaiti Courier Led to Bin Laden." Associated Press, May 3, 2011. Accessed October 25, 2015. abcnews.go.com/US/wirestory?id=13512344.

Goldschmidt, Arthur Jr. *A Concise History of the Middle East*. 7th ed. Cambridge: Westview Press, 2002.

Goodson, Larry P. *Afghanistan's Endless War: State Failure, Regional Politics, and the Rise of the Taliban*. Seattle: The University of Washington Press, 2001.

Griffin, Michael. *Reaping the Whirlwind: Afghanistan, Al-Qa'ida and the Holy War*. Sterling: Pluto Press, 2003.

Heibert, Frederick Talmage. *Origins of the Bronze Age Oasis Civilizations in Central Asia*. Cambridge, MA: Harvard University Press, 1994.

Hendawi, Hamza. "Osama bin Laden Dead: Muslim Scholar Says Al Qaeda Leader's Sea Burial 'Humiliates' Muslims." *The Huffington*

Post, May 2, 2011. Accessed October 11, 2015. http://www.huffington post.com/2011/05/02/osama-bin-laden-sea-burial-muslim-scholars_ n_856315.html.

Hersh, Seymour. "The Killing of Osama bin Laden." *The London Review of Book*, May 21, 2015. Accessed October 11, 2015. http://www .lrb.co.uk/v37/n10/seymour-m-hersh/the-killing-of-osama-bin-laden.

Hildinger, Erik. *Warriors of the Steppe: A Military History of Central Asia, 500 B.C. to 1700 A.D.* New York: Sarpedon, 1997.

Hopkirk, Peter. *The Great Game: The Struggle for Empire in Central Asia.* New York: Kodansha America, Inc., Reprint Edition. 1994. (Author's note: First published in Great Britain in 1990 as *The Great Game: On Secret Service in High Asia* by John Murray Publishers, Ltd.)

Imatiz, Saba. "Key Al Qaeda Operative Lived in Abbottabad in 2003." *The Tribune*, May 2, 2011. Accessed April 30, 2014. http://tribune.com .pk/story/161650/key-al-qaeda-operative-lived-in-abbottabad-in-2003/.

Johnson, Kay. "Afghanistan Presidential Election Set for Second Round Runoff." *The Huffington Post*, April 26, 2014. Accessed April 30, 2014. http://www.huffingtonpost.com/2014/04/26/afghanistan-elec tion-runoff_n_5218446.html.

Jones, Ann. *Kabul in Winter: Life without Peace in Afghanistan.* New York: Metropolitan Books, 2006.

Kaplan, Robert D. "Afghanistan Postmortem." *Atlantic Monthly* 263, no. 4 (April 1989): 26–29.

Kaplan, Robert D. "The Coming Anarchy." *Atlantic Monthly* 273, no. 2 (February 1994): 44–76.

Kaplan, Robert D. "The Lawless Frontier." *Atlantic Monthly* 286, no. 3 (September 2000): 66–80.

Kaplan, Robert D. *Soldiers of God: With Islamic Warriors in Afghanistan and Pakistan.* New York: Vintage Departures Edition, 2001.

Keegan, John. "The Ordeal of Afghanistan." *Atlantic Monthly* 256, no. 5 (November 1985): 94–105.

Kroft, Steve. "Osama on bin Laden: The Full 60 Minutes Interview." *60 Minutes*, May 4, 2011.

Landsberg, Mitchell. "Dalai Lama Suggests Osama bin Laden's Death Was Justified." *The Los Angeles Times*, May 4, 2011. Accessed April 30, 2014. http://articles.latimes.com/2011/may/04/local/la-me-0504-dalai-lama-20110504.

Lewis, Bernard. *The Middle East: A Brief History of the Last 2,000 Years.* New York: Scribner, 1995.

Londoño, Ernesto. "Study: Iraq, Afghan War Costs to Top $4 trillion." *The Washington Post*, March 28, 2013. Accessed October 15, 2016. https://www.washingtonpost.com/world/national-security/

study-iraq-afghan-war-costs-to-top-4-trillion/2013/03/28/b82a5dce-97ed-11e2-814b-063623d80a60_story.html?utm_term=.5cf92e52d3f9.

Longstreth, Andrew. "Analysis: Legal Questions Remain over bin Laden Killing." *Reuters*, May 5, 2011. Accessed April 30, 2014. http://www.reuters.com/article/2011/05/05/us-binladen-usa-legal-id USTRE7442NA20110505.

Maley, William, ed. *Fundamentalism Reborn? Afghanistan and the Taliban*. New York: New York University Press, 2001.

Maley, William, and Contributors. *Fundamentalism Reborn? Afghanistan and the Taliban*. New York: New York University Press, 1998.

Maloney, Sean M. *Enduring the Freedom: A Rogue Historian in Afghanistan*. Washington, DC: Potomac Books, Inc., 2005.

Man, John. *Genghis Khan: Life, Death, and Resurrection*. New York: Thomas Dunne Books of St. Martin's Press, 2004.

Mansfield, Peter. *A History of the Middle East*. New York: Viking, 1991.

Margolis, Eric S. *War at the Top of the World: The Struggle for Afghanistan, Kashmir, and Tibet*. New York: Routledge, 2000.

Marozzi, Justin. *Tamerlane: Sword of Islam, Conqueror of the World*. Cambridge: De Capo Press, 2004. Originally published: London: HarperCollins, 2004.

Marsden, Peter. *The Taliban: War, Religion, and the New Order of Afghanistan*. New York: St. Martin's Press, Inc., 1998.

Martin, Chris. *Beyond Neptune Spear: The (Open) Secret History of SEAL Team Six, Post-9/11*. Ebook: Imprint Smashwords Edition, 2012.

Mason, Colin. *A Short History of Asia: Stone Age to 2000 A.D.* New York: St. Martin's Press, 2000.

Matinuddin, Kamal. *The Taliban Phenomenon: Afghanistan 1994–1997*. Oxford: Oxford University Press, 1999.

Meyer, Karl. *The Dust of Empire: The Race for Mastery in the Asian Heartland*. New York: The Century Foundation, 2003.

Miller, Greg. "Al-Qaeda Is Weaker without bin Laden, but Its Franchise Persists." *The Washington Post*, April 28, 2012. Accessed October 25, 2015. http://www.washingtonpost.com/world/national-security/manhunt-details-us-mission-to-find-osama-bin-laden/2012/04/27/gIQAz5pLoT_story.html.

Mohmand, Abdul-Qayum. *American Foreign Policy toward Afghanistan: 1919–2001*. Ann Arbor, MI: ProQuest Information and Learning, 2007.

Moore, Robin. *The Hunt for Bin Laden: Task Force Dagger*. New York: Random House, 2003.

Morgan, David. *The Mongols*. Cambridge: Blackwell Publishers, 1986.

Mulrine, Anna. "Military Interrogators: Waterboarding Didn't Yield Tips That Led to bin Laden." *The Christian Science Monitor*, May 5, 2011. Accessed October 25, 2015. http://www.csmonitor.com/USA/Military/2011/0505/Military-interrogators-Waterboarding-didn-t-yield-tips-that-led-to-bin-Laden.

Myrdal, Jan, and Gun Kessle. *Gates to Asia: A Diary from a Long Journey.* New York: Pantheon Books, 1971.

Nauman, Qasim. "U.S. Links Pakistan to Group It Blames for Kabul Attack." *Reuters*, September 17, 2011. Accessed October 25, 2015. http://www.reuters.com/article/2011/09/17/us-pakistan-usa-haqqani-idUSTRE78G1RM20110917.

Nawa, Fariba. *Opium Nation: Child Brides, Drug Lords, and One Woman's Journey through Afghanistan.* New York: Harper Perennial, 2011.

Nawid, Senzil K. *Religious Response to Social Change in Afghanistan 1919–29.* Costa Mesa: Mazda Publishers, 1999.

9/11 Commission Staff Report. "Improvising a Homeland Defense," Staff Statement No. 17. Accessed April 30, 2014. http://govinfo.library.unt.edu/911/staff_statements/staff_statement_17.pdf.

Nojumi, Neamatollah. *The Rise of the Taliban in Afghanistan: Mass Mobilization, Civil War, and the Future of the Region.* New York: Palgrave, 2002.

Padgett, Tim. "The Interrupted Reading: The Kids with George W. Bush on 9/11." *TIME Magazine*, May 3, 2011. Accessed October 25, 2015. http://content.time.com/time/magazine/article/0,9171,2069582,00.html.

Partlow, Jonathan. "Osama bin Laden Is Killed; Afghanistan Reacts." *The Washington Post*, May 2, 2011. Accessed October 11, 2015. https://www.washingtonpost.com/national/osama-bin-laden-is-killed-afghanistan-reacts/2011/05/01/AFioA9VF_story.html.

Pfarrer, Chuck. *SEAL Target GERONIMO: The Inside Story of the Mission to Kill Osama bin Laden.* New York: St. Martin's Press, 2011.

Pitts, Michael W., and Mark Roberts. *Fairweather Eden: Life Half a Million Years Ago as Revealed by the Excavations at Boxgrove.* 1st ed. New York: Fromm International, 1998.

Randal, Jonathan. *Osama: The Making of a Terrorist.* New York: Knopf, Distributed by Random House, 2004.

Rashid, Ahmed. *Decent into Chaos: The U.S. and the Disaster in Pakistan, Afghanistan, and Central Asia.* New York: Penguin, 2008.

Rashid, Ahmed. *Jihad: The Rise of Militant Islam in Central Asia.* New Haven, CT: Yale University Press, 2002.

Rashid, Ahmed. *Pakistan on the Brink: The Future of America, Pakistan, and Afghanistan*. New York: The Penguin Group, 2012.

Rashid, Ahmed. *Taliban: Militant Islam, Oil, and Fundamentalism in Central Asia*. New Haven, CT: Yale University Press, 2000.

Richter, Paul. "U.S. Cool to Karzai Plan on Taliban." *Los Angeles Times*, January 29, 2010. Accessed October 25, 2015. http://articles.latimes.com/2010/jan/29/world/la-fg-afghan-meeting-29–2010jan29.

Risen, James. "U.S. Identifies Vast Mineral Riches in Afghanistan." *The New York Times*, June 13, 2010. Accessed October 25, 2015. http://www.nytimes.com/2010/06/14/world/asia/14minerals.html?pagewanted=all&_r=0.

Roberts, Fiona. "'For God and Country—Geronimo, Geronimo, Geronimo': The Words the SEAL Who Killed Osama Bin Laden Radioed Home—And Why No-One Will Ever Know His Identity." *The Daily Mail*, August 2, 2011. Accessed October 25, 2015. http://www.dailymail.co.uk/news/article-2021260/Osama-Bin-Laden-Full-details-raid-catch-Al-Qaeda-leader-know-SEALs-identity.html.

Rosen, James. "Gates Says U.S. Forces in Afghanistan for 'Years' to Come." *Fox News*, September 2, 2010. Accessed October 25, 2015. http://www.foxnews.com/politics/2010/09/02/gates-start-afghanistan-troop-pullout-debate/.

Rosenberg, Joel C. *Inside the Revolution: How the Followers of Jihad, Jefferson, and Jesus Are Battling to Dominate the Middle East and Transform the World*. Carol Stream, IL: Tyndale House Publishers, 2009.

Roy, Oliver. *Islam and Resistance in Afghanistan*. 2nd ed. Cambridge: Cambridge University Press, 1990.

Roy, Oliver. *The Politics of Chaos in the Middle East*. New York: Columbia University Press, 2008.

Rubin, Barnett R. *The Fragmentation of Afghanistan: State Formation and Collapse in the International System*. 2nd ed. New Haven, CT: Yale University Press, 2002.

Rubin, Elizabeth. "Karzai in His Labyrinth." *The New Yok Times*, August 9, 2009. Accessed 25 October 2015. http://www.nytimes.com/2009/08/09/magazine/09Karzai-t.html?_r=0.

Russel, Malcolm B., and Ray Cleveland. *The Middle East and South Asia*. 39th ed. Harpers Ferry, WV: Stryker-Post Publications, 2005.

Saikal, Amin. *Modern Afghanistan: A History of Struggle and Survival*. 1st ed. London; New York: I.B. Tauris & Co., 2006.

Sargent, Greg. "John McCain to Bush Apologists: Stop Lying about bin Laden and Torture." *The Washington Post*, May 12, 2011. Accessed October 25, 2015. http://www.washingtonpost.com/blogs/

plum-line/post/john-mccain-to-bush-apologists-stop-lying-about-bin-laden-and-torture/2011/03/03/AF10AnzG_blog.html.

Sarin, Oleg, and Lev Dvoretsky. *The Afghan Syndrome: The Soviet Union's Vietnam.* Novato, CA: Presidio Press, 1993.

Schroen, Gary C. *First In: An Insider's Account of How the CIA Spearheaded the War on Terror in Afghanistan.* New York: Presidio Press, 2005.

Seiff, Kevin. "A Fight for Afghanistan's Most Famous Artifact." *The Washington Post*, December 29, 2012. Accessed October 25, 2015. http://www.washingtonpost.com/world/a-fight-for-afghanistans-most-famous-artifact/2012/12/29/ab2dc394–51cb-11e2–835b-02f92c0daa43_story_1.html.

Shahzad, Asif. "Pakistan Condemns US Comments about Spy Agency." *The Associated Press*, September 23, 2011. Accessed October 25, 2015. http://news.yahoo.com/pakistan-condemns-us-comments-spy-agency-044440789.html;_ylt=A2KJ3vVYX3xOdRkA9EZXNyoA?rnd=00568125300417493071441 3.

Shelala, Robert M., et al. "U.S. and Iranian Strategic Competition: The Impact of Afghanistan, Pakistan, India, and Central Asia." *Center for Strategic and International Studies (CSIS)*, June 26, 2012. Accessed October 25, 2015. http://csis.org/files/publication/130626_AfPak_Asia.pdf.

Sief, Martin. "Terrorist Is Driven by Hatred for U.S., Israel." *The Washington Times*, August 21, 1998. Accessed October 25, 2015. https://www.highbeam.com/doc/1G1–56776487.html.

Smucker, Philip. "Taliban Talks Open Rift in Kabul Leadership." *The Washington Times*, April 9, 2007. Accessed October 25, 2015. http://www.washingtontimes.com/news/2007/apr/8/20070408–111652–7309r/.

Stewart, Jules. *The Khyber Rifles: From the British Raj to Al Qaeda.* Stroud, UK: Sutton Publishing, 2005.

Stossel, Sage. "Understanding Afghanistan." *Atlantic Monthly*, October 2001, 24–32.

Stroup, Herbert. *Founders of Living Religions.* Philadelphia, PA: The Westminster Press, 1974.

Tang, Alisa. "Afghan 1,423 Afghan Artifacts Return to Kabul." *The Washington Post*, March 18, 2007. Accessed October 25, 2015. http://www.washingtonpost.com/wp-dyn/content/article/2007/03/18/AR2007031800207.html.

Tanner, Stephen. *Afghanistan: A Military History from Alexander the Great to the Fall of the Taliban.* New York: Da Capo Press, 2002.

Tapper, Jake. *The Outpost: An Untold Story of American Valor.* New York: Little, Brown, and Company, 2012.

Thapar, Romila. *Asoka and the Decline of the Mauryas*. New York: Oxford University Press, 1960.

Tomsen, Peter. *The Wars of Afghanistan: Messianic Terrorism, Trial Conflicts, and the Failures of Great Powers*. New York: Public Affairs, 2011.

Wahab, Shaista, and B. Youngerman. *A Brief History of Afghanistan, Second Edition*. New York: Infobase Publishing, 2010.

Walsh, Declan. "Osama bin Laden Killing Prompts US and Pakistan War of Words." *The Guardian,* May 4, 2011. Accessed October 25, 2015. http://www.theguardian.com/world/2011/may/04/osama-bin-laden-pakistan-us.

Walsh, Declan. "Osama bin Laden Mission Agreed in Secret 10 Years Ago by U.S. and Pakistan." *The Guardian*, May 9, 2011. Accessed October 25, 2015. http://www.theguardian.com/world/2011/may/09/osama-bin-laden-us-pakistan-deal.

Warrick, Joby. "Bin Laden's Last Stand: In Final Months, Terrorist Leader Worried about His Legacy." *The Washington Post*, April 30, 2012. Accessed October 25, 2015. http://www.washingtonpost.com/lifestyle/food/bin-ladens-last-stand-in-final-months-terrorist-leader-worried-about-his-legacy/2012/04/30/gIQAStCjsT_story.html.

Weatherford, Jack McIver. *Genghis Khan and the Making of the Modern World*. New York: Crown Publishers, 2004.

Weaver, Mary Anne. *Pakistan: In the Shadow of Jihad and Afghanistan*. New York: Farrar, Straus and Giroux, 2002.

West, Bing. *The Wrong War: Grist, Strategy, and the Way Out of Afghanistan*. New York: Random House, 2011.

Whitaker, Brian. "Bin Laden's Body Buried at Sea." *The Guardian*, May 2, 2011. Accessed October 25, 2015. http://www.theguardian.com/world/2011/may/02/bin-laden-body-buried-sea.

Wimmel, Kenneth. *The Alluring Target: In Search of the Secrets of Central Asia*. Fairfax, VA: Trackless Sands Press, 1996.

Woodcock, Andrew. "MP 'Shocked' at bin Laden Pakistan Discovery." *The Independent*, May 2, 2011. Accessed October 25, 2015. http://www.independent.co.uk/news/world/asia/mp-shocked-at-bin-laden-pakistan-discovery-2277941.html.

Woodward, John, ed. *Afghanistan: Opposing Viewpoints*. Farmington, NM: Greenhaven Press, 2006.

Woodward, John. "Death of Osama bin Laden: Phone Call Pointed U.S. to Compound—And to 'the Pacer.'" *The Washington Post,* May 6, 2011. Accessed October 25, 2015. https://www.washingtonpost.com/world/national-security/death-of-osama-bin-laden-phone-call-pointed-us-to-compound—and-to-the-pacer/2011/05/06/AFnSVaCG_story.html.

Yousaf, Mohammad, and Mark Adkin. *Afghanistan——The Bear Trap: The Defeat of a Superpower*. Havertown, PA: Casemate, 2001.

Zangorin, Adam, and D.S. Hilzenrath. "Unreleased: Probe Finds CIA Honcho Disclosed Top Secret Info to Hollywood." *POGO.org*, June 4, 2013. Accessed October 25, 2015. http://www.pogo.org/our-work/articles/2013/unreleased-probe-finds-cia-disclosed-secret-info.html.

Index

Note: page numbers in *italics* indicate photos.

About the Author

Meredith L. Runion is a Program Manager for the Department of Defense. As a freelance writer, Meredith has authored several articles on leadership, national security, and global strategy. Her published works include Greenwood's *History of Afghanistan, First Edition* (2007).